How to Winter

life

How to Winter

Harness Your Mindset to Thrive

on Cold, Dark, or Difficult Days

KARI LEIBOWITZ, PhD

PENGUIN LIFE

VIKING
An imprint of Penguin Random House LLC
penguinrandomhouse.com

A Penguin Life Book

Grateful acknowledgment is made for
permission to reprint the following:
"Útilykt" by Fischersund used with permission of Fischersund.
Student reflections on pages 174, 192 used with permission
of Alexandra Daily-Diamond and Hardik Nagrecha.

LIBRARY OF CONGRESS CATALOGING-IN-PUBLICATION DATA

Names: Leibowitz, Kari, author.
Title: How to winter : harness your mindset to thrive on cold,
dark, or difficult days / Kari Leibowitz, PhD.
Description: [New York] : Penguin Life, [2024] |
Includes bibliographical references.
Identifiers: LCCN 2024009833 (print) | LCCN 2024009834 (ebook) |
ISBN 9780593653753 (hardcover) | ISBN 9780593653760 (ebook)
Subjects: LCSH: Environmental psychology. |
Winter—Psychological aspects. | Seasonal affective disorder.
Classification: LCC BF353 .L45 2024 (print) | LCC BF353 (ebook) |
DDC 616.85/27—dc23/eng/20240412
LC record available at https://lccn.loc.gov/2024009833
LC ebook record available at https://lccn.loc.gov/2024009834

Printed in the United States of America
1st Printing

Designed by Amanda Dewey

For Nanny and for Rob

One must have a mind of winter
To regard the frost and the boughs
Of the pine-trees crusted with snow;

And have been cold a long time
To behold the junipers shagged with ice,
The spruces rough in the distant glitter

Of the January sun; and not to think
Of any misery in the sound of the wind,
In the sound of a few leaves,

Which is the sound of the land
Full of the same wind
That is blowing in the same bare place

For the listener, who listens in the snow,
And, nothing himself, beholds
Nothing that is not there and the nothing that is.

"The Snow Man"

WALLACE STEVENS

CONTENTS

Part Three

Get Outside

INTRODUCTION

F OR A LONG TIME, it would have seemed like a hilarious joke
that I'd be telling anyone "how to winter." When I moved to
the Arctic city of Tromsø, it was in spite of a lifelong bias against
the season. Growing up at the Jersey Shore, an hour south of
New York City, I hated winter. As a high school senior, I'd re-
fuse to drive my little brother—a freshman—to class unless he
preheated my car to a toasty warmth each morning. But from
2014 to 2015, I was a researcher and Fulbright Scholar at the
University of Tromsø—the northernmost university in the world.
There, I lived through the Polar Night, a two-month period in
which the sun never rises. I was drawn to the Arctic to try to
understand how people who live through some of the darkest
winters on Earth cope with the season. As I immersed myself in
a culture that celebrates winter's opportunities, I conducted re-
search to investigate what I was seeing around me. My study
assessed how people in Norway think about winter: what I call

their wintertime mindsets. Along the way, I learned a new approach to the season and fell in love with winter myself.

After a year in northern Norway, I headed to sunny California to complete my PhD in psychology at Stanford University— not exactly the best place to hone winter expertise. To put a bow on my time in Scandinavia, I wrote an article about my experience and research. I figured this would enable me to move on toward what awaited me in the Stanford Mind & Body Lab, where I would study how our mindsets influence our health and well-being in medical contexts. "The Norwegian Town Where the Sun Doesn't Rise" appeared in *The Atlantic* in July 2015. Despite being an essay about wintertime mindsets published in the US summer, it was the most popular article of the day, prestigiously beating "I Made the Pea Guac." Satisfied with my accomplishment and having shared my story, I was ready to dive into my new work, and my new life, in Palo Alto.

But that article didn't put a bow on my time in Norway; it cracked my experience wide open. It revealed a hunger, almost a desperation, for a better approach to winter. Since then, I've received hundreds of requests from journalists who, in advance of the end of daylight saving time and the onset of winter, want advice on how people can find something other than gloom and depression in the season's darkness. My research has been covered in outlets from *National Geographic* to *The Guardian* to *Forbes*. I was invited to be on *Skavlan*, a Norwegian-Swedish television talk show, one week after Adele appeared on the program. (I couldn't go, I was at a conference in San Diego. Also, I didn't realize how big of a deal it was.) A *Fast Company* article, "The Norwegian Secret to Enjoying a Long Winter," became the number-one most popular leadership story of the year, spawning yet another piece by the same author: "The Norwegian Secret to Getting an Article Shared 300,000 Times."

People from all over the world have written to me, recounting what they love about winter, what they hate about winter, their happy childhood memories of snow days, the way winter drags them down. Rather than put wintertime mindsets behind me, I spent the next decade augmenting my original research with further study on how our mindsets work and why they matter, exploring cultural strategies for thriving during the darkest season, and sharing stories of my time in Tromsø and lessons of my research with international audiences. It seems that from Seattle to New York, Dublin to Bucharest, Sydney to Tokyo, people struggle with winter.

At the same time, there are places worldwide—including Tromsø—where winter is anticipated and savored. My stint in the Arctic taught me that winter doesn't have to just happen to us: we can shape how we experience the season. Yet while there were plenty of researchers to consult about how to manage seasonal affective disorder or discuss how daylight saving time shifts our circadian rhythms, there were shockingly few experts providing strategies for people who want to enjoy winter more. I started asking: What does it look like to embrace the season? How can we find opportunities in the darkness, the cold, and the wet? And what can winter teach us about the ways our mindsets help create our reality?

I found myself uniquely suited to answer these questions. As a reformed winter-hater, I knew what it was like to change my own winter mindset. My time living in northern Norway, a personal foray into a challenging but enchanting winter, was eye-opening, a crash course in learning to actively embrace the season.

And my academic training—informed especially by the collective wisdom of the Stanford Mind & Body Lab—gave me the scientific expertise to parse decades of research about how to deliberately change our perspectives, behaviors, and mindsets.

Ultimately, my search for the answers to these questions led to the book you hold in your hands.

AT ITS BEST, winter conjures images of cozy snow days and hot chocolate with marshmallows. Reading in front of the fireplace with a dog in your lap, skiing from rustic lodges, sledding at top speeds, and snowball fights. Presents under the Christmas tree, latkes fried in oil, sparkly New Year's Eve parties.

But many of us don't inhabit these idealized winters for most of the season. Winter also means deicing your windshield before driving to work, walking through frigid wind tunnels to get to school or the office. Leaving for work in the dark and coming home in the dark. The sky pressing down in an endless string of gray days. Sleet that gets down the back of your neck and leaves you cold for hours. That gross snow that piles up and turns brown on the edges of highways and city streets. Feeling tired and lethargic, sniffly and melancholic.

Winter poses many challenges. Depending on where you live, winter might bring bitter cold and mountains of snow. Or the season might be full of lashing rain, sleet, and hail. It could be a dull, monotonous gray for weeks on end; chilly, constant drizzle; wind that steals your words and whips your hair into a knotted mess. Unless you live near the equator and don't experience much winter at all, it undoubtedly brings darkness: early sunsets, long nights. These climatic conditions affect us; the darkness can make us feel sluggish and tired, unable to focus. Cold, wet weather discourages outdoor activity and movement, further compounding our lethargy. We might feel less social, less like our best selves. And with climate change, winters are becoming less predictable, bringing more cold to places unused to freezing temperatures and transforming snowy winters into rainy ones, requiring our approach to the season to adapt to new conditions. These problems are, on the surface, issues of weather and climate. But they reflect much more: how disconnected we are from yearly cycles of light and dark. How desperate we are to fit the natural world to our own schedules rather than to shift our rhythms seasonally. The way we have absorbed narratives about what we can and can't enjoy when it's dark, wet, or cold.

Winter is associated with death. In poetry, literature, and metaphor, winters are harsh, fallow periods. The antithesis of goodness, light, and growth. Colorless seasons, robbed of joy. In psychological research, winter is most often studied in conjunction with seasonal affective disorder, or wintertime depression. It feels natural, to many, that winter would be a dangerous time of year for mental health. Some view winter as innately depressing. I once asked a five-year-old named Alma what her favorite season was, and she responded: "Don't laugh at me. It's winter." Even a five-year-old knows it's not cool to like winter.

YET RESIGNING OURSELVES to trudging through the season costs us. At best, we're missing the joys and delights of a special time, one unique in its opportunities for contemplation, connection, and delight. At worst, though, we're sleepwalking through a third of the year or more—meaning we're opting out of fully embracing months of our lives. Whether we're aware of them or not, our mindsets impact our experience of winter.

In Norway, I was surrounded by people who approach winter differently. There, despite the long, dark, cold winters, these Northerners find joy, comfort, and excitement in the season. My research in Norway found that many people there have what I call a "positive wintertime mindset." Those who appreciate winter generally orient toward the season's wonders: coziness and gathering around a fire, crisp air and starry skies, slowed-down rituals and a chance for rest. For people with this mindset, winter is not a limiting time of year to dread but a time full of opportunity to anticipate. In Norway, I learned that we are not condemned to waste the winter months, throwing away the season, wishing for spring. We can change our mindsets and, as a result, change our experience of winter—and of our lives.

This wintertime mindset isn't magic, and you don't have to have a Scandinavian upbringing to adopt it. For more than a decade I've been studying how people can change their mindsets and embrace winter. To understand how to winter, I've combined my psychological expertise with personal experience, cultural observation, and conversations with people all over the world. I've lived in—and traveled to—some of the most extreme winters on Earth. I've gone weeks without seeing the sun rise. I've fielded questions from journalists in dozens of countries. And I've spoken to thousands of people about how a different approach to winter can unlock a new way of being year-round. In response to requests from schools, businesses, and winter festivals, I developed my Wintertime Mindset Workshop—an interactive workshop that shares concrete strategies for cultivating more adaptive mindsets about winter. I've brought this workshop to the Winter Cities Shake-Up conferences in Saskatoon and Edmonton, Canada, and The Great Northern festival in Minneapolis, Minnesota; to tech companies on their winter retreats; to the staff of major news organizations; to psychology classes, continuing education students, and wellness centers at universities; to museums and arts centers and nonprofits; and, once, to a bird sanctuary. Year after year, I heard from people who wanted help enjoying winter, and who, subsequently, were able to find more meaning and pleasure in the season by shifting their mindsets. I've seen firsthand that changing your thoughts about winter isn't just possible—it's transformative.

Because how we approach winter is a pretty good litmus test for how we approach other dark, difficult seasons in our lives. How do we respond to situations out of our control? How do we react to circumstances we did not choose? Do we shrink and wither, or do we turn inward with intention and cultivate moments of joy? Do we focus on frustration, or do we seek wonder and connection to get us through? And, most important, which mindsets are motivating us, consciously or unconsciously? Are our mindsets holding us back or propelling us forward? Winter isn't just a season in nature. Winters—times of challenge, struggle, or grief—can come into our communities, our homes, and our lives in unexpected ways and at unexpected times. The strategies I observed in my research on how people around the world uplift winter can help us weather any storm—snow or otherwise. The same practices that help us embrace and enjoy winter can also help us through difficult seasons of life.

I STARTED TO see changing our mindsets about winter as an entry point: an entry point to deliberately cultivating useful mindsets, wielding our attention and language intentionally, and leaning into weather and darkness that we can't control. I saw the power in wintertime mindsets to transform not only people's experience of the season, but of their lives year-round. I wrote this book to share everything I've learned. I hope it helps you see winter differently. If you are already a winter-lover, I hope it helps you find even more ways to celebrate the season. If you are a winter-hater, as I once was, I hope it helps you find moments of lightness amidst the dark and guides you to create such moments yourself. Most of all, I hope this book begins to reveal to you the unseen ways that our mindsets shape our experiences, and how they are a powerful, underutilized resource for navigating whatever challenges life throws our way.

How to Winter

Prelude

MY JOURNEY TO
THE LAND OF WINTER

L OCATED MORE than two hundred miles north of the Arctic Circle, Tromsø, Norway, is home to an extreme and special winter, when the world often appears blue-tinted, snow cloaks the city in quiet, and the northern lights dance in the sky. During the Polar Night, which lasts from late November to late January, the sun doesn't rise at all. At this time of year, Tromsø gets, at most, about six hours of diffuse twilight light each day as the sun skirts below the horizon. On the shortest day of the year, full darkness lasts for almost nineteen hours: the light at four p.m. looks no different than the light at two a.m.*

It was the Polar Night that drew me to Tromsø in the first place. In 2013, I was a recent college graduate looking for research experience before applying to PhD programs in psychology. In search of an opportunity to explore my interests in

---

*After the Polar Night ends, the days progressively lengthen until the Midnight Sun period, from May to July, when the sun never sets.

positive psychology and mental health—and to satisfy my sense of adventure—I was drawn to the work of Joar Vittersø. Joar, a professor of psychology at the University of Tromsø, is one of the world's leading experts on human happiness. His research distinguishes between hedonic well-being, things that feel pleasurable and enjoyable, and eudaimonic well-being, things in life that give us meaning and purpose. Joar has studied life satisfaction and personal growth, researching what it means to live a fulfilling life.

Fascinated by his work and with daydreams of fjord adventures, I contacted Joar to ask if he might collaborate with me on a study and mentor me should I be awarded funding. Joar generously agreed and mentioned, somewhat offhandedly, that his university, also known as The Arctic University of Norway, is the northernmost in the world.

Tromsø is so far north that it's home to many of the world's northernmosts: the northernmost botanical garden, the northernmost outdoor swimming pool, the northernmost mosque, the northernmost traffic light, the northernmost aquarium, and the northernmost Burger King and 7-Eleven, to name just a few. I also learned about Tromsø's extreme winter and the Polar Night. It struck me as interesting that Joar, one of the world's foremost scholars of well-being, lives in a place where the sun doesn't rise for two months each year. I suggested that Joar and I study seasonal variation in well-being to understand how Tromsø's winter affects people's mental health—negatively, I presumed. Joar responded by saying something along the lines of: "You could certainly try that, but research hasn't found much difference in mental well-being between seasons in Tromsø."

◆

AS AN AMERICAN, I assumed that Tromsø's long, dark winters would be harmful to mental health. Growing up on the Jersey Shore, I was steeped in a culture that believed—that knew—that summer was unequivocally the best season. So much of what makes my hometown special—going to the beach, getting ice cream on the boardwalk, attending outdoor concerts—are things we did only in summer. Winter was the season of limitations: the time of year we were stuck inside, when I shivered in my jeans, when going to school required defrosting my windshield, and when the liveliest hangouts were abandoned until Memorial Day. I went to university in Atlanta, Georgia, partly to escape northeastern US winters.

In fact, I assumed that rates of seasonal affective disorder, or wintertime depression, would be high in Tromsø. Seasonal affective disorder is a pattern of clinical depression that manifests seasonally, most often in winter. Because light therapy is an effective treatment for the disorder, psychologists reverse-engineered a theory: the cause of wintertime depression must be the lack of daylight in winter. The "latitude hypothesis" of seasonal affective disorder states that as latitude increases and wintertime daylight correspondingly decreases, rates of seasonal affective disorder should rise. Based on this, it would be reasonable to assume that people living through Tromsø's two-month Polar Night—and six-to-eight-month winter—must suffer from high rates of wintertime depression.

But the research I found supported Joar's claim and calls the latitude hypothesis of seasonal affective disorder into question. Despite the city's high latitude and winter darkness, research has shown that residents of Tromsø have surprisingly low rates of seasonal depression. This doesn't mean that they don't experience winter depression in Tromsø; they just don't experience it at the rates we would expect considering how extreme their winters are. One analysis of almost nine thousand residents of Tromsø found no meaningful seasonal variation in mental distress—meaning that people in Tromsø didn't seem to be more tense, depressed, or hopeless in winter than during the rest of the year. The authors of this study concluded that the negative impact of winter on mental health is more of a popular myth than a scientific fact. We'll talk more about seasonal affective disorder in chapter 2, but the research suggests that residents of northern Norway don't experience much of the wintertime suffering experienced elsewhere—including, paradoxically, in warmer, brighter, more southern locations.

After speaking with Joar and looking at the research, I realized my study should focus not on winter depression but the lack thereof. I wanted to know: How do the residents of northern Norway protect themselves from wintertime woes? Why *aren't* they more depressed during such intense winters? And could I identify strategies that people use to cope with winter in Tromsø that might be applicable elsewhere, to the same beneficial effects?

In April 2014, I was awarded a US-Norway Fulbright research grant to study these questions in Tromsø, and my hypothetical adventure was suddenly my very real future. Was I really going to pack up my entire life and move to the Arctic?

I ARRIVED IN TROMSØ in August 2014 a little bit excited, but mostly afraid. Afraid of moving to a foreign country where I didn't know a soul. Afraid of navigating a new culture in a language I didn't understand. And, yes, certainly a bit afraid of the winter and the cold. In preparation, I'd read everything I could find on the small city. Most tourist guides talked about how beautiful it was: the fjords, the mountains, the northern lights. But as I rode the Number 42 bus from Langnes Airport to my apartment, I was struck by a pervasive grayness. The sky was overcast; a drizzly mist fell without vigor. All I could see were gray clouds, gray water, gray mountains. A fellow American researcher living in southern Norway later documented the Norwegian shades of gray on her blog: downy-fill gray, goodbye-daylight gray, pavement-of-sadness gray, heavy-frost gray, mid-November-noon-sky gray. The buildings along the bus route seemed industrial and utilitarian. Where were the colorful wooden houses I'd been promised? Where was the rustic Norwegian architecture?

When I got to my new home, a student apartment I'd be sharing with three roommates, the first thing I did was learn that there was no Wi-Fi. The second thing I did—when I realized that meant I had no way to tell my family I had arrived, or to contact anyone at all—was cry the panicked tears that marked the start of a new adventure across the world, when you've thrown your knapsack over the fence and have no choice but to figure out how to climb over after it. The third thing I did—my first attempt at climbing the fence that was my new life in Tromsø—was rearrange my bedroom. The room's finest feature was its windows: one small and high, through which you could see only clouds, and one large and square. From the larger window, you could gaze at the always-lit blue sign of the Ahlsell building across the street (the leading Nordic distributor of installation products, tools, and supplies!) and then the fjord, a narrow strip of water, and, beyond that, the mountains of the mainland rising to meet the sky.

The room was arranged so that while lying in bed you were treated to a view of the door. Tears under control, I rotated the bed 90 degrees so that I could lie down and take in the view outside. When I think of my time in Norway, I think of sitting in that bed, watching boats great and small chug to and from Tromsø's harbor: speedboats Norwegians use to get to their weekend cabins, commercial fishing boats, and the mighty Nordic cruise ship *Hurtigruten*. As the lush greenness of late summer gave way to the first frosts of fall, I saw clouds let loose fine, misty drizzles and fat, heaving downpours, gentle flurries and raging whiteouts. I saw the days shorten and the nights lengthen—sometimes to pitch black, but sometimes to a soft, diffuse blue reflecting off of snow and water. If I opened the window and stuck my head out, I sometimes saw the northern lights ripple across the sky. Once, in a blizzard, I saw a man out for a run in a pair of shorts.

TROMSØ IS A SMALL ISLAND, roughly the same size as Manhattan, nestled between the Norwegian mainland to the east and the much larger Kvaløya ("Whale Island") to the west. If it wasn't labeled on the map, you'd be hard-pressed to find it: it's virtually indistinguishable from the hundreds of other islands dotting Norway's coast. Home to approximately eighty thousand inhabitants, Tromsø is the third-most populated city north of the Arctic Circle. The city has a bustling downtown with everything a person could need—a mall, three main shopping streets, and a few movie theaters. But it still felt isolated and wild to me.

I wondered how much my knowledge of the map—of Tromsø sitting high atop the globe—contributed to my feeling like I was now living at the edge of the Earth.

The psychology department at the University of Tromsø welcomed me to the Arctic, easing my initial loneliness. When Joar and I met in person after almost a year of email correspondence, his first words to me were, "So, you exist!" Joar also introduced me to a colleague who would become one of my closest Norwegian friends, and whose wisdom appears throughout this book, Dr. Ida Solhaug. Ida was the first of many people I met in Tromsø who countered the stereotype that Scandinavians can be cold and standoffish. In typical Ida fashion, she immediately invited me to her house for her birthday party.

The next evening, I arrived at my first Norwegian gathering nervous. As I stood awkwardly at the end of the room, a man with thick black glasses introduced himself to me as Thor-Eirik (names I'd heard only in mythology are commonplace in Norway), and I introduced myself, in my New Jersey accent, as Kari.

"What is your name?"

"Kari. Kah-REE."

"Can you spell it?"

"K-A-R-I."

"Oh! CAR-ee! Did you know that is a very common Norwegian name?"

My jaw dropped as Thor-Eirik explained that the name "Kari"—an unusual spelling of Carrie, by American standards, is not just common: it's prototypically Norwegian. The way Americans might use "Jane" to signal a generic girl's name, Norwegians would use "Kari." I felt something shift within me, a signposting of potential belonging. I don't put much stock in fate or destiny, but as someone with no Norwegian heritage, whose family had never been to Norway, this information provided a boost. I was suddenly over the fence and into my new life: Kari of Norway.

OVER SEVERAL MONTHS, Joar and I laid the groundwork for our study, expanding upon the background research I'd conducted before coming to Tromsø. As I became more at ease in my foreign surroundings, I discovered an additional benefit of my study topic: everyone I spoke with—in casual conversations, at parties, over psychology-department lunches at the university—had a theory as to why their city flourished during the Polar Night. Some people swore by cod-liver oil or told me they used lamps that simulated the sun by brightening progressively each morning. Others attributed their winter well-being to community involvement, Tromsø's wealth of cultural festivals, or daily commutes by ski. Most residents, though, simply talked about the Polar Night as if it wasn't a big deal. Many even expressed excitement about the upcoming season and the unique opportunities it would bring: for skiing, being cozy at home, and resting.

However, it wasn't until October, several months into my project, that I realized that by focusing on a lack of seasonal depression I might be asking the wrong questions. At Ida's party, Thor-Eirik had invited me to join his weekly meditation group. Our Tuesday evening gatherings were an early lesson in how people in Tromsø are undaunted by the weather: in daylight, in darkness, in snow and in rain, we ventured out to sit together in silence. One such Tuesday, I stood outside the red building on the Tromsø harbor with my new friend Fern. Fern Wickson is an Australian who had been in Tromsø for more than five years.

When she wasn't working in her ecological biotech job as scientific secretary for the North Atlantic Marine Mammal Commission, Fern was teaching yoga classes out of her home studio, the Peaceful Wild, which overlooks a fjord on Kvaløya, or riding her motorcycle around the islands of the Arctic. On this Tuesday evening, Fern was asking how long I planned to stay in Tromsø. Although my grant ended in May, I told her that I hoped to stay through as much of the summer as possible. "It would be a shame to make it through the winter only to leave right before the best season," I said.

Without pausing, Fern replied, "I wouldn't necessarily say summer is the best season."

FOR PEOPLE IN TROMSØ, Fern's comment probably wouldn't be very surprising. But I was astounded: Fern was insinuating that *winter* was the best season?! Tromsø has only two real seasons: a long winter and a brief summer that arrives suddenly between late May and late June, at the start of the Midnight Sun period. Not only that, whenever I told anyone in the US that I was moving to the Arctic for the year to study winter, the most common responses I heard were "I could never do that," "I would get so depressed," "I just hate the winter," and, my personal favorite, "Do you think you're going to go to Norway to study why they're not depressed and get winter depression yourself?"

Yet Fern's comment crystalized a theme I'd been hearing in my conversations but hadn't fully processed: that, in Tromsø, winter is something people look forward to. I saw my research with a newfound sense of clarity. The assumptions of my original proposal had been off. I was asking why people in Tromsø weren't more depressed, thereby assuming that winter was inherently depressing, and they were somehow immune. But people in Tromsø seemed to hold a different view of the season: that winter is something to be enjoyed, not endured. According to my friends, winter in Tromsø would be full of snow, skiing, the northern lights, and all things *koselig*, the Norwegian word for "cozy." As the blink-and-you'll-miss-it autumn transformed, I started glimpsing Tromsø's winter magic. By November, open-flame candles adorned every café, restaurant, and home. Even in the break room at the university, we gathered for lunch by candlelight. I strapped on my first pair of cross-country skis and followed the Lysløpa, a well-lit walking and skiing path the length of Tromsø island, gliding, and often falling, through snow-laden pine trees. The whales came back to Tromsø, their last chance to feed before their journey south to give birth, and every walk by a fjord became a game of "wave or whale"? as we scanned the sea for emerging fins. I had my first encounter with the northern lights and learned their different forms: streaky and undulating, like a stripey curtain, or diffuse and hazy, like a green mist in the sky.

As I grew to enjoy life in Tromsø, I began to see past the gray I had felt closing around me like iron bars on that first homesick bus ride into town. I learned firsthand that, far from a period of absolute darkness, the Polar Night is a time of beautiful colors and soft, indirect light. Fern told me she refused to call the Polar Night by its typical Norwegian name, the *mørketid*, or "dark time," preferring instead to use its alternative name, *blåtid*, meaning the "blue time," to emphasize its color. After hearing this, I couldn't help but pay more attention to the soft blue haze that settled over everything, and I consciously worked to think of this light as cozy rather than dim. As I waited at bus stops, layered in woolen undergarments, my breath fogging rhythmically before me, I marveled at the sky, which, thanks to the never-rising sun hovering below the horizon for hours, was often painted with streaks of pink, purple, pale yellow, and every shade of blue. My Norwegian friends would walk or ski to our meetups, arriving alert and refreshed from being outdoors, inspiring me to bundle up and spend time outside on even the coldest days. One day in mid-November, my troupe of international student friends and I journeyed to Kvaløya to see the sun shining on the tips of the mountains for the last time, alighting their points in bronze, copper, and gold. When I got home, I placed candles on every available surface of my bedroom and turned the heater down to compensate for their warmth.

MY ORIGINAL RESEARCH questions were colored by my own culturally biased perspective of winter. I decided to include a questionnaire in my study that would capture the potential benefits of winter and focus on the season's positives. But I hit a snag: Aside from the assessment surveys used to identify seasonal affective disorder, no standardized psychological questionnaires about attitudes toward winter existed. (We'll discuss this more in chapter 2, but previous research on seasonal affective disorder in Tromsø used a mix of the standard SAD-assessment surveys and more general surveys measuring mental distress.) While there were questionnaires that asked about seasonal depression, distress, and sleep disorder in winter, there were no surveys that made room for the potentially positive aspects of the season.

This not only created problems for my study, it hinted at biases in the larger scientific framework for researching winter. If we can only study what we can measure, the fact that there were no existing instruments to capture winter's benefits suggested that we weren't used to looking for or thinking about people's positive experiences of the season, even as thousands of research articles addressed winter depression. In focusing, admirably, on helping people who suffered during winter, academics, researchers, and clinicians may have inadvertently created a conversational bias in the psychological literature, perpetuating the idea that we must all be vigilant against winter's negative mental health effects. No one seemed to be talking about the people around the world who thrive during winter.*

AROUND THIS TIME, as I was exploring psychology graduate programs, I flew back to the US and visited Stanford University. There, I met Alia Crum, a professor of psychology, who later became my PhD adviser. Alia, or Ali as we call her, runs the Stanford Mind & Body Lab, where she leads pioneering research investigating how our mindsets influence our well-being, performance, and physiology. Ali defines mindsets as "core assumptions about the nature and workings of things in the world": we can think of them as the lenses or frames of mind through which we perceive and understand information. Our mindsets influence what we notice and what we expect, and while we're not always aware of our mindsets, research is showing they can have a profound effect on our behavior, health, and happiness. As we chatted about her research and my own work

---

*Since my time in Norway, Kelly Rohan, a clinical psychologist at the University of Vermont who studies seasonal affective disorder, developed the Seasonal Beliefs Questionnaire, a measure of maladaptive thoughts about winter and darkness. While still mostly focused on identifying patients at risk of seasonal affective disorder, this scale does much more than previous measures to capture potentially positive relationships with the winter months.

in Norway, Ali suggested that mindsets might play a role in the wintertime flourishing I was observing in Tromsø.

Ali follows in the footsteps of psychologist Carol Dweck, who also mentored me at Stanford and whose work examines mindsets about our ability to grow and improve in domains including intelligence and athletics. In her research and her book, *Mindset: The New Psychology of Success*, Carol details the ways a "growth mindset" (the belief that traits such as intelligence and talent can be developed through sustained effort over time) leads to greater success than a "fixed mindset" (the belief that individual qualities are set for life). Those in a fixed mindset, her research finds, often fail to see feedback as an opportunity for learning and are more likely to view criticism as a personal attack. Conversely, those with more of a growth mindset tend to be more open to learning from mistakes, taking risks, and pursuing self-improvement. In the case of an academic failure, for example, students with growth mindsets, motivated to get smarter, might feel they need to try harder or use a different strategy, leading to increased effort and engagement. A student with a more fixed mindset, conversely, might feel that this failure confirms their lack of intelligence. Motivated to make sure others don't realize this, they may shy away from challenges or become disengaged. Students with growth mindsets generally have a greater appreciation for academics, more motivation to succeed, improved performance after setbacks, and higher GPAs. Carol's influential research also demonstrates that our mindsets can change, and that a person can move from a fixed mindset to a growth mindset. Her and her colleagues' intervention studies show that it's possible to help students deliberately adopt growth mindsets, and that academic benefits often follow. And simply making people aware of their mindsets is a powerful tool for helping people cultivate more useful ones.

Ali's work expands on these ideas by investigating how mindset influences not only achievement and success, but also physical health. In one of her studies, for example, employees of a large financial institution were experimentally exposed to an adaptive mindset toward stress, coming to view it as enhancing rather than debilitating. These employees later experienced fewer negative health symptoms and better work performance during the 2008 financial crisis and recession. Changing their mindsets seemed to change how these people reacted to the stress in their lives. In another randomized controlled experiment, hotel room attendants who were informed that their job was good exercise saw decreases in body fat and blood pressure compared with those who continued to simply view their jobs as work. Ali's research illustrates that it's not only fixed and growth mindsets about our abilities that influence us: mindsets related to health, performance, and well-being can be helpful or unhelpful, constructive or destructive.

The mindsets in these studies are all true—intelligence can increase with effort; stress can have beneficial effects for our health and performance; cleaning several hotel rooms a day exceeds exercise recommendations for an active lifestyle. However, they are also biased: a specific perspective of a more complex truth. Intelligence has both genetic set points and can be improved through study and learning. Stress can have negative health effects even as it prepares us mentally and physiologically to meet challenges. Scrubbing hotel rooms is healthy movement and also hard, taxing work. Mindsets help people make sense of ambiguity: What does a failure in school say about my abilities? How will stress affect my performance? Should I worry if I'm sore after a cleaning shift? Reality is multifaceted, and many mindsets fall along a continuum. But by helping people selectively focus their attention and energy on a particularly useful facet of a complicated reality, shaping mindsets can improve health, performance, and well-being in a variety of situations.

WINTER, I REALIZED, is similarly multidimensional and ambiguous: there are parts of winter that are unpleasant, and parts that are delightful. Perhaps people in Tromsø are just better at recognizing and pursuing the season's pleasures. Perhaps their winter well-being is due, in part, to their mindsets.

This led me to ask: Could we measure positive or negative mindset toward winter? And might this wintertime mindset have something to do with Tromsø residents' psychological well-being during the Polar Night? My hope was to add an overlooked, more positive dimension to the conversation on winter mental health, one that had previously been missed in research on seasonal affective disorder. Instead of focusing on why people weren't depressed, I now wanted to concentrate on trying to understand what allowed people in Tromsø to flourish during the darkest, coldest time of the year.

Joar and I developed a Wintertime Mindset Scale, which aimed to measure mindsets and attitudes about winter by asking respondents to rate how strongly they agreed or disagreed with statements such as "There are many things to enjoy about the winter," "I enjoy doing many things I only do during the winter," and "I find the winter months dark and depressing." Our goal was to understand the relationship between what we

called wintertime mindset—whether respondents viewed the
season as full of opportunities to enjoy or limitations to dread—
and other aspects of psychological well-being, including life sat-
isfaction and positive emotions.

A random sample of more than two hundred Norwegian
adults responded to our survey. The group was almost evenly
divided between respondents living in southern Norway, north-
ern Norway, and Svalbard, an Arctic island located halfway be-
tween northern Norway and the North Pole. Thanks to the
warm current of the Gulf Stream, Tromsø is considered "sub-
arctic" despite its northern location: average winter tempera-
tures hover around 25 to 30°F, which is more temperate than
its latitude suggests. Svalbard, however, is probably closer to
what most people think of when they imagine the Arctic: With a
population of only about 2,500, the island's main town, Long-
yearbyen, has only one grocery store. And, if residents leave
Longyearbyen, they are required by law to carry guns to pro-
tect themselves in case they encounter a hungry polar bear. In
winter, many residents travel by snowmobile. In terms of both
light and temperature, Svalbard feels much more extreme than
Tromsø; average January temperatures range from -4 to 8°F,
and the Polar Night of Svalbard is significantly darker than in
Tromsø, lacking even indirect sunlight, with almost no change
in light to mark months of passing days.

Our survey results suggested that wintertime mindset may
be at least partially responsible for winter well-being in Nor-
way. In our study, wintertime mindset was positively associated
with every measure of well-being we examined, including the
Satisfaction with Life Scale (a widely used survey that measures
general life satisfaction, or the sense that our lives are unfolding

the way we would want), positive emotions (pleasure, satisfaction, and happiness), and the Personal Growth Composite (a scale that measures openness to new challenges). The people who had more positive wintertime mindsets, in other words, tended to be highly satisfied with their lives, experienced positive emotions more frequently, and pursued personal growth.

We also found that wintertime mindset was significantly correlated with latitude in Norway—those living farther north tended to experience winter more positively and enjoy it more. With its extreme climate, Svalbard is almost certainly home to a self-selecting group; many residents live on the island for only a few years at a time. And you wouldn't move to Svalbard if you detest winter. But even when the residents of Svalbard were excluded from the sample, people living in northern Norway still had a more positive wintertime mindset than those living in southern Norway. It's not as if people in southern Norway don't experience winter: Oslo resides at roughly the same latitude as Anchorage, Alaska, and winters there are cold, dark, and long, particularly by American standards. But Oslo receives significantly more winter daylight than Tromsø: even on the solstice, the sun still rises. Yet despite a lighter, brighter winter, southern Norwegians don't seem to experience the season as positively as their compatriots in the north.

ONCE I REALIZED that people in Tromsø had this positive wintertime mindset, I started noticing it everywhere. The environment and culture of Tromsø facilitate an appreciation and enjoyment of winter. The city has infrastructure to keep roads clear of snow and restaurants warm even when it's blustery outside. Every restaurant and coffee shop has soft lighting and open-flame candles (something Americans aren't always used to—while visiting, my father accidentally set a restaurant menu on fire by inadvertently holding it too close to the flame), and cafés often have heat lamps and blankets at outdoor tables so that people can enjoy coffee outside year-round. People dress with an eye toward practicality—sleek and stylish coats that are warm and waterproof, boots with woolen inserts and thick soles, and chunky woolen sweaters. In Tromsø, winter is celebrated culturally with an abundance of community events and festivals: the Tromsø International Film Festival, the Polar Night Half Marathon, the Northern Lights Music Festival, and Sami Week, which celebrates northern Norway's Indigenous Sami population.

It might be easier to love winter in Tromsø, where so much of the culture treasures winter and the season is uniquely magical. My best friend, Becky, a fellow summer-lover who grew up surfing at the Jersey Shore and who visited me in Norway, said, "If winter was a place, it would be Tromsø." Tromsø lives up to fantasies of Disney's *Frozen*: I never got used to walking home from the bus stop and seeing the northern lights dancing in the sky. And I want to be careful not to overstate the impact of our study. As far as we are aware, Joar and I were the first to examine wintertime mindset. Given that this was a correlational study, we can't say with certainty that having a positive wintertime mindset causes people to have greater life satisfaction, or vice versa—only that these things are associated. But research on other mindsets—about stress, intelligence, or the nature of illness—suggests that when people adopt useful mindsets, benefits to health, well-being, and performance often follow.

The lessons I learned in Tromsø showed me that winter misery is not inevitable. Even as some aspects of the culture can't be exported, there are simple but meaningful steps you can take to experience the season more joyfully. Regardless of where you grew up—in a winter-celebrating or a winter-bashing culture—you can consciously cultivate an appreciation of winter to enjoy the season more. This doesn't apply just to places with freezing, snowy winters: if you live somewhere gray and misty where winter treats you to steady drizzle, or even somewhere temperate where winter days are still shorter and darker, your perception of winter influences you, and you can benefit from learning how to adapt to, and enjoy, winter.

HOW TO WINTER

Inspired by what I observed in Tromsø, I embarked on an around-the-world tour of winter locations while writing this book. I reveled in the coziness of Copenhagen, swam in frozen rivers in Finland, and inhaled Reykjavík's frosty air. I felt the wind sting my face on the Isle of Lewis, off the coast of Scotland, biked in the rain alongside the canals of Amsterdam and relaxed, steaming into the night, in onsens in Yamagata, Japan. My tour of places that do winter well was not comprehensive—the more I learn about winter traditions and rituals, the more I see unique and specific ways cultures all over the world savor the season. But it was a collection of places with their own interesting relationships to winter, places where I immersed myself in winters wet and stormy, sunless and snowy, cozy and curious.

In the next pages, I'll take you along with me as we unpack the psychological science supporting the winter practices I observed in each place.

There are as many ways of celebrating winter as there are types of winter weather: some cultures luxuriate in hot baths and saunas, others are obsessed with candles; in some countries, learning to ski is like learning to walk; in others, winter swimming draws crowds of would-be polar bears. In some communities, gathering around fire is sacred; elsewhere, film festivals give comfort to the long nights. But in locations rainy and windy, snowy and icy, I noticed three general strategies for embracing the season. The first is to **Appreciate Winter**: look at winter for what it is, and let it be a time for slowing down. Adapt to the season, using your words and attention to lift up winter's pleasures. The second is to **Make It Special**: lean into the activities and feelings that are unique to this time of year. Revel in coziness, enjoy delights made possible by winter's darkness, and create and savor rituals that imbue the season with meaning. The third is to **Get Outside**: layer up and enjoy the outdoors in all weather, experiment with winter bathing, and take advantage of the ways your town or city celebrates the season. Together, these three broad approaches help us find opportunities in winter, transforming it from a season of limitation to one full of possibility for meaning, connection, and fun.

How to Winter is organized around these three broad strategies, combining practical techniques for transforming your experience of the winter months with cutting-edge, evidence-based research on how to cultivate the mindsets that will serve you best. Each chapter dives into a specific winter-focused strategy— expecting the onset of the season, adjusting the way we talk about winter, developing rituals, practicing winter bathing—with supporting scientific evidence. Each of these practices can not only help you embrace and enjoy winter, but also reveals something about how our mindsets work: how they influence our attention, or our emotions, or our motivation. By reading this book, you'll gain both a functional approach for increasing your winter joy and learn how our mindsets can help us through any difficult season of life.

Each chapter ends with a series of Winter Practices: strategies that you can implement no matter what the winter is like where you are.* Many of these are supported by psychology research, and I think of these practices as experiments: try them with an open mind and see what works for you. The recommendations in this book are not one-size-fits-all. Rather, they are a smorgasbord of psychological tools and winter strategies that anyone can use, wherever you live, to cultivate more adaptive mindsets and embrace the darkest time of year. You can pick and choose which ones speak to you; you can try them out of order; you can keep the ones that help and discard the ones that don't. I hope you come back to the resources in these pages again and again, share passages with friends and family, and use the words in this book to write your own winter stories for years to come.

---

*These practices are designed for the winter months, so if you're reading this book during other seasons, you might want to bookmark your favorites to come back to this winter.

Part One

Appreciate
Winter

1.

WELL, WHAT DID
YOU EXPECT?

M Y TIME IN TROMSØ didn't just change my mindset about winter. It showed me how strong and stubborn our expectations about the season are. Before I ever inhaled Norwegian air, before I experienced the Arctic or Polar Night myself, my expectations screamed that such a frigid, sunless winter would be miserable. These expectations were formed over a lifetime of seasonal struggle and reinforced by what I heard from the people around me, whose words about Tromsø's assumedly depressing winter echoed in my ears.

For some people I've spoken to in the far north, the hardest time of the year is the onset of winter: late October, early November, as the days are getting darker and the darkest days are still ahead, everything feels heavy. In below-freezing climates, this is the time before snow; it's all darkness, no reflected light, and no snow-related winter activities yet. Kelly Rohan, a professor of psychology at the University of Vermont and an expert in treating seasonal affective disorder, told me that this is a particularly difficult time of year for people suffering from winter depression. In her research, she tries to identify "the script that people follow in the fall as the seasons change": specific cues that trigger their depression. For her patients, Halloween and the end of daylight saving time, markers of the oncoming winter, are basically "really strong, conditioned stimuli." Recognizing these cues can be helpful if it motivates adaptive coping strategies, or harmful if it triggers spirals of anxiety about seasonal affective disorder.

But it's not only people with seasonal affective disorder who—consciously or otherwise—anticipate winter misery. The onset of winter, particularly the shortening daylight and increased darkness, often impacts our mood. It's not just the darkness itself, which, on its own and temporarily, might be bearable. It's the embodied knowledge that it's only going to get darker before it gets lighter again. It's the spiral that begins with the expectation of how dreadful winter will be.

In many cases, our anticipatory powers serve us well. They help us envision what it will be like when we go to work, to the grocery store, or to a party. We have general expectations about what these events will entail (and how to prepare for them), which come from the people around us, our previous experience, and our mindsets. But when they're overly negative, they can heighten our suffering. They increase our distress not only during negative experiences, but in anticipation of them as well. They are designed to help us be vigilant and avoid unpleasantness, but they can backfire. Because our expectations don't just reflect reality; they also create our reality.

EXPECTING THE WORST

After my year in Tromsø, I was the first incoming PhD student of Ali Crum, who started at Stanford the year before I did. She was building and growing the Mind & Body Lab, and I was ecstatic to be a part of it: to undertake new research on how our mindsets influence our health and well-being, form new connections in the department and across the university, and be part of creating a lab community. Stanford was, for me, a phenomenal place to be a graduate student.

Stanford is not, however, a phenomenal place to study winter. Located in Palo Alto, California, it can get chilly (even down into the 40s Fahrenheit), but overall, even the coldest months are usually warm and sunny. Spring often arrives in February, when winter rains cause verdant grass and orange poppies to sprout practically overnight. In a wet year, the rainy season might bring sixty days of rain, which leaves about ten months devoted to sunshine. It hasn't snowed on Stanford's campus since 1976. So, initially, I turned my research efforts toward other domains where our mindsets matter. By diving into research on the placebo effect, I started to see how our expectations might be influencing our experience of winter before the season even begins.

PLACEBOS ARE INERT TREATMENTS—often sugar pills—labeled as real medications. They are most often researched in the context of randomized controlled trials, in which new drugs or treatments are compared against placebos to determine whether they're really effective. The goal is to ensure that any treatment benefit isn't due to the placebo effect, allowing us to see the impact of the active ingredients once we subtract out "everything else." But psychologists like myself, my colleagues in the Stanford Mind & Body Lab, and other researchers in the Society for Interdisciplinary Placebo Studies (there's even a placebo conference I attend every other year, which inspires lots of jokes about whether it's a "real" conference) are asking questions like: "What exactly is this 'everything else'?" and "What causes placebo effects?"

Because the placebo effect works. It's difficult for new drugs to pass trials, in part because the placebo effect provides benefit that can be hard to outperform. One large-scale review, published in *BMJ*, found that placebos can account for 50 to 75 percent of the benefit from pain-relieving medications. And it's not just pain: placebos can alleviate anxiety and depression. They can quell parkinsonian tremors. They can decrease asthma and allergies. They can reduce blood pressure. They can strengthen the immune system and treat Alzheimer's. If the placebo effect was a singular drug, it would be the most effective drug, across conditions, of all time.

What's causing these improvements? It's not the sugar in the sugar pill or the saline solution in the syringe. There are no "active ingredients" in these placebos. Instead, placebos activate the healing mechanisms in the body. The mechanisms by which they work depend on the condition they're treating and patients' beliefs about what they'll do. When patients are given a placebo and told it will relieve their pain, the body responds by activating endogenous opioids and dopamine—pain-relieving, feel-good chemicals in the brain. Placebos can reduce overactive neuron firing in the sub-thalamus to quiet parkinsonian tremors. In patients with depression, placebos have been associated with metabolic increases in brain regions responsible for cognitive processing and control, including the prefrontal and anterior cingulate cortex. In other words: the effects of placebos vary based on what people *expect* the placebo will do.

Our expectations impact our experience in measurable ways. In one study conducted by my colleagues in the Stanford Mind & Body Lab, participants were brought into the lab and induced to have an allergic reaction. They were pricked on the forearm with a drop of histamine, which causes an itchy, raised bump called a wheal, similar to a mosquito bite. Then a medical provider administered cream for their allergic reaction. For half the participants, the provider said it was an antihistamine: a cream that would reduce their allergic reaction. For the other half of participants, the provider said it was a histamine agonist: a cream that would increase their allergic reactions. Truthfully, it was unscented hand lotion for both groups. But the expectations the provider instilled determined what happened: compared with participants who were told that the cream would increase their reaction, participants who were told that the cream would help their allergic reaction had a smaller physical wheal size six minutes later.

Placebo effects can help treatments work better. When patients expect to benefit, these expectations can increase relief and healing. But the placebo has an evil twin: the nocebo effect.

Nocebo effects are when treatment is harmful because people have negative beliefs about its impact. This usually refers to side effects: those who expect side effects from a medication are more likely to have them. Sometimes just telling people about possible medication side effects increases their occurrence—in one study, men who were taking a medication for prostate gland enlargement were almost three times as likely to have sexual dysfunction when they were informed it was a possible side effect. Outside influences can also affect our expectation of side effects, like what our friends and family say or what we see in the media. In New Zealand, after a nationwide drug switch to a generic version of an antidepressant, two major news outlets ran stories about the generic version of the drug causing particular side effects. A study on this switch found that side effects for the drug increased more than 300 percent after this media coverage; the reported increase was strongest for the specific side effects mentioned in the news.

THE PREDICTIONS of our own minds, shaped by our mindsets, are meant to be helpful and prepare us for what comes next. But as research on placebo effects shows, they also make the reality we expect more likely. When we have the mindset—subconscious or otherwise—that "winter is dreadful" or "winter is limiting," we expect that winter will be lifeless and boring. By expecting winter to be terrible, we might be nocebo-ing our way into the season. In my workshops on wintertime mindset, the first thing I do is ask people to fill in the following sentence: "Winter is _____." For such a simple phrase, I get a wide variety of answers. Some people orient straight to the positive: "cozy," "magical," "fun." But most of the answers skew negative. Not just answers that are objectively true, like "cold," "dark," and "wet," but also words that are subjective, negative interpretations: "depressing," "bleak," and "miserable." The truth, of course, is that winter can be any of these things—it can be magical or depressing, fun or miserable. But when the very thought of winter conjures only pessimism, this isn't just reflecting what winter can be like: it increases the chance that our winter *will* be gloomy. Thanks to confirmation bias—our tendency to look for and process information that supports our beliefs and mindsets—these expectations make us more likely to notice and engage with either winter's delights or its hardships, which, day by day, shapes our actual experience of winter. When we expect winter misery, every shiver, soggy commute, or gray morning leaps out at us, confirming our fears and etching our mindsets more deeply. But when we expect winter wonder, our attention and behavior reorient accordingly. The cold becomes a reminder that it's time to make soup, our commutes become chances to observe the rain fall, and gray mornings become aesthetic backdrops for coffee drinking.

When we adopt the mindset that "winter is wonderful" or "winter is full of opportunity," contemplating the arrival of winter changes. We no longer focus on the things we can't do. Instead, we imagine winter's pleasures: our favorite sweaters, steaming mugs of tea, crisp morning walks. And even as our mindsets influence our expectations, our expectations can shape our mindsets. Focusing on what we look forward to can strengthen the mindset that winter will be fun. We can cultivate positive wintertime mindsets by targeting our expectations about the season: welcoming winter deliberately, preparing for the season proactively, and imagining what delights lie ahead. The act of looking forward can change winter before it starts.

SAVORING THE END OF DAYLIGHT SAVING

While the first day of winter is officially December 21 or 22, the date of the winter solstice (that's in the Northern Hemisphere;

it's June 20 or 21 in the Southern Hemisphere), we can choose to mark the beginning of winter at other times. For some, it might be when the first snow falls. For many in the US, it might be the day after Thanksgiving, when Christmas preparations begin, lights are strung, and trees are decorated. My personal marker for the start of winter is the shortening of days, which happens most dramatically when we end daylight saving time.

The end of daylight saving time—in late October or early November—is an abrupt shift: from one day to the next, the day is blunted. The change is usually met with initial relief at getting an extra hour of sleep, and then a lot of grumpiness the following week, punctuated by remarks of "It gets dark out so early now" and "It's only six thirty!? It feels like nine p.m.!"

One of the biggest problems with the end of daylight saving time is how, like so much of winter, it sneaks up on us. Now that our phones update the time automatically, it's even possible to sleep through the shift without realizing: while writing this book, I visited a local coffee shop the morning after the clock change. When I asked the barista if she enjoyed her extra hour of sleep, she replied, "Oh, is that why my cat woke up early this morning?" Our schedules don't accommodate the change in daylight: we don't end work or school earlier or adjust our routines. It's registered as almost a nonevent, and rarely planned for in advance. There are no cultural celebrations or rituals centered around the end of daylight saving time. As a result, we are blindsided by the darkness, shocked at how tired we feel, frustrated that the world around us has shifted suddenly and unnaturally.

But rather than responding passively, we can set our expectations around this harbinger of winter by preparing for the time change. We can actively anticipate, and even welcome, the end of daylight saving time.

THE FIRST STEP is to acknowledge and anticipate the transition. The same way we plan ahead and schedule time for holiday meal prep or prepare mentally and physically for the start of school or summer camp, we must look ahead to see when daylight saving time ends. Mark it on the calendar in advance, so it becomes part of the rhythm of fall. This can also alter our emotions around the shift: we anticipate and prepare for things we love—birthdays, holiday celebrations, vacations. By registering the onset of winter as a real event, we elevate it in our hearts and minds.

This practice is also a chance to bring nuance into our expectations. Not only can our expectations be overly negative, focusing our attention on the worst parts of winter, they can also fail by not being properly calibrated. If our expectations aren't at least somewhat aligned with reality, they can't help us anticipate the future. Expecting that winter will be wonderful doesn't mean deluding ourselves into thinking it will be warm, or that the sun won't set until eight p.m. Trying to adopt positive expectations like "The time change won't affect me" or "I will feel energized when it gets dark out early!" will not be useful unless they are true. Expectations, like mindsets, are not all-powerful, and can't will something into existence that isn't there. When talking about the power of mindsets versus objective circumstances, Ali Crum says: "It's always both. The total effect of a thing is the *combined* effect of the objective properties of that thing *and* your mindset about it." In other words: the reality of what we're facing affects us, and is not always beneficial or pleasant. But our mindset also plays a role—one that we frequently overlook.

We almost always account for the objective properties of something: how a medication will relieve our headache, how the darkness might make us tired. But we often underestimate the impact of mindset: the effectiveness of a pain reliever is influenced not only by the active ingredients of the medicine and the severity of the pain but also our expectations of relief. The increased darkness may, objectively, affect our energy. But so will our mindsets about it. Both expectations and mindsets orient us to a slice of what is true, thereby amplifying that truth. They can bias us either toward opportunities for early bedtime and showers by candlelight or toward evening lethargy and a lack of interest in heading out after dark.

We have to acknowledge that the end of daylight saving time might have consequences. It's unreasonable to think that a sudden one-hour change in daylight won't affect us physically or emotionally; at the very least, this abrupt shift disrupts our circadian rhythms, messing with our sleep schedules in a way similar to jet lag. Light also helps us feel alert and improves cognition, which boosts our mood, so losing an hour of afternoon luminosity can have a mild depressant effect, especially when we're not prepared for it. We may have less energy in the week after the clock change, have our routines disrupted, and feel less like socializing or being active. It may take us time to adjust. The goal is to reconcile the possible unpleasant effects of the time change with the desire to anticipate winter with hopeful enthusiasm. We can expect that the week post-clock-change will be a transition week: an in-between period bringing us from one season to another. It's fair to cut ourselves some slack—it's not a week to be operating at the highest level. Allow yourself this time to ease into a new rhythm and give yourself space to adjust.*

TO FACILITATE THIS TRANSITION, and to give myself something comforting to look forward to, I plan in advance for a lighter week after the end of daylight saving time, scaling back on unnecessary meetings and appointments. I know that I'll feel more tired, so I try not to overload myself. Not all of us are able to adjust our schedules significantly, but if you can reduce meetings or after-work commitments to enable more flexibility to listen to your physical and emotional needs during this time, it can feel wonderful. If you have kids, it can be especially helpful to lighten their schedules this week: the change in daylight can make sleep schedules wonky and throw things out of whack for them too.

Anticipating this transition gives us room to adjust with intention. It is an opportunity to practice living with nature rather than fighting it. Many people bemoan the change in daylight, complaining about feeling tired. Rather than seeing this as a problem, it can be a week to catch up on rest. If you're sleepy, you can have a cozy night in or allow yourself to go to bed earlier. If you go to bed earlier and still wake up at your normal time—great, you got more sleep than usual, and your body must have needed it! If you go to bed and wake up earlier than usual, then you're adjusting to the sun's new schedule and you have more time for your morning.

For some people—especially those with kids, working long

---

*The beginning of daylight saving time, in the spring, can also be a transition week, but people usually have an easier time adjusting to more evening daylight than to more evening darkness. However, planning ahead for the loss of an hour of sleep can be helpful.

hours, or with other caregiving responsibilities—getting more sleep can be easier said than done. (While this is true for many, it is painful to live in a world where a few extra hours of sleep is viewed as a luxury only for the privileged.) But making a little extra space for rest during this transition—whether sleeping more or simply slowing down a bit—can sustain us so that we can keep doing the things we need and love to do. Attending a restorative yoga class, taking a long bath, cooking a comforting meal, or rewatching a favorite movie are all low-stimulation ways to replenish ourselves this week.

We can also reframe the feeling of "It's only six o'clock!?" as a gift: How often do you realize that it's earlier than you thought, and the night is still young? I relish the clock change when I can think it's nine p.m., realize it's only seven, and have time ahead for leisure or productivity and still get to bed early. The feeling of more evening time is a bounty of the clock change, and seeing this as a boon, rather than a punishment, changes the experience entirely.

Many people dislike the early darkness that follows the end of daylight saving time. To counteract this, we can give our-selves things to look forward to. In advance of the time change, try readying supplies for a sunset ritual to mark the end of the day: enjoying a cup of coffee or a pot of tea, lighting candles, or putting on fuzzy socks. Those of us commuting as it gets dark can enjoy the sunset colors on our way home from work or can take a sunset or early dusk walk after the workday ends. We can enjoy the darkness: movie nights can begin at six p.m., dinner can be by candlelight, evening workouts and showers can use soft lighting, these activities made cozy by the lack of sun. If we clear our schedules of unnecessary obligations during the transition week, it makes room for special activities. For those needing downtime, plan a special night at home: a new video game or book, favorite takeout, or family slumber party in the living room. For those who need to socialize to energize, meet friends for dinner or have people over for game night. The key is to make it special: whether by yourself or with family or friends, make it a real plan and give yourself something to anticipate. Call it your daylight saving time activity or your darkness celebration. When done successfully, you may even find yourself counting down the days to the shift in daylight. And making the end of daylight saving time fun is a practice in deliberately and playfully meeting oncoming challenges. Acknowledging and preparing for an approaching change gives us the chance to make it our own.

THE END OF DAYLIGHT saving time is a practice run for the season. Those first two weeks after the time shift are a microcosm of winter: as we're plunged into darkness, we're forced to confront our thoughts and feelings about winter—good or bad. How you respond to the clock change can set the tone for the following months. By anticipating it, making space for the transition, and finding ways to make the shorter days feel special, we can make the shift easier and more fun and also start to see—in a small but meaningful way—how possible it is to transform our experience of winter darkness, putting us on a path to enjoying the season to come.

PREPARING FOR WINTER

Growing up, I loved back-to-school season. The excitement of a new year brought with it the actions that prepared me: getting the school lists and doing back-to-school shopping, picking out brand-new pens, pencils, and fresh, blank notebooks that represented a chance to start again. Asking older students about my teachers; hunting through my closet for the perfect first-day outfit. And it all began not on the first day of school, but in the weeks leading up to it, when anticipation thrummed through me.

We can expect winter not just mentally, but physically as well: by engaging in pre-winter rituals that prepare us for the season, we start daydreaming about winter. In Tromsø and other places with extreme winters, active anticipation is a necessity. People switch out summer and winter wardrobes in autumn, pulling out sweaters and jackets and reflective vests that have been stored away while the summer sun shone, and packing up T-shirts, shorts, and dresses. Candles are purchased or brought out of storage to provide light and ambiance on winter evenings. String lights are hung to add soft radiance to the darkness.

Ashley Bredemus spends the lead-up to winter preparing her cabin for the cold. Two years before the world heard of COVID-19, Bredemus quit her engineering job and moved from sunny, swampy Florida back to her home state of Minnesota, land of 10,000 lakes. But she didn't move back to Grand Rapids, where she grew up. Instead, she moved into the Pepper Shack— a one-room cabin built by her parents and grandparents in the early 1980s. The Pepper Shack sits on land where Bredemus, her father, and her husband run Birchwood Wilderness Camp, a summer camp for boys, bordering Minnesota's Boundary Waters Canoe Area. Before Bredemus, the Pepper Shack was a camp director's cabin, where muscular and messy twenty-year-old men spent the summer. Until she moved in, no one had ever overwintered there before.

The Pepper Shack has electricity but is primarily heated by a wood-burning stove. And even though Bredemus enjoys summers spent helping campers make magic memories and swimming in the lake, she loves the prelude to winter the most. "Between the fall equinox and winter solstice is my favorite time of year," she told me. For Bredemus, it starts with the chopping and gathering of firewood: the physical manifestation of preparing to turn inward. "Gathering firewood, there's something so peaceful about it. You're moving your body, so that conscious, chattering mind has something to focus on. And you are methodically putting away this firewood that's going to keep you warm all winter." As Bredemus and her husband engage in physical preparation for winter, their minds get the call to slow down.

IF YOU LIVE IN A HOME heated by a wood-burning stove, in a place that experiences the Polar Night, or where roads can be blocked by snow for months, you have no choice but to physically prepare for winter. The extremity of these conditions forces planning and groundwork; your survival may depend on it. But those of us who live through more moderate winters, surrounded by modern conveniences, are not required to spend as much time preparing for winter, mentally or physically. It becomes easy to slip into the season mindlessly, only to be frustrated and disappointed when our routines fall apart, our energy dips, or our mood takes a tumble.

But we can use physical preparation to help us expect seasonal change wherever we live. Small acts prepare us for winter in mind as well as body.

One widely practiced pre-winter ritual involves putting up seasonal home decor. In my home growing up, we marked shifts in seasons with the changing of the tchotchkes: at the first whisper of fall, my mom (an elementary school teacher for forty years, which might have something to do with this) would swap out Fourth of July and beach-themed hand towels in the bathroom and red, white, and blue M&M's in the candy jar for pumpkins, pine cones, and candy corn, which eventually gave way to her outrageous snowman collection, which goes up in December and stays up through March (one time my brother and I counted more than sixty snowmen around the house).

How else can you deliberately prepare for winter? Pull your sweaters, coats, hats, and scarves to the front of the closet, and move thick socks and flannel pajamas to the top drawer. Eagerly await the first day that the temperature drops and make a favorite soup to enjoy with family and friends. Restock your tea and coffee supplies to prepare for hot-beverage season. Switch your bedding to the warmer duvet or add extra blankets at the first sign of frost. Swap light, gauzy summer curtains for thicker, heavier ones that insulate and keep your house warm. Put out candles when daylight saving time ends. Rather than waiting for the season to sneak up on us, proactively preparing for winter can help us align with the changing seasons while ensuring that the items we need to be comfortable—blankets and coats and winter sweaters—are accessible. As we use our feet, hands, and actions to prepare our nests for winter, our minds are given time to wander toward the season, readying us for its arrival.

SETTING OUR EXPECTATIONS FOR WINTER, embracing the end of daylight saving time, and preparing with our actions give us the chance, every year, to be pragmatically eager and to use our foresight to make winter more comfortable. In doing so, it helps us hone the skill of deliberately harnessing our expectations, grounding them in reality but with an eye toward hope and joy; it helps us recognize when and how a bit of foresight and preparation can transform the mundane or miserable into the manageable and magical. It can alleviate underappreciated sources of winter agony: dreading the season before it even begins, and bemoaning inevitable seasonal changes as they arrive. It's also a low-stakes chance to practice meeting transitions head-on. Ritualizing periods of change, wringing joy from the passage of time, and actively embracing shifts in external circumstances outside of our control are practices that can aid us during some of life's most poignant and bittersweet moments. Like winter's darkness, we will all face unwanted changes—or wanted changes that still hurt—at some point. Learning to meet these changes is learning to accept both the rhythms of the year and the rhythms of our lives. Preparing for what lies ahead while pinpointing opportunities for delight, comfort, and fun is a skill that will serve us in winter and beyond.

WINTER PRACTICE:
LOOKING AHEAD

· **Set positive winter expectations:** As fall wanes, make a list of five specific things you're looking forward to about winter, big or small. This can be a written list, a vision board, or a collection of saved social media content. The most important thing is taking time to think about what you enjoy that winter will bring.

· **Plan a daylight saving time celebration:** Mark the day of the clock change in your calendar and schedule a special event: the first candlelit dinner of the season, a movie night, a new book or video game. Whatever you do—on your own or with family or friends—make it in honor of the early darkness.

· **Prepare your nest:** When the clocks change, choose at least one physical action to help ready your home for winter. Restock your hot cocoa, coffee, and tea; pull your sweaters to the front of the closet; move your warm socks to the top drawer; switch your bedding for warmer covers; if you have a fireplace, get wood for the season; put up twinkly lights and set up spots for candles. Prepare now to facilitate winter comfort later.

2.

LEANING IN,
LYING DOWN

F OR TEN DAYS, my husband Rob and I bounced between Ha-
nukkah parties on Long Island, log-cabin Christmas in New
Jersey, and a New Year's Eve rager outside Philadelphia, com-
pleting what we have affectionately dubbed the "diplomacy
tour," in which we spend our brief stints on the East Coast visit-
ing every relative living in the New York tri-state area. In be-
tween, we were trying to fit three months' worth of bulky layers
into our carry-on suitcases to embark on a global tour of winter
wonder. I'd be researching cultural approaches and strategies
for embracing the season, interviewing winter experts, and
writing. Rob would come along for adventure, insight, and to
make sure I got enough sleep in between drafting sprints and
research excursions.

As usual, Rob's snooze protection proved invaluable. After
concluding the diplomacy tour, we began our travels in Copen-
hagen, the birthplace of *hygge* and international winter coziness
capital, and I arrived utterly exhausted. The crush of moving

around, the loving insanity of the holidays, and the stress of getting ready for our trip took everything out of me. On top of my serious case of jet lag, I lost two and a half hours of daylight; in New York the sun rose at seven a.m. and set around five p.m.; in Copenhagen it rose after eight thirty and set before four. Even in the brightest of times, I am a clinically sleepy person. But the jet lag, darkness, and post-holiday exhaustion trifecta imbued me with a deep weariness. I spent several days in a bed piled high with blankets, wedged into the corner of a very pink Airbnb bedroom, barely able to open my eyes. I wasn't just sleeping at odd hours; I was sleeping *so much*. A twelve-hour night felt like a catnap, and with very little effort I could sleep for fourteen hours. Even after my jet lag passed and I resumed a semi-normal schedule, the pallid drizzle of Copenhagen made it hard to shake my fatigue. I explored the city's candlelit cafés, visited the Danish design museum, and strolled around the candy-colored harbor, but spent many hours a day abed.

After eight nights in Copenhagen, Rob and I returned to Tromsø in mid-January, eight years after I originally lived there. We went from Copenhagen's short, gray days to Tromsø's full Polar Night. It was the time of year when, in Tromsø, the sun never rises, but you can feel her lingering. On clear days, the sky was alight with sunrise and sunset colors between ten a.m. and two thirty p.m.; the bracketing hours of this diffuse light were deeply blue. Yet it was true nighttime for about sixteen hours a day. I reveled in the peaceful darkness and blue time of the Polar Night, but I was *just so sleepy*. I would take a long afternoon nap only to get in bed a few hours later. I abandoned my routine of carefully modulating caffeine intake, drinking multiple cups far past the time that would usually trigger insomnia. In Tromsø, the darkness and the caffeine seemed to negate each other; I had no problems falling asleep.* Coffee helped especially when I sat down in the afternoons to write and felt my eyelids hang heavy.

Rob's role as snooze protector developed, in part, because I've spent my entire life ashamed of my need for sleep. Only in my early thirties was I diagnosed with "delayed sleep-wake phase disorder," a circadian rhythm disorder that means I live perpetually in a jet-lag-like state, where my natural tiredness kicks in only very late at night and my natural wake time is in the late morning or early afternoon. In addition to this sleep-phase disorder I was also told I had hypersomnia, which is characterized by excessive daytime sleepiness. In a culture that equates forgoing sleep with dedication and moralizes being a morning person, my profound need to snooze has, at times, made me feel lazy, weak, and broken.

Rob's efforts to help me rest without guilt were aided by Copenhagen and Tromsø, which provided logical excuses for my tiredness. I was jet-lagged. The days were short. It was so *dark*. My need for sleep no longer reflected something deformed about me—anyone would be tired in that situation! And so my sleep-shame sloughed off me. I was able, at least temporarily, to accept my tiredness. I gave myself permission to adjust to the Arctic darkness.

In losing my self-judgment of my sleep patterns, the tiredness took on an almost pleasant quality. In not fighting it, I could listen to my body with kindness and respond more adaptively.

---

*The average Norwegian has four to five cups of coffee a day. In fact, all the top coffee consumers in the world seem to be in dark, wintery places: the top ten, per capita, are Finland, Norway, Iceland, Denmark, the Netherlands, Sweden, Switzerland, Belgium, Luxembourg, and Canada. These also include some of the happiest countries in the world—coincidence?

Rather than thinking about how much more I could get done if only I didn't need so much sleep, I went to bed early so that I could wake in morning darkness to be up during the brightest part of the day. I was happy while awake, active in the Arctic air and enjoying the little light we got, and content and ready for bed after several hours of darkness each evening.

The darkness of winter in Tromsø and Copenhagen gave me the chance to embrace rest, helping me reframe my normal sleepiness as a natural response to the external world.

Winter's darkness can make you more tired. Emerging research suggests that we might need more sleep in winter: one study found that REM sleep—which is essential for learning and memory consolidation and emotion regulation—tended to be about thirty minutes longer in winter than in summer.* But this is not inherently problematic. The trouble arises when we fight the effects of winter or, worse, pathologize a natural response to the season. When we start to see normal fluctuations of energy as a sign that we're depressed, or that we struggle in the winter, we're taking an ambiguous symptom—winter tiredness—and coming to an unhelpful conclusion—that there's something wrong with us or the season. We can cultivate a more useful winter mindset by recognizing that seasonal change is both adaptive and essential, and leaning into winter as a time for rest.

---

*This study was conducted in patients with sleep disorders—a good first test because these patients are already having their sleep tracked. While this research needs to be replicated with healthy subjects, it's also possible that the seasonal changes could be even greater in people who don't have sleep disorders, since over one third of the patients in this study suffered from insomnia.

SAD OR JUST SEASONAL?

Part of our resistance to seasonal behavior change likely comes from warnings about seasonal affective disorder. Every September, my inbox pings incessantly with requests from journalists about the topic; there are hundreds of articles written each autumn about the looming risk. It's made its way into the common vernacular and pop culture.* There's even a *Seasonal Affective Disorder for Dummies* book ("An accessible approach to stopping SAD thoughts and looking at the brighter side of life")! Estimates vary, but research generally suggests that in the US, somewhere between 0.5 percent and 3 percent of people suffer from the disorder. Yet despite being relatively uncommon, seasonal affective disorder seems to have an outsized effect on our culture and dominates our narratives about winter.

SEASONAL AFFECTIVE DISORDER was first described in the US in the early 1980s by psychologist Norman Rosenthal. It's defined as a subtype of clinical depression: one that usually appears as the days get shorter and then remits each spring when the temperature warms and the sun returns. (It's possible to have summertime seasonal affective disorder, but it's much less common.) Modern best practice dictates that, to receive a clinical diagnosis, a person must *first* meet the threshold for clinical depression. Only then can we look for the seasonal pattern that indicates seasonal affective disorder.

---

*My favorite is a reference to it on *30 Rock*, in which Tina Fey's character asks, "Oh, is that where the word 'sad' comes from?" and Alec Baldwin's character replies, "What? You think 'sad' is an acronym invented by psychologists?"

The *DSM-5*, or *The Diagnostic and Statistical Manual of Mental Disorders* 5th edition, is the gold standard for diagnosing mental health disorders. In the DSM-5, to be diagnosed with major depression, patients must have *at least five* of the following symptoms *nearly every day for two weeks*:

- depressed mood or feeling sad
- loss of interest and pleasure in usual activities
- significant weight loss or gain
- significant increase or decrease in sleeping
- observable speeding up or slowing down of speech or movement
- fatigue
- feeling excessively worthless or guilty
- decreased concentration
- suicidal thoughts

In addition, these symptoms cannot be explained by substance abuse or other life circumstances, such as a recent breakup, loss of a job, or death of a loved one. Finally, and perhaps most importantly, these symptoms must cause "clinically significant distress or impairment in social, occupational, or other important areas of functioning." In other words: these symptoms must disrupt your daily quality of life. (If this feels like you, or if you feel like you have many of these symptoms and they are impairing your life, that's a sign to seek professional guidance.)

Looking at the list above, it's clear that feeling more tired, more cranky, and less sociable in the winter are not enough to warrant a diagnosis of seasonal affective disorder. The vast majority of people who self-diagnose winter depression likely have a far milder version of the "winter blues." Unless someone can't get out of bed for days at a time, is unable to take care of basic needs like feeding themselves or showering, is ignoring deadlines and missing work, or can't meet other responsibilities like childcare, it is unlikely that they have clinical winter depression.

But seasonal affective disorder has taken on a disproportionate role in our collective culture, making true winter depression seem more common than it actually is. Well-meaning efforts to help people suffering from clinical seasonal depression have had the spillover effect of pathologizing behavior change in response to winter—even as these behaviors might be reasonable and warranted.

The pathologization of changing sleep, eating, and socializing habits in winter is inextricably linked to the initial discovery, description, and diagnosis of seasonal affective disorder. The original diagnostic tool, developed by the psychiatrists and researchers who first described winter depression, is the SPAQ: the Seasonal Pattern Assessment Questionnaire. The tool has largely fallen out of favor: Kelly Rohan told me that the most clinically rigorous strategy is to focus first on "full blown major depressive episode criteria with all the associated impairment." However, the SPAQ is still highlighted in the official manual for seasonal affective disorder and defined our understanding of the disorder and its prevalence. The scale asks people how much their sleep length, social activity, mood, weight, appetite, and energy level change with the seasons. It also asks during what months of the year people feel best, gain and lose the most weight, and eat, socialize, and sleep the most and least. These questions are designed to measure a person's "seasonality," or how much their behavior shifts seasonally.

When it comes to mental health, anything extreme can be considered problematic: major, rapid fluctuations in behavior *can* be signs of a mental illness episode, but are not always. Yet the very nature of the SPAQ items suggest that there's something wrong with too much seasonality; if you significantly shift your eating habits, how much you socialize, and how much you sleep in the winter, the SPAQ highlights this as problematic. But the measure contains no assessment of what the seasons are like where respondents live. If someone lives in a place with tremendous variation between seasons, couldn't even major seasonality be an appropriate response to the environment? If the day length shifts by six hours (as in Chicago, Denver, Boston, Buenos Aires, Beijing, and Madrid),* what's more reasonable: adjusting behavior with the seasons, or expecting people to have the same sleeping, eating, working, and socializing patterns year-round?

LOOKING AT EXTREME PLACES can provide insight for the rest of the world. Like other towns in the high north, Tromsø experiences major seasonal variation: residents go from two months without direct sunlight in the winter to two months of twenty-four-hour sunlight in the summer. Would it really be reasonable to suggest that this change shouldn't affect people? In Tromsø, it's considered normal to sleep more and socialize less in winter. In the summer, you're likely to be more active and social and sleep less. Rather than being seen as problematic, this is viewed

---

*If you live farther north than these Northern Hemisphere cities, or farther south than these Southern Hemisphere cities, the summer-to-winter change in daylight is even larger.

as living in tune with nature.* When I speak with her, Rohan confirms my observation that winter changes can be adaptive. She says that if you have these seasonal changes, "it doesn't mean that they're impairing, or that they're a problem. In fact, maybe embracing them could be a really healthy response."

By classifying a wide range of seasonal behavior change as winter depression, seasonal affective disorder may have historically appeared more widespread than was warranted. Current scientific thinking includes significant skepticism of the disorder, with some researchers going so far as to state that it is not a meaningful subtype of depression. Outside of the US, research in places like Norway, Iceland, and the Netherlands—all with longer and darker winters than most of the US—has been calling the ubiquity of winter depression into question for decades, suggesting that it may be more of an American than a global phenomenon and highlighting how increased winter darkness doesn't necessarily lead to an increase in mental illness.

Research in Tromsø has found no evidence of a wintertime increase in depression and low mental distress in the season overall. A study of more than five thousand Dutch residents found no evidence of higher depression or lower mood in the winter; this study found that only highly neurotic participants demonstrated any effect of seasons on mood, and even then only found that these participants had a slight mood boost in

---

*In *Winter Blues*, Norman Rosenthal's comprehensive guide to seasonal affective disorder, he writes this about Tromso: "Inhabitants of northern Norway talked a lot about their sunless 2 months every year but insisted the lack of light didn't bother them," and then makes a logical leap to write: "Perhaps the stoicism of the North prevents many of these people from acknowledging their difficulties." My take? Maybe they just have a different relationship with seasonality, darkness, and winter itself.

spring, with no differences found between summer, autumn, and winter. This is despite the Netherlands' long, gray, wet winters. (Amsterdam is located farther north than Calgary, Canada.) Another study found that rates of seasonal affective disorder were lower in Iceland than on the East Coast of the United States—a surprising result given that Iceland's winters are considerably darker, lengthier, and harsher than anywhere in the northeastern US. This doesn't mean that winter is without challenges, or doesn't affect people's moods or energy. But, particularly in places with intense winters, seasonal adaptation may be necessary and helpful, not a sign of mental illness. If these populations had been measured with the SPAQ, rates of seasonal affective disorder may have appeared high. But using the more rigorous DSM criteria—including significant distress in response to symptoms—allows people to demonstrate seasonality without a diagnosis of winter depression. Studies that use this more precise screening method usually find lower rates of seasonal depression or no evidence of winter depression at all.

Recent large-sample studies in the US indicate that even American statistics on winter depression may be inflated. If seasonal affective disorder is a common subtype of depression, we would expect to see seasonal variation when looking at large samples of people who suffer from major depressive disorder. Yet two studies of American populations—one with more than 1,700 respondents with significant depression and one with almost 5,500 respondents with mild depression—found no significant effect of season, latitude, or daylight on either mild or major depression. And Rohan herself has been a coauthor on a study that found no overall seasonal effect on depression in children and adolescents, although she told *The New York Times* that this doesn't mean that seasonal affective disorder doesn't exist, just that it can be difficult to see the small subset of seasonal patterns amidst larger depression data.

EVEN AS EVIDENCE ACCUMULATES that winter might not cause depression as much as we think, the popular story remains strong: winter makes people depressed. Seasonal affective disorder has emerged as the dominant—and perhaps only—framework for understanding the psychology of winter. And so when people feel more tired or less social in the winter, they have a top-of-mind explanation for their grumpies. Because many of us have the very real lived experience that winter *does* affect us: if you feel like you have the winter blues, or like the season's darkness impacts you, you're not alone, and these effects *are* real. But the *meaning* of these effects remains open to interpretation. Is sleeping more in the winter a sign of depression or seasonal adaptation? Is wanting to stay home, snug in our burrows, problematic or normal? Is craving rich, warming foods cause for concern, or healthy? Mindsets help us make sense of ambiguity. If, when faced with uncertainty about the meaning of our seasonal mood and energy changes, the only existing cultural narrative about winter is that it is depressing, your experience may be filtered through that lens. But, armed with another way of looking at the season, a different interpretation can emerge.

Beliefs about winter matter: the stories we tell ourselves are consequential, and the interpretation of how we feel in the winter can determine whether dark days feel gloomy and monotonous or cozy and restful. Rethinking our approach to the season can be useful for both those who have mild winter blues and those who struggle with clinical winter depression. We need a new way of interpreting and understanding winter's effects on us, and a new way of responding adaptively.

A TIME TO REST

Here is an ambiguous situation ripe for influence from our mindsets: What does it mean if we feel more tired when it gets dark early? What does it mean if winter is affecting us? If we hold the mindset—consciously or otherwise—that "winter is dreadful," then winter's impact is interpreted through this lens. It must be a bad thing if we feel sleepier in winter. There must be something wrong with us if the onset of winter influences our mood, energy, or appetite.

This underlying, usually unhelpful, mindset often results in a reluctance to adapt to winter. If winter is dreadful, and its effects unwelcome, why would we try to work with the season? Better, perhaps, to soldier on and power through as usual.

Rather than adjust, we deceive ourselves into believing that we control the seasons with our schedules and plans; if only we find the right routine or muster enough willpower, we can master the darkness. We pretend we are not animals like any other, as if aligning with nature is a personal or moral failure. But this is a fallacy, and when we look at it plainly, we can see how nonsensical this view is.

Almost every other living thing—plant or animal—changes its behavior in winter. Leaves drop, flowers die, the earth hardens. Some animals migrate, others spend the entire summer making an acorn pantry or stuffing their faces and bulking up for a big snooze. The animals that sleep for months opt out of winter entirely; in the slumber of hibernation, animals toe the line between life and death. Others go in and out of torpor, a hibernation-like state associated with decreased heart rate and metabolism, which allows animals to exist in a near-coma for hours, days, or weeks at a time. (If you see a frog that looks like it's frozen to death in the winter, it might just be in torpor.) Some animals grow new coats to keep themselves warm or blend in with the landscape, and others huddle together in nests and hovels to keep out the chill. Researchers have found that the inner parts of reindeers' eyes morph* between seasons to allow them to see better during the sunless blue and gray months in the Arctic. All these animals are adapting their behavior in some way. All are living in a yearly rhythm, where energy and recreation ebb and flow.

Next to the obvious gains of spring's sowing, summer's growing, and fall's reaping, winter's critical function is less visible. For plants, what looks like an off-season is a vitally important time. The freeze cycles improve soil and kill pests and diseases, resetting the environment for spring. In places with four distinct seasons, many native plants evolved to need winter: in a process called vernalization, some plants require hundreds of hours of cold temperatures to germinate successfully in springtime. Apples need among the most "chill hours" to grow properly when the weather warms, but apricots, peaches, nut trees, and berry bushes all require prolonged cold to bloom.

---

*In summer, the tapetum lucidum of their eyes is gold, which is optimized for taking in all the colors of the midnight sun period. In winter, this part of the eye changes to blue, making their eyes more sensitive to the shades of blue that dominate during the Polar Night.

Bulbs like tulips, daffodils, and hyacinths also need months of cold dormancy to grow and flower. This chill cycle is not only critical, it is in danger: warming temperatures and more unpredictable winters are threatening plants that rely on vernalization. In the 2022 to 2023 season, a too-warm winter caused peaches in the state of Georgia to develop early, which made them vulnerable when temperatures later dropped below freezing, destroying an estimated 90 percent of the crop, which, the year before, was worth $34 million. This winter warmth was so catastrophic that US federal officials designated much of rural Georgia as a natural disaster area.

Snow is one of nature's best insulators: it covers the ground and shields the soil, keeping it moist and protecting plant roots and bulbs from freezing or drying out during the most frigid times of the year. A few weeks after my return to Tromsø, I visited Japan, where I harvested special radishes from beneath snowdrifts, digging them out by hand. "The radishes grown under the snow are sweeter than those grown under the summer sun," I was told. The blanket of snow encases them, and the longer growing time packs them with nutrients while allowing sugars to develop. These prized vegetables are shipped from snow-filled regions to Tokyo as a delicacy. Overlooking winter's contributions to life in other seasons is to overlook the foundation on which the rest of the year relies.

Looking at nonhuman life on Earth, it becomes apparent how foolish the notion is that we can enter and exit the winter without changing our sleep, diet, or social behavior. Instead, we can take our cues from nature and adopt our own seasonal rhythms. As Katherine May writes in her memoir, *Wintering*,

"Plants and animals don't fight the winter; they don't pretend it's not happening and attempt to carry on the same lives that they lived in the summer. They prepare. They adapt. They perform extraordinary acts of metamorphosis to get them through. But that's where the transformation occurs. Once we stop wishing it were summer, winter can be a glorious season in which the world takes on a sparse beauty and even the pavements sparkle. It's a time for reflection and recuperation, for slow replenishment, for putting your house in order." Like these plants and animals, we can appreciate this "glorious season" for being the time of year in which we get to do less.

PERHAPS ANOTHER REASON the narrative of seasonal affective disorder persists is that many modern cultures are more amenable to the idea of a personal problem—individual winter depression—than a societal one, in which current structures are recognized as incompatible with adaptive seasonal change. My ability to accept my sleepiness and rest more in Copenhagen and Tromsø was facilitated by my circumstances: as a writer and researcher, I made my own schedule, with the freedom to start later or end the day earlier. At that time, I had no childcare or other caregiving duties. My days were full: meetings and interviews, daily word-count goals, catch-ups with old friends. But I had the autonomy to sketch my days according to my needs and to accommodate extra sleep.

Many of our problems with winter are actually problems with a society and setup that don't allow for seasonal adaptation, and so much winter suffering is manufactured by expectations that are increasingly divorced from the rhythms of nature.

Our work may require us to spend every hour of winter daylight indoors, looking at screens, so that winter sun remains perpetually out of reach. Despite feeling naturally more tired when the days are shorter, school schedules remain the same, requiring many teenagers to wake in darkness. In my hometown, winter sunrises range from 6:32 to 7:19 a.m.; when I was in high school, my first class of the day started at 7:25.

We can begin to examine which of our personal seasonal problems are perhaps cultural, manufactured ones. Is the problem that you're more tired in the winter, or that school and work hours fail to shift according to the seasons? Is the problem that you can't get up in the morning, or that our institutions assume a sudden one-hour clock change has no effect on our bodies or sleep patterns? Is the problem that you're low energy, or that we're expected to have the same productivity and output regardless of what's going on in the world around us?

When our work schedules, school calendars, and responsibilities don't fluctuate with the seasons to make room for rest, we're fighting the natural world. We suffer from living in a culture that is out of sync with yearly rhythms of light and dark. We turn our ire toward winter, blaming the season for making us feel this way, rather than pointing fingers at a civilization organized with no regard for the changing light, at jobs without flexibility, at norms that mean we're raising children without the support needed to make it less relentless.

This is, naturally, worsened by living in a culture obsessed with productivity. In *How to Do Nothing*, Jenny Odell writes about the difference between "exponential growth" and "maintenance." Exponential growth is the idea that we should never stop moving forward, growing, and developing, while maintenance is required merely to preserve and sustain what already exists. Odell explains how maintenance is regularly overlooked and undervalued in many "developed" cultures. This is true not only on a societal level, as companies race to build self-driving cars while public transportation languishes, but also on an individual level: we value the new, the exciting, and the challenging over the constant, the steady, and the nourishing.

It is easy to mistake the fallowness of winter for wasted time and space. But this view obscures the necessity of winter for sustaining the whole cycle, dismissing how crucial dormant times are for the growth and beauty that comes later. It ignores the critical work being done under the surface. It pretends that we can all go nonstop, all the time, working and living and loving at full capacity, unceasingly. But we can't, and there is much to be gained by not trying, and by gifting ourselves a season to restore.

Some of these societal and structural forces are beyond our control: we can't change school schedules so that they start later in the winter; we can't convince our workplaces that they should give less work so we have more space to slow down. We can't ignore our caregiving responsibilities. But that doesn't mean we're completely without agency. Winter gives us a natural, yearly opportunity to pump the brakes. If we heed the darkness, we can look to the season as a chance to ease up wherever we can. We can examine what may be unnecessary, superfluous. We can say no to invitations and activities unless we really, really want to say yes.

We can take winter as a chance to value maintenance as much as we value growth, and to recognize the necessity of this kind of care. We can make this a season of slowness.

◆

ONE OF THE MOST INSPIRING proponents of rest is Tricia Hersey, the founder of an organization called The Nap Ministry. Hersey preaches the gospel of rest, and her book *Rest Is Resistance* details how "rest is about much more than naps." In her words, rest is a powerful tool for dismantling capitalism and white supremacy. This work is based on the historical legacy of the US, founded on slavery, in which her ancestors were never allowed to rest. That history has led to a system today that affords many people too few sick days, not enough vacation, and little opportunity for leisure. This has led to a culture of overwork, burnout, and normalized exhaustion, because there is always more money to be made, another side hustle to start, another hour to be productive, and the chance that falling behind could have disastrous consequences. For Hersey, resting is a way to push back against the unceasing demand to do more, where in particular, those with less—especially black and brown people who have historically been systemically excluded from opportunities—have to work longer hours for less pay to get by. In this context, in this culture, to rest is to resist these structures.

As the Nap Bishop, Hersey writes extensively about the guilt people often experience when they listen to their bodies and slow down. Her words resonated with my struggles and the mixed feelings I have when my need to rest conflicts with my instinct to *be* more by *doing* more. Rob and I call it "snooze guilt": the uniquely terrible feeling of shame brought on by sleeping away the morning or the afternoon. But reading and meditating on Hersey's words, coupled with Rob's snooze-positive support, makes me wonder why I internalized that listening to my body was lazy and wrong. Fighting our winter tiredness—or any tiredness—is to fight our fundamental human needs. I don't get mad at myself when I need to go to the bathroom, nor do I feel ashamed about needing oxygen. So why do I see it as a moral failing when I need sleep?

As Hersey writes, "You are worthy of rest. We don't have to earn rest. Rest is not a luxury, a privilege, or a bonus we must wait for once we are burned out." So often it feels like rest is the reward for ticking things off our to-do lists, but instead, rest is the foundation that makes everything else possible. I've learned this many times: there's no point pursuing my other goals if I'm exhausted and sleep deprived. Without enough rest, the whole system breaks down.

And research supports this view: one study found that viewing leisure as "wasteful" and "unproductive" undermines enjoyment of relaxing or fun activities, even as leisure itself has been shown to lower blood pressure, reduce risk of depression, and strengthen social relationships. Worse still, viewing this downtime as wasteful is associated with lower happiness, greater depression, and more stress and anxiety. This effect was strongest for leisure activities that are not in service of other goals (like exercising or meditating), but whose sole purpose is enjoyment (like relaxing, watching TV, or pursuing hobbies). It turns out snooze guilt might be bad for our health.

Hersey's view of rest is as expansive as it is urgent. She's clear that rest can be anything that fills us up with slowness and peace. Meditating, mindful bathing, drinking tea, connecting with loved ones, and listening to music can all be forms of rest. My favorite example that she gives is not responding to text messages or emails right away—a suggestion that is revolutionary in its simplicity, in how obvious it is once someone else says it aloud. This generous view of rest can be especially helpful for people with busy jobs, caretaking responsibilities, or small children, for whom the idea of a quiet, leisurely winter feels like a laughable dream. Where can you reframe small moments in your day as cup-filling snatches of rest? What restorative activities—besides sleep—can you seek out more of: short, slow walks that give kids time to explore closely, coloring alongside little ones, stretching in the morning, merely taking a few deep breaths?

Hersey emphasizes the need for rest year-round. At the same time, winter is a perfect season to explore what Hersey calls "crafting a rest practice." Can we hibernate not out of depression or avoidance, but intentionally, with winter as a container? It can be easier to go deep into rest practices when they are bounded by a season: winter allows us to experiment more boldly, protect our time more firmly, and rest more guiltlessly, because we know there will be another season to pick up again all that we've put down.

LEARNING TO ACTIVELY resist all that is telling us that we shouldn't rest is a skill we can practice, a muscle we can build. There will be other seasons of life where we must give ourselves permission to retreat: seasons of illness, of caregiving, of grief, of exhaustion. Times we need to slow down and recover: from burnout, childbirth, surgery, loss, or change. Seasons that call for maintenance rather than growth. Paradoxically, learning to rest in this way is a kind of growth, a new achievement to unlock, but one that is worthwhile in and of itself. The freedom of guiltless rest, of understanding rest's foundational importance, will be something for us to fall back on in dark, fallow seasons for years to come.

SLOW HOBBIES

To embrace winter's slowness requires appreciating how clearing away unnecessary tasks and commitments makes space for what gets crowded out in other seasons. Alongside the literal rest of sleeping more, winter is a time for cultivating other rest practices described by Hersey. As we retreat into our winter selves, it is the perfect chance to find nourishment in small comforts, creative pursuits, and quiet delights.

This is a gift of winter's darkness, which asks us to fill our days with indoor diversions. It is a time of year especially for unhurried crafts, for pastimes that rejuvenate by letting our mind wander. When I think of the opportunities afforded by long nights, I think of Becky making sourdough: the time required for the starter to double, the hours necessary for the dough to rise, the precise turning and folding and flattening and baking that alchemizes yeast and flour and water into what my grandmother biblically called the staff of life. "Without rest," Becky says, "the dough cannot rise." I think of myself in the pottery studio with clay at the wheel, cautiously centering and pulling and turning, and the times I rushed and pressed too hard, applied pressure unevenly, nicked the side with my nail, deformed my bowl in my haste. I think of my dad, a meticulous woodworker, who claims he is no more skilled than any other, only more patient: his purpleheart-and-rock-maple cutting boards are smooth and silky, perfectly joined, the place where one wood meets another undetectable after hours of sanding.

The Scandinavians, especially, love to knit. When I visited Finland, my host, Kaisa, talked about how she takes her knitting out when it gets dark in the fall, knits in the evenings all winter long, and then promptly puts her supplies away each spring as she returns to outdoor activities in the longer daylight. Over the past ten years, I've given workshops on embracing winter all over the world. In these talks, I ask audiences to come up with a list of the activities they enjoy in winter. So many of people's favorite winter activities invite presence and slowness: listening to music, reading, making cookies, baking bread, sitting by the fire, crafting, going to art classes, bingeing TV, reading the Sunday paper, puzzles, cuddling, tree pruning, sending holiday cards, sharing a big pot of soup with friends, having dinner parties, sauna, ice fishing, home decorating, making music, painting, yoga, Qi Gong, quilting, sewing, knitting, playing games, and "sitting on the porch swing with a blanket and hot toddy."

These hobbies are an antidote to cultures that reward urgency, where everything feels like an emergency. When we find arts that refuse to bend to our desire to hurry, we rehearse allowing things to be slow, practice patience, and remind ourselves to be present and enjoy the process. Refining our ability to revel in small comforts, to make our own joys during the long nights, empowers us to find micromoments of happiness in any season.

UPWARD SPIRALS

When do our mindsets matter most?

Jer Clifton thinks about this a lot. A researcher at the University of Pennsylvania and instructor in the university's Masters in Applied Positive Psychology, Clifton studies mindsets by another name, what he calls "primals": "extremely basic beliefs about the world as a whole." These are fundamental, and often deeply entrenched, mindsets: beliefs like "the world is good," "the world is beautiful," and "the world is safe" vs. "the world is bad," "the world is ugly," and "the world is dangerous."

In our conversation, Clifton highlighted two features of primals that align with research by Ali Crum and others about how mindsets work. The first is that they impact us most when we're around, or in, the object of our belief. Clifton explains it this way: "Your beliefs about the school that you go to should probably only impact what you do, how you feel, and how you behave when you're at the school or doing homework."

But, said Clifton, "if you had a belief about a place that you never leave, based on all that we know about beliefs, that should impact almost everything you do to some degree." According to this theory, our mindsets about winter impact nearly every action we take during the season because it's a situation that we're in all the time. Even if we're indoors, we're still "in" winter, with its associated darkness and cold.* And so our mindsets are always relevant.

Clifton continued, "Situations that you never leave are uniquely likely to impact you, *and* that impact is uniquely likely to go overlooked, because you're in it all the time." When you're in a situation—like winter—constantly, there's no break to provide a comparison or reference point. Our winter mindsets may have affected our relationship with the season for our entire lives, yet gone unnoticed: only when they are made explicit is their impact obvious.

---

*We may temporarily "escape" winter on warm-weather vacations, but short of moving to tropical climates year-round, we eventually return to winter.

◆

THE SECOND FEATURE of how primals and mindsets work is that they matter most in ambiguous situations. These "core beliefs," according to Clifton, "are used to fill in the gaps of your information, how you interpret things." When a situation is unclear, our mindsets leap into action to help us make sense of what we're experiencing: Is this stress I'm feeling helping me or harming me? Is this darkness depressing or cozy? Is my fatigue during exercise a sign I'm weak or that I'm getting stronger? Is the sleepiness I feel problematic, a sign of winter depression, or is it adaptive, a natural response to the changing seasons? When faced with uncertainty, our mindsets come online to help us make meaning. Because so much of life, and the world, is painted not in black and white, but in shades of gray, we fall back on our mindsets more often than we realize.

Our interpretations of ambiguous winter experiences, like sleepiness, can strengthen our beliefs about the season. If feeling tired is a chance to pursue rest or comfort or alone time, then winter becomes a season full of opportunities for slowness and restoration. If our fatigue is seen as a problematic barrier to well-being, it strengthens the view that winter is unproductive, unenjoyable, miserable. Maybe these beliefs lead to a further self-fulfilling spiral, one where, before winter even begins, we believe we will spend the season battling exhaustion. Then, not only do we still feel tired but we also feel down on ourselves for succumbing to weakness and down on winter for making us feel this way.

But if we view winter tiredness as seasonally adaptive and natural, we may accept, and make space for, sleeping more in the winter. As a result, we get more rest. Maybe we also pursue other rest practices, other ways of rejuvenating and restoring. Maybe this helps us enjoy winter more or look forward to the rest that winter brings. This belief leads to an upward spiral of acceptance and adaptation.

MINDSETS ARE NOT SIMPLY the "power of positive thinking." There *is* an aspect of cultivating a more adaptive wintertime mindset that involves finding the positives of winter and deliberately focusing on them (and in this book, I do sometimes refer to "positive wintertime mindsets"). But adopting useful mindsets is more than merely looking on the bright side. Looking on the bright side might be focusing on ideas like "Winter will be over soon" or "Winter makes spring and summer that much sweeter." Looking on the bright side might mean comparing winter where you live to somewhere you perceive as even worse: "At least I don't live where the sun doesn't rise!" This "positive thinking" may be comforting in the moment, but doesn't help us engage with winter differently. In fact, this kind of positive thinking reinforces negative mindsets about winter: looking ahead to other seasons and comparing our winter to worse both strengthen the belief that winter is dreadful. These perspectives provide no road map for how to make winter better, today, where you live.

Nor do these address genuine winter struggles: fatigue, decreased interest in socializing or going out, feeling grumpy. Trying to deny these realities or focus on unrelated positives doesn't channel effort into accepting them and doesn't provide clues of how to work with them.

But a more adaptive mindset directs our energy differently. When we hold the mindset that winter is full of opportunity, we look at our winter tiredness and ask: What is the opportunity here? The opportunity to rest more. We look at our decreased interest in socializing and even our winter crankiness and ask what opportunities they provide: perhaps a chance to enjoy more solo creative pursuits, to socialize more selectively and intentionally, to be gentle with ourselves and pursue soothing activities that soften our mood.

Cultivating your mindset about winter can provide insights for shifting your mindset in related, but no less important, domains. The shift in mindset about rest that I experienced thanks to winter helps me year-round: I'm working on releasing the mindset that "rest is unproductive" or "rest is lazy" and instead adopting the perspectives "rest is healthy" and "rest is vital." All of these *could* be true interpretations: certainly sometimes I am resting when it would better serve me to be working. But using winter as an entry point, I'm able to better experiment with Hersey's framework of "rest as resistance." This view imbues the rest with profundity; rest becomes not only inherently valuable, but something that allows Hersey to achieve other goals—pushing back against unsustainable and exploitative systems, connecting with herself and her ancestors. And adopting the mindset that rest is inherently worthwhile, that it is part of being human, changes the meaning of rest.

Winter meets two of the specifications for a time when mindsets impact us most: it's a situation we never leave (except, perhaps, for warm-weather vacations*), and many of its qualities are not objectively positive or negative. We always have

---

*Also: warm-weather vacations are perfectly compatible with a "winter is wonderful" mindset. This mindset is about enjoying whatever climate you're in, when you're in it: taking a break somewhere warm and sunny can help you enjoy the cold and dark more when you return.

mindsets, and these mindsets impact our daily lives. There's no such thing as not having a wintertime mindset. So becoming aware of—and shifting—our winter mindset is particularly powerful: it has the potential to dictate our interpretations of nearly everything we experience for several months a year.

WHEN WE FOCUS on adopting mindsets that are *useful*, they have the added advantage of being robust to contradictory information. The understanding that mindsets are intentionally selective allows us to confront conflicting evidence without dissonance. The mindset that "winter is full of opportunity" or even "winter is wonderful" is not negated by irritating winter experiences. When we're out in the bitter cold, or clearing the snow off our car, or overheating in our layers on the bus, we can acknowledge that there are unpleasant aspects of winter. But that does not contradict that winter is also wonderful and full of opportunity. Similarly, when we feel tired, or like we don't want to leave the house, we no longer have to take this as evidence that winter is depressing. Instead, we can see that winter is the time to indulge these feelings by staying in and resting more: not reflexively, out of misery, but intentionally and fulfillingly. When we are aware of our mindset, and aware that this mindset is an adaptively chosen perspective, those mindsets become more resilient. We can integrate discrepant information without our mindset crumbling, because we are deliberately focusing on the most useful facet of a nuanced reality without denying that other perspectives might hold truth as well.

FOSTERING A CONSTRUCTIVE winter mindset can also lead to a broader shift toward seeing seasonal change as natural and

valuable. I let summer be a time for eating dinner late, after the
sun has set, and going to bed later; a time for swimming and
picnics and high energy; ripe tomatoes and grilled corn. I enjoy
these seasonal delights while they last; I say goodbye to them
with sadness even as I eagerly anticipate the crispness of autumn
and the quiet of winter. It's more useful for me to change with
the seasons, to allow myself to be a human animal affected by
light and temperature, than to try to maintain a consistent rou-
tine year-round. Winter has been an entryway to greater sea-
sonal living. This has helped me view the season not as lacking
what I love about summer, but as a time for special winter qual-
ities: quiet, coziness, slowness; a time of year for recuperation,
and for practicing listening to my body and saying no to the out-
side world so I can say yes to my inner world.

Adapting to winter is also practice adjusting to whatever is in
front of us. There are seasons of the year—and seasons of life—
for putting ourselves out there, for pushing ourselves, for striv-
ing and learning and growing. And there are seasons for going
inward, for slowing down, for healing and taking stock. There
will be months and years of great joy and bounty and months
and years of hardship and sadness. Learning to accept, even em-
brace, wherever we are, whenever we are, is the practice of a
lifetime. Knowing when to slow down and when to speed up is
wisdom. The ability to listen to ourselves, to match the natural
world, to work with circumstances rather than fight against
them are skills that will aid us in every venture we undertake.
And winter gives us the chance to rehearse every year.

WINTER PRACTICE:
EMBRACING REST

· **Designate a winter adaptation week:** As it gets darker, pick a week to say no to extraneous requests and activities and fill your calendar with deliberate space. For this week, set an earlier bedtime or arrange for a later wake-up in the morning. Let yourself do less to transition into the season. How does making space to adapt to winter change your response to winter tiredness?

· **Take a family nap:** Declare it a snooze day, stay in your pajamas, and pile up pillows and blankets in the living room. If you have kids at home, call it a daytime slumber party and watch a movie while drifting off. Indulge in being horizontal for as long as possible.

· **Find rest in new places:** Spend a week inviting small, peaceful moments into your day: sit and listen to a song before heading out the door, drink tea slowly, luxuriate in baths or showers, stretch before bed. Add one deliberate rest practice to every day, even if each is only a few minutes long. If you have small children, try letting things take longer together: extended bath time, slower meals, coloring, and unhurried walks. Where else can you expand your definitions of rest?

· **Explore slow hobbies:** Pick one indoor, slow hobby to dive into this winter, and use the long nights and desire to stay home as a chance to enjoy this pastime. Lean into activities you already love (baking, woodworking, playing music, puzzles) or pick up new a new hobby you've been meaning to try (watercolor, sewing, bread making).

· **Institute a winter sabbath:** Pick one day a week or month to observe as a self-defined sabbath. Maybe for you this means not working and not checking email; maybe you turn your phone off entirely or eschew all screens. Maybe you outlaw "logistics discussions" in your household (future planning, coordinating, or organizing). Whatever markers you set for your sabbath, deliberately designate time to focus on maintenance and rejuvenation.

3.

WHAT YOU SEE IS
WHAT YOU GET

N THE WINTER, you can walk on water.

The village of Ii—just shy of ten thousand residents—sits a half hour's drive north of Oulu, Finland, and about two hours south of the Arctic Circle. Rob and I went to Ii to investigate the Finnish approach to winter, where we stayed with Kaisa Kerätär and Antti Ylönen, who founded the KulttuuriKauppila Art Centre. Next to Antti's woodworking studio, across from their historical, three-chimneyed house, and amid the sounds of his saw whirring and jazz music playing, they have a three-rooms-and-a-sauna cabin to host artists and writers in residence. This tiny red cabin, front awning frosted with icicles, was our home in Ii.

On a cloudless day in late January, Kaisa and Antti, generous hosts, took us on a field trip. The sky was clear and Kaisa remarked that it was "the most sun we've seen since November," although the 9:45 a.m. sunrise and 3:15 p.m. sunset made for a short winter's day. The four of us loaded into the van, armed with provisions, and headed to the sea.

Or, what was the sea a few months ago and what would be the sea again come summer. In the heart of winter, the Baltic Sea meets the Finnish shoreline in a vast, glittering plain, entrancing in its pure whiteness. There, in the Gulf of Bothnia, you can walk straight across the water to Sweden.

We went for a picnic, and in an hour's time we'd make a fire in the simple metal pits provided by the park, burn our fingertips eating eat hot sausages smeared with spicy mustard squeezed out of a metal tube like toothpaste, and drink hot chocolate out of the small wooden cups Kaisa brought along. But upon arrival, we were drawn to the ice.

The flat expanse was a marvel. The sun hung low in the sky—it was after two p.m., almost sunset—a brilliant, tangerine orb setting the horizon aflame. Where the sky met the sea, a saffron glow gave way to the faintest line of green, then tapered from periwinkle to a richer, deeper azure. Lines crisscrossed the snow that lay upon the ice: tracks from skiers out for a jaunt, or from snowmobiles carrying miniature cabins, just large enough for a single fisher to sit in over a hole drilled in the ice. The sea had become a winter gathering place for those drawn by the sun, undaunted by the cold: other picnickers, kids playing, people ice fishing.

In some ways, it was a simple landscape: level, continuous. Snow on ice. Setting sun. Trees in the distance. But by turning our powers of attention to the scene before us, wonders appeared. The snow glinted and glimmered, and where the sun hit it, it sparkled. Kick a bit of the fluff into the air and the powdery crystals exploded into shimmering fairy dust. Use your foot or a gloved hand to sweep it away: notice how the ice is bumpy, its surface closer to sandpaper than glass. *How thick is the ice*, I wondered, finding a fishing hole to see how far down it went before slushy water appeared. The ice cracked, creaked, and grumbled, sometimes frighteningly loudly, although I was assured by Antti that those noises were not relevant to our safety. Up above, a single, wispy cloud was painted pink by the setting sun, the only one of its color against the orange-yellow-blue sky. In front of the line of trees on an island across the way, the fog created a strange effect, a thin gray whisper of smoke suspended, perfectly horizontal, slashing a line against the dark woodland. As we grilled hot dogs, I realized that the rush of air from underneath the suspended firepit was creating an updraft that pulled and melted the snow, which refroze into concentric circles of tiny, fragile ice spikes, as if all the crystals were in worship to the god of fire above.

Between noticing these wonders, other, less appealing sensations nagged at my attention. It was a brisk 7°F. My fingers were cold; my nose ran constantly. The layers keeping my core warm made it clunky to move. Peeing in the sparse, frigid bathroom necessitated a wrestling match between me, my coat, and my pants. My forehead itched where my hat rubbed against it. I could go on, listing the day's irritations. Yet the cold causing these annoyances also enabled the alchemy of ice and snow and Arctic light. Whether I focused my awareness on the discomforts or the delights changed nothing about the temperature or what time the sun set. But it changed everything about my experience.

SELECTIVE ATTENTION

Our mindsets shape our attention: by influencing what we believe winter fundamentally *is*—dreadful or delightful, boring or fascinating—and what we expect winter will be like, our mindsets subconsciously orient us to one version of reality or another. My day on the Baltic Sea was objectively freezing. It was also magical. But which I paid more attention to in the moment—cold discomforts or winter wonders—influenced how I experienced our field trip. If I had spent most of my time noticing the numbness in my fingertips or the itch of my woolen leggings, those sensations would have ruled the day. But, in part because I spent most of my time noticing the sparkly snow and the ever-changing light, the cold barely registered.

Mindsets are true, but biased: they zoom in on one slice of complicated phenomena. Similarly, our attention is selective: it's meant to filter. Attending to every light, sound, and physical sensation at all times would put you in sensory overload. We can't notice and observe everything, so our mental shortcuts—including our mindsets—help determine our focus. When we're in love, we only notice the wonderful things about the object of our heart's desire; when we're in a fight, all we notice is how loudly they chew. Some people are able to concentrate on the positives in any situation; for others, no matter how wonderful things are, imperfections snag their attention, attuning them to the deficient. Research finds that people who struggle with anxiety are more likely to pay attention to threatening signals in the environment, which is associated with perceiving ambiguous items negatively and overestimating the likelihood of unfavorable events. Our attentional biases are shaped by many factors: our personality, our upbringing, our culture, our mood, and our mindsets.

If we believe that winter is boring, we are more likely to notice the times we feel bored. If we believe that winter is fascinating, we are more likely to notice the parts of winter that are engaging. One of the ways mindsets become self-fulfilling is by directing our attention, making us more likely to observe winter's negatives or positives. When it's gray and rainy, it's equally true that the world is hushed and reflective as it is that you'll have to avoid puddles and feel a bit damp. The winter light can make us more tired, but it can also fall in unusual, soft shadows. The cold can chill and numb, and it can awaken and refresh. Our mindset can determine which of these truths we notice.

Our attention then reinforces our mindsets: if we hold the mindset that winter is dreadful, and, as a result, disproportionately notice winter's unpleasantness, it strengthens our beliefs about the season. We pay more attention to the parts of winter we find disagreeable, and the spiral continues. But our attention can be a tool for kicking off a new spiral: one of winter admiration. Because attention is a tool we can wield deliberately.

In the introductory psychology course at Stanford, students watch a now-classic video of a basketball team practicing and are asked to count how many times the ball is passed from one player to another. Focused on the task of keeping their eyes on the ball, most students completely miss the person in a giant gorilla suit who walks onto the middle of the court, does a little dance, and shimmies away. When the video is replayed and the gorilla is pointed out, students are astounded that they missed something so absurd and obvious. But such is the power of deliberate, selective attention: it allows us to focus and concentrate, but also to filter out anything we think is irrelevant to the task at hand. What if we make the attentional task at hand falling in love with winter?

In an unending cycle, our mindsets focus our attention, and our attention informs our mindsets. To change one, we can change the other: by shifting our mindset, we alter what we notice. Likewise, we can use our attention to deliberately adjust our mindset: by changing what we attend to, we change our experience. When we do this over and over again, this noticing becomes easier and more automatic. We can go from needing to effortfully direct our attention to having winter's pleasures grab our attention automatically.

IN VERMONT, one psychologist is using our powers of attention to change people's beliefs about winter—and treating their seasonal affective disorder as a result.

SEEING WINTER DIFFERENTLY

Kelly Rohan landed in my inbox in September 2020, saying, "I cannot believe we haven't met." A particularly popular article about my research on wintertime mindset had just come out in *The Guardian*: according to the author, it reached more than a million readers. After a colleague sent the article to Rohan, she reached out to me, and it became obvious that our meeting was indeed long overdue.

Rohan—the professor of psychology at the University of Vermont I wrote about in chapter 2—is doing research that is bringing us out of the dark ages of treatment for seasonal affective disorder.

Historically, the most effective treatment for seasonal affective disorder has been light therapy with sunlamps. This therapy—sitting in front of a light box, which can be purchased online for anywhere from twenty dollars to upward of two hundred dollars—is still the most studied, most popular, and widely used treatment for winter depression. Internet searches return thousands of options for purchasing light boxes, and publications from *The New York Times*'s Wirecutter to *Consumer Reports* put out lists of the best sunlamps on offer.

But Rohan takes a different approach to helping her patients who suffer from winter depression. Rather than focusing on remedying winter's lack of sunlight, Rohan uses cognitive behavioral therapy (CBT) to identify and change patients' negative beliefs about the season. While most of the field historically viewed seasonal affective disorder as being primarily caused by a lack of sunlight affecting the body's circadian rhythms, Rohan didn't think that alone was enough. People are not "passive organisms who just surrender to their biology," she says. "They're active observers of their experience." In her hundreds of interviews with patients suffering from winter depression, she noticed the cognitive hallmarks of depression but with a unique winter focus: a lot of rumination about the meaning of winter's onset. "They learn that 'I have this pattern,'" Rohan explained. Maladaptive thoughts about winter's inevitably depressing effects arise in the fall; the shortening days reduce patients' interest and enjoyment in the world around them. These patients are likely to strongly agree with statements like "There's something wrong with me in the winter" or "It's difficult to feel good on dark, dreary days." Rohan suspected that cognitive behavioral therapy could interrupt these rumination cycles and create more helpful winter narratives.

Her new approach had hurdles to overcome from the start: the preference for light therapy—which almost all patients have heard of—is so strong that Rohan spends the first two of her twelve CBT sessions merely outlining the treatment rationale. Then Rohan can move into the substance of the therapy, which focuses first on shifting patients' attention toward enjoyable activities they can do in winter. The goal is "behavioral activation"—getting patients to engage with winter differently. "We look for things that will get people to develop new, strong associations with winter that are more pleasurable," Rohan told me. "It takes a lot of creativity," she says. This is a population that "is very summer specific in what they like to do." Activities like gardening and beachcombing are high on patients' lists. "So we're all the time reminding people: Lake Champlain doesn't go anywhere, it's still here." The idea is to help people identify their favorite summer pastimes and envision modifying them for winter enjoyment: beachcombing while bundled up, or snowshoeing over the bike path instead of cycling. Indoor activities work too: "I don't personally push people to go outside if someone's just really averse. So we have plenty of people choosing indoor activities: yoga, gym memberships, taking a class, joining a club, learning something new, cooking. Knitting circles are huge here in Vermont," Rohan said. The specific activities are not nearly as important as having a number of options that become part of daily winter life: "As long as they find a good menu of things that are mood enhancing, I think of them as natural anti-depressants." The goal is to infuse winter-positive activities into people's routines until they become natural.

After Rohan and her team encourage patients to think differently about their winter behaviors, they dive into harnessing the power of attention and mindset. "Patients keep thought diaries, they record the buzz terms, or automatic thoughts, that they have, and moods that they're feeling in response to those thoughts. And then eventually, we get around to using the cognitive restructuring of: What's the evidence for that thought? How could you say it instead, that's a little bit more neutral in tone? What effect does that have on your mood? And we do this for many, many sessions," Rohan told me. By directing patients' attention to their thought patterns, inviting them to notice when they're overly pessimistic, and observing how these thoughts impact their mood, these techniques encourage patients to recognize how negative beliefs about winter orient them toward a negative reality. Hallmarks of a maladaptive wintertime mindset, such as focusing only on winter's limitations, tend to be common for patients suffering from seasonal affective disorder: "The thoughts that are discussed, some of them are along the lines of negatively appraising the environment, the day length, the weather, the things they can't do in the winter."

For Rohan, these thoughts are merely symptoms of an underlying core belief—or mindset—about winter. "A metaphor that we use that works really well to articulate this is a dandelion. Automatic thoughts are like the part of the dandelion that's visible, above the ground. With training through cognitive therapy, we can bring attention and get in touch with what our moment-to-moment spontaneous thoughts are," she explained. But, critically, "What is driving that is what's below the surface, the root of the dandelion, which is where the core beliefs and broad thoughts about self, world, future, and others are.* And winter, in the case of seasonal affective disorder, is the root of those automatic thoughts that are wreaking havoc on mood. So we need to uproot the dandelion, deal with what's there. So hopefully, those weeds won't continue to grow back over time." These general beliefs about winter are at the heart of this seasonal suffering, responsible for the automatic thoughts making people feel depressed. By drawing attention to them, and using that attention to observe and consciously reframe these thoughts, Rohan is changing these patients' mindsets about winter.

RESEARCH SUGGESTS that Rohan's approach—using CBT to reframe people's negative beliefs about winter—has advantages when compared with traditional light therapy. While patients are in treatment, both therapies seem equally effective. But once the studies end—and patients don't have someone standing over their shoulder making sure they continue treatment—the superiority of Rohan's approach becomes apparent. One study followed patients for two winters after they participated in a clinical trial where they were randomized to receive either Rohan's winter-focused CBT or light therapy. Two years later, patients who had received the CBT treatment were 50 percent more likely to be in remission from seasonal affective disorder than patients who received sunlamp treatment. This may be

---

*This is similar to how we can think about the relationship between thoughts and mindsets: our mindsets influence our thoughts, and our thoughts reflect our mindsets. But much of what we consciously experience as our thoughts is really driven by the underlying mindset.

because of light therapy's major drawback: if you stop doing it, it stops working. People prefer light therapy because it "is perceived to be easier," Rohan said. "I just, you know, passively sit in front of this light box a minimum of thirty minutes a day. I get magically transported to the beach. It sounds pretty great." But the reality is not as bright. Rohan explained that the logistics of incorporating light therapy into your morning are often more difficult than people expect: it requires waking up earlier, getting in a thirty-minute session before going to work or getting kids ready for school. Additionally, while effective, the feel of sitting in front of a harsh light first thing in the morning, day after day, becomes monotonous: it has none of the warmth of sitting in real sunlight. It's often difficult for people to stick with light treatment, and most patients stop using the light lamp once they finish their clinical trial. And if people won't use it, it doesn't matter how effective it is.

But Rohan's CBT approach changes people's beliefs about winter and helps them see the season in a new way, planting seeds that grow long after patients finish formal therapy, so the positive effects of treatment persist even after sessions end. Patients leave treatment equipped with skills for experiencing winter more positively and a new set of beliefs about what the season means for them. As a result, they may notice things like winter's golden, diffuse light instead of attending only to the darkness. Rather than focusing on dry skin and chapped lips, they may begin to see how the cold can make indoor hobbies feel extra cozy. They may start to recognize that they have more control over their reaction to the season than they realized. By inspiring this noticing, this treatment can make winter more manageable—or even enjoyable—for the people who used to suffer the most when the days grow shorter.

Even if you don't struggle with full-blown seasonal affective disorder, Rohan's approach may help strengthen your positive wintertime mindset. By noticing what we enjoy about winter, we can start writing a story about embracing the season, one that focuses on all there is to love. What I—and so many others—appreciate about cognitive behavioral therapy is that it helps us recognize distorted thoughts. It asks us to question the validity of the unhelpful observations whispered by the voice in our head. When we practice noticing which of our thoughts and beliefs about winter hold us back from seasonal joy, it trains this muscle. Soon, noticing our maladaptive thoughts about winter might become noticing our destructive thoughts about ourselves or our capabilities, or noticing when we're being held back by our internal narratives. Getting in the habit of questioning our negative thoughts—whether they're about winter or anything else—can help us tweak and nudge our automatic reactions until they are kinder and more helpful. This kind of mental awareness is the cornerstone not only of CBT, but also of contemplative practices, like mindfulness, that have been employed by people around the world to find more peace for millennia. Observing our thoughts about winter can be just the beginning.

ROHAN ISN'T THE ONLY one studying how looking at things differently impacts winter well-being. Farther north, in Edmonton, Canada, Holli-Anne Passmore is finding that the mere act of noticing the nature around us can transform our experience of winter.

NOTICING NATURE

When Holli-Anne Passmore gets excited about a research idea, she claps her hands together in glee and—when our conversation is flowing—tries to restrain herself by clamping her fingers over her mouth. A professor of psychology at Concordia University of Edmonton in Canada, Passmore is a world-leading expert in how nature influences well-being. Her research underscores how our attention is key to the relationship between nature and mental health.

Passmore and colleagues developed what she calls the "Noticing Nature Intervention"—a title that's *almost* self-explanatory. "This is a very straightforward, simple intervention," Passmore explained to me. "The entire instructions are: pay attention to how the everyday nature you encounter in your daily routine makes you feel."

In this intervention, Passmore and her team ask people to do two things for two weeks: (1) notice the nature in their everyday lives, and (2) pay attention to how they *feel* in response to that nature. In practice, this means that while driving to work, going to the grocery store, taking the bus, looking out your bedroom window, or riding your bike, first notice what nature you see: the grass that pokes through sidewalk cracks, the trees alongside the highway, vines snaking up city buildings, clouds in the sky. Then pause, and ask yourself: What does it feel like to pay attention to this nature? What emotions, thoughts, or sensations does looking at these plants or vistas inspire? Control participants, by comparison, were asked to notice human-made objects in their environment and how those made them feel.

Across multiple randomized controlled studies in the US and China, Passmore and her colleagues find that noticing nature increases positive emotions, including profound, sometimes hard-to-come-by emotions like awe, wonder, and inspiration. The intervention also increased participants' life satisfaction and sense of meaning and made participants feel more connected, both to nature and to other people. At the same time, the Noticing Nature Intervention decreased negative emotions, depression, anxiety, and stress. Participants in the studies often express surprise at how strongly nature affects their feelings. They reflect that "nature impacts me more than I thought."

One of the most brilliant aspects of Passmore's Noticing Nature Intervention is how small the ask is, and how *natural* (pun very much intended) it is. "It's not about changing your routine. It's paying attention to how everyday nature makes you feel," Passmore described. The intervention doesn't require participants to go backpacking or hiking, or spend a half hour walking outdoors every day, or find a forest for solitude. In fact, it's so accessible, Passmore said, "I haven't encountered anybody so far who has not been able to do this."

PEOPLE OFTEN WANT TO KNOW: What's the smallest dose of nature that "counts"? How much time in nature is enough to see improvements in well-being? Some studies say just twenty minutes is enough. But Passmore prefers to think about quality over quantity. "Moments, not minutes." The analogy she uses is that of sitting in school. Imagine, she says, two students: one who sits in class for six hours a day, but doesn't pay attention—they're on their phone, they're zoning out, they're sleeping. And another student who sits in class for three hours a day but really pays attention—taking notes, asking questions, engaged. Who do you think is going to learn more?

Harnessing our attention deliberately and having a corresponding moment of self-reflection might allow us to do more in a few meaningful moments than if we spent many more minutes surrounded by nature without attention or connection.

In Passmore's intervention, attention isn't only directed externally, at the nature that surrounds us. It's also directed internally: Asking people to specifically attend to the emotions evoked by nature greases the wheels of this self-fulfilling intervention. Encouraging people to mindfully notice their emotions—particularly when there's reason to believe these emotions will be positive—creates a self-reinforcing cycle in which people start to realize that nature makes them feel good. Noticing this pattern might motivate them to start paying even more attention to nature, or seek out more nature as a result, compounding the intervention's benefits.

OTHER SCIENTISTS, the media, and the general public started to recognize the success of the Noticing Nature Intervention. People were excited by the idea that noticing nature in our everyday life improves well-being. But over and over, Passmore was asked: "What about in winter?"

A typical response to learning about this research, she told me, is something like, "Well, that's great, but I can't do that in the winter." Or: "I can't access nature because it's so cold." And so, Passmore thought: *Okay, let's put this to the test here. Because we also know that oftentimes well-being drops in the winter.*

Passmore also had personal motivation for testing the impact of noticing nature in winter. Born and raised in Edmonton, she has always enjoyed the season. "I get that that's a very unpopular position," she said to me. It felt important to put the Noticing Nature Intervention to the test in Edmonton, "where people really do consider winter to be difficult."

Passmore herself has a rare, severe neuropathy and, after several hip surgeries, impaired mobility. She walks with a cane or crutches and commutes to the university on what she calls her "old lady scooter."* Since winter's icy sidewalks and slushy puddles can prove challenging for those with mobility issues, I'm somewhat surprised to hear her talk about how much she loves the season. "It's a big adventure to me," she said. "It makes you feel so alive."

THIS STUDY WAS RUN with community participants in Edmonton during the first winter of the COVID-19 pandemic, and finds that attending to winter nature can boost feelings of hope and resilience in even difficult times. Passmore shared the anonymized responses with me, and I was struck by how often small interactions with nature provided moments of transcendence. The weight of that first long COVID-19 winter was evident in participants' responses: people commented on the difficulty of living with uncertainty, the loneliness and isolation of social distancing, and feelings of sadness and despair. Yet these emotions were often mentioned alongside hope and comfort brought on by interacting with nature.

Looking at a tree, one participant wrote, *"This tree made me*

---

*Passmore rides her mobility scooter as long as it's above around 7°F, after which point she takes the bus.

feel humbled and small. I was also struck by how it seemingly touches the sky. I think I was looking at it in those terms because a dear friend of mine just died 2 days ago from COVID and I'm heartbroken and thinking about things beyond us and this world. The tree seems to be reaching for the heavens and I found it comforting."

Another participant wrote, *"This moment reminded me of the fact that I am surrounded by incredible beauty and that I am part of my environment. It made me feel small in some ways, but also part of something bigger than me."* This idea of something bigger was shared by many: *"I feel peaceful, calm, and protected when I see this image. There is something about the slanting light and tree shadows that make me feel like I'm part of something bigger." "This made me think about how we are shaped by our environment just like these mounds of snow were shaped by the forces of nature and created something beautiful."*

It's easy to view winter nature as dead, or at least dormant. But really focusing our attention reveals the opposite: how the natural world has an incredible resilience, and how things that appear inactive are actually preparing to bloom again. Attending to winter nature is a reminder that the seasons are always changing, and that even in the depths of winter, spring is coming: *"Around noon I was taking a walk as a break at work and noticed these little green shoots beginning to grow. The snow is recently gone (which actually makes me a little sad as I have really enjoyed the winter this year). Yet these shoots provided a bit of hope as spring is on the doorstep (a bit cliche, I know). However, it is also a promise of change and a bit reassuring that regardless of the human-caused craziness, nature marches to her own drum. I like to listen to her beat."* Looking at a bare tree, one participant said, *"I think the most prominent feeling that I have looking at this scene is anticipation—anticipation for the change and growth that is to come. The bare branches of the tree are a symbol and image of the spring that is to come and the leaves that will soon cover the trees. Simultaneously, there is awe at how the tree subtly and yet obviously grows every year."*

Passmore is one of the first people to specifically investigate a nature and well-being intervention in winter. And yet even in Edmonton, when the trees weren't in bloom and the flower seeds were gathering strength underground, the Noticing Nature Intervention provided meaningful benefits. Two weeks of noticing nature in winter led people to feel increased positive emotions and connection to nature, experience more awe and inspiration, and feel more motivated and capable of achieving their goals. Noticing nature in the winter reminds us that even when some living things are in hibernation, we can see nature all around us.

While bare trees might seem hopeless, winter can also be viewed as the most hopeful season: all promise and potential, hidden growth, stored-up energy. If winter is the season of rest and hibernation, it's also the season that enables the growth of the rest of the year, a time for us to contemplate what lies ahead. And when we look for it, we can see the reminders—the barest leaf bud, a shoot of grass, an animal's footprint—that this too shall pass. The moments spent noticing nature, during a difficult season of the COVID-19 pandemic, helped these keen observers notice more than nature—it helped them see these fundamental truths, and to take solace in them. Turning our attention toward small, mundane moments of beauty in challenging times strengthens our emotional resilience and helps us appreciate the wonder that accompanies being alive. Doing this in winter—when perhaps nature's beauty is less obvious and requires more intention to really notice—strengthens our tendency to do this automatically even when times are hard. How might noticing nature more help us all during our darkest seasons?

I BELIEVE THAT the Noticing Nature Intervention is so effective because it does something Passmore and colleagues didn't initially intend. By demonstrating how easy it is to see nature as part of our everyday life, this intervention may expand our definition of what "counts" as nature. It might take us from the mindset that "nature is inaccessible" to "nature is all around us." It can help us realize that even when we can't plan a camping trip or spend a whole day hiking or even make it to the park, we can still connect with nature daily. Most profoundly, it helps us recognize the boost nature gives us, setting off a virtuous cycle: now that we know that nature makes us feel better, and how easy it is to find nature around us, we might find ourselves connecting with and appreciating nature more easily and more often.

If you want to try this at home, it's simple. As Passmore says, there are only two steps. First, notice the nature in your everyday life: the plant on your desk, the sky out your window, the trees on your commute. Then pay attention to how noticing that nature makes you feel. Particularly in the heart of winter, how does consciously shifting your awareness to the nature in your daily life change your experience? Does anything surprise you as you contemplate the natural world in winter? Are your feelings in response to noticing nature differently—in type or in magnitude—than you might have thought? Bonus points if you snap a picture of the nature you see each day, or share your observations with friends and family.

As Passmore says about winter, "This is part of your life. Why would you not want to embrace it?"

AND WITH PLANTS and animals in hibernation, tree branches bare, winter is the perfect time of year to notice other aspects of nature: the sky, wind, clouds, snow, and rain that can make winter weather some of nature's most exciting performances.

WATCHING THE WEATHER

One March, I was on a trip in Yosemite National Park when I awoke to a surprise: our surroundings blanketed in white. In my enthusiasm, I screamed so loudly that my friends in the adjacent hotel room texted, "We're guessing you just saw the snow." That morning we enjoyed a leisurely breakfast, feeling as though we were sitting inside a living snow globe, fat flakes swirling outside the windows. As we strategized about the day's adventures, our cheerful, chatty waiter, David, gave us his insider tips and recommended we drive up to Tunnel View, an iconic Yosemite overlook from which you can see the whole valley spread out in its glory—granite, waterfalls, and Half Dome. With the snow blowing and the blustery gray sky, we wondered aloud whether it would be worth going, or if the winter weather would ruin the view. Quite the opposite, David quipped: "Sure, you can go when it's sunny, but I love the drama."

Our trip to Tunnel View that day did reward us: the clouds clung to the granite, adding depth and mystery to the landscape. During our thirty minutes at the top, the mist shifted this way and that, sometimes obstructing Half Dome, sometimes hugging it like a foamy skirt, sometimes dissipating to let the sun shine on the stone.

And David's observation about loving the drama is one that I have made time and time again: "bad" weather is so much more *fascinating* than "good" weather. I love a sunny day. But the days when a storm rolls in, when the wind blows and roils the sea, when the leaves on the trees jump and dance, when mist hangs low, when rain wallops—those are the days when the weather itself is a spectacle and when looking out the window offers its own entertainment.*

As I child, I spent what felt like hours in the back seat of the car watching raindrops race one another down the windows—how they joined and separated, whether one I picked would make it out of my sight line before another, how they seemed all the same but upon closer inspection were all different. But—like so many of us—as I grew older I lost my interest in watching the way water moved, or the way clouds drifted, or how I could smell a storm coming. Bad weather can invite this kind of fascination back into our lives. By observing, noticing, and watching the change in the weather, we can come to know the patterns of wind and rain and sleet and snow and to feel wonder at the sight of them. In the Outer Hebrides, ragged islands off the coast of Scotland, Jon Macleod talks about the changeability of the

---

*In San Francisco, the "bad" weather is even personified: the San Francisco fog is named Karl. Karl The Fog.

ocean, which goes through seasons like a forest, if only you know how to read the water: "If you didn't know what season it was, you could look at the sea and say 'this is spring' or 'this is winter,' simply because of the color."

WE OFTEN NOTICE only the downsides of winter weather: the cold that hits us in the face when we walk outdoors, the wind that whips through the streets and makes our hair all crazy, the rain and sleet that soaks through any clothing beyond our raincoats' borders. But winter weather—and perhaps especially challenging winter weather—can engage and fascinate us if we pay attention to it. Good weather is all alike; all "bad" weather is bad in its own way.

Winter weather is a full sensory experience. Sometimes those sensations can be unpleasant—wet socks and frozen toes. Yet we can take a page out of Passmore's book and notice nature by really attending to winter weather with all of our senses. Trees rustle in the whistling wind; rain splats and patters; ice crunches and crackles; snow muffles sound while shushing under our feet. Rain turns the streets into mirrors, reflecting the glow of lampposts, and transforms the sounds of passing cars into a gentle, hypnotic whooshing. The light of winter is varied and vast, especially at more northern latitudes. It can be wan and thin, but also soft, luminescent. When the sun hangs lower in the winter sky, the light diffuses differently. Sunlight comes in at a beautiful, slanting angle. The rays spread, gilding the landscape. Shadows are elongated and soft, falling dramatically and unusually. In winter, it can be golden hour all day long. After sunset, it's blue hour, the time when the world is tinted soft cobalt: the farther from the equator you are, the bluer blue time is.

And the closer we are to the winter solstice, the better sunsets are. The angle of the sun around the solstice increases the time it takes to set, so watercolor sunsets last longer. And clouds—the true and unsung heroes of sunset—are more likely to be well-defined in the winter, providing the necessary backdrop for a ROYGBIV sky.

When it drops below freezing, a new world of winter fascination appears. Ice can appear in a dizzying array of shapes, sizes, and formations: it can frost grass so delicately that the first rays of the sun melt it away as if it never existed. Freezing rain coats everything it touches, encasing branches and lampposts in ice; I've made a game of trying to surgically separate leaves from sheets of ice, marveling when I'm able to extract a ghostly, ephemeral ice leaf. Frost flowers occur when thin layers of ice are extruded from slits in plant stems: the ice curls outward and upward in delicate, intricate patterns. Ice rings can form in puddles or ponds when water freezes around an object—like the base of a tree—in concentric circles. Hair ice forms only on deadwood, usually in broadleaf forests between 45 and 55° north, because it relies on the fungus *Exidiopsis effusa*, and looks like the fine, silvery hair of a troll doll. Currents and eddies can form ice circles, lily pad–like ice often seen in moving rivers. On Senja island in northern Norway I saw pancake ice, formed when moving water freezes into flat, blob-like pancakes, which gently nudge each other to create raised, slushy edges. Icicles drip drip drip down into fragile stalactites, to be admired from all angles except directly below. Even the dirty icicles that form on my car's bumper make a pleasing tinkle when kicked.

The magic and fascination of winter weather is owed, at least in part, to its temporality. Nowhere have I experienced this more strongly than when I traveled to Iceland, where the weather is harsh, extreme, and whiplash-inducingly changeable. I spent one afternoon reading a book amidst the coffee fumes of Reykjavík Roasters and witnessed periods of blue skies and brilliant sunshine, where the mountains were visible in high definition, sandwiched between the slate-gray ocean and the cerulean sky; gentle snowfall, peaceful and quiet; wind-whipped snow, a blustery blizzard with big fat flakes, which had people pulling their hoods over their heads and hunchbacking in protection; Dippin'-Dots hail, bouncing off windows and sidewalks. I could barely read my book for fear of missing this natural spectacle, and I longed to hold on to each turn of the weather, to soak it up with my attention and memory.

But part of embracing winter is learning to love something that is fleeting, to pay attention while it's there and then let it go, and to learn that lesson over and over again.

OUR ATTENTION CHANGES the very nature of winter weather: when we relax our face and our shoulders and breathe deeply, the cold can transform from unbearable to pleasant. When we stop pushing against it and observe what it really feels like, asking ourselves "How intolerable is this, really? Am I in danger or am I just a bit uncomfortable?" the quality of the cold shifts and we find that maybe it's not as bad as we thought. On clear days, we can turn our faces upward and seek apricity, the warmth of winter sun. When indoors, we can enjoy what is called *gluggaveður* ("window weather") in Icelandic: weather that is enjoyable to watch from inside. Even then, the weather is usually fleeting: the snow will fall for a little but, eventually, it always stops. This is true even in places like rainy Scotland, where the

word for damp, wet, gray weather—*dreich*—is also a synonym
for drawn-out or wearisome: the kind of weather that appears
constant and seems unceasing. But in reality, the weather is al-
ways shifting: the rain falls harder or softer, the wind whips
faster or slower, the sun breaks through the clouds for a few
moments. When people complain about unending weeks of
gray, monotonous drizzle, I wonder: Is it really that unchanging
and monochrome, or are we just failing to notice the texture of
the clouds, the sun's brief appearances, the times when the rain
pauses for a few hours? When we succumb to the narrative that
winter is always colorless and rainy, or when we look on the
weather app and see rain clouds all week, we close ourselves off
to the curiosity of seeing how the weather changes minute to
minute, hour to hour, day to day. Anne Campbell, an artist I
met on the Isle of Lewis in Scotland, told me how sad she would
be to travel during winter to learn that she missed the biggest
storms and sea swells while she was gone. Even the harshest
winter weather can be a thing of beauty, something to savor,
because we never know when it will arrive nor when it will de-
part. All we can do is pay attention while it's there.

Amidst all of this, we know that winter itself—like any
season—will not last. Whether early or late, spring will arrive.
The days will lengthen. The temperature will rise. The snow
will melt and the buds will bloom. Why deny the invitation to sit
beside and within winter while it's there? Instead, pay attention
to its variance, its changeability, and, in so doing, find more fas-
cination. We can also, just maybe, learn to notice how all things
come and go—how the storm that threatens to pull us under
will pass like any other. How what seems like it will last forever
will not, and there is both comfort and sadness in that. Watch-

ing the weather—with openness, curiosity, and mindfulness—is a practice in being present with whatever is really in front of us, in finding enchantment even alongside discomfort. Winter weather has so much to delight us with—and to teach us—if we are willing to pay attention.

THE ATTENTION INTENTION

If you're trying to cultivate a more positive wintertime mindset, harnessing your powers of attention is a great place to start. Using our attention has two huge advantages: the first is that we're *already noticing selective aspects of winter all the time.* We might not be doing this intentionally or even consciously, but any time we're awake, we're paying attention to something, either internal or external. Since our attention influences our experience so strongly, it can be impactful if we make even small strides in noticing the world around us more deliberately. The second advantage is that attending to the world differently doesn't require time; it only requires intention. Using our attention to see things deliberately is something we can do in micromoments, which makes it a simple practice to incorporate into daily life.

Once you start using your attention to focus on winter's delights, you might start asking yourself where else your powers of observation could be harnessed to improve your well-being. In what aspects of your life—your relationships, your job, your living situation—are you focusing too much of your attention on what you don't like instead of what you do like? Where is this creating cognitive distortions or rumination? Where can you notice more wonder, more comfort, more joy? There will always be unpleasantries to notice, but among those we can also attune mindfully to: What is pleasant here? How can you direct your attention deliberately to appreciate more of what there is to love around you—no matter how small?

Leveraging our attention like this doesn't mean overlooking or ignoring problems, or turning a blind eye to the upsetting or irksome. Instead, consciously strengthening our attentional abilities can help us recognize the opportunities in even difficult situations, and can also give us the emotional and mental fortitude required to tackle issues we notice. Observing what we enjoy and find comforting or meaningful can also give us solutions to work toward: instead of just noticing what we don't like, when we see what we *do* like we can use these signals as blueprints to build the home, community, and world we want to live in.

How we attend to things shapes our existence. Our attention is a powerful tool, and it plays a tremendous role in our everyday experience. What we attend to becomes what we see, and what we see becomes what we engage with, and what we engage with becomes our life.

WINTER PRACTICE:
ACTIVE ATTENTION

- **Capture the moment:** Take one picture a day of something you noticed that brings you winter-related delight. Seasonal foods, warm clothing, holiday decorations, and winter nature are all fair game; the important thing is taking a moment to pause and capture.

- **Question your negative thoughts:** Write down your negative perceptions of winter, and ask yourself: Is this thought an exaggeration? A distortion? Is it grounded in reality? For each perception, write down a gentler, more helpful way you could reframe this observation.

- **Notice nature:** Try noticing nature—and then how that nature makes you feel—in your everyday life. On your commute, inside your home, or walking outside, notice where nature is present, what is unique about that nature in winter, and what emotions that nature inspires.

- **Watch the weather:** For one week, attend to the weather as often as possible; look out your window in between meetings or tasks, take several short outdoor breaks a day, or just notice the weather whenever you find yourself outside. How does the weather you observe compare with the forecast? Is it more constant—or more changing—than you thought it would be? Are the stories you tell yourself about what the weather is "like" in winter supported by your observations?

- **Engage your senses:** Pay attention to the sights, smells, and sounds of winter. How is the light in winter different from or similar to other times of year? How does the winter air smell? How does winter weather—snow, rain, fog, sleet—sound on the street, or change the color of the ground or sky? How does winter engage your senses differently than other seasons?

4.

USE YOUR WORDS

I MET RANNVEIG KRISTJÁNSDÓTTIR in a perfume shop. I wandered into Fischersund, a "family-run perfumery and art collective," in Reykjavík, Iceland, because a travel writer I follow listed it as her "favorite store in the world." The small shop is dark and mysterious, with black shelves and unidentifiable vegetation preserved in test tubes. Unearthly music plays. Dried herbs and plants dangle from strings. The walls are made of worn brick and moss, and the wooden plank floors are the color of spring mud. It feels like a witchy apothecary, it smells delightful, and I was immediately intrigued.

I'd traveled from Finland to this island nation in the North Atlantic to spend eight days immersed in the Icelandic winter and writing at Gröndalshús, a museum devoted to Icelandic naturalist and writer Benedikt Gröndal, the bottom floor of which now houses a cozy, red wood-paneled apartment. Rannveig works at Fischersund, and we got to chatting; I told her I was staying at the writer's house across the street and explained the premise of this book. She immediately replied, "Oh, I love winter."

Even after hearing this sentiment repeatedly throughout the Nordics, I was caught off-guard by her enthusiasm. The Icelandic winter can be extreme. When Rob and I picked up our rental car, the agent carefully informed us that the insurance does *not* cover car doors being ripped off by the wind: a common enough occurrence to bear warning. Our drive through Iceland's countryside felt like being on a very wet moon. We navigated roads sandwiched between snarling seas and towering lava rock mountains. At times, the snow whipped across the asphalt like desert sand, and in an instant, the conditions could progress to a total whiteout, forcing me to creep along. Then, just as quickly, the swirling snow would abate, revealing patches of clear blue sky. It's enough to make anyone dizzy and the combination of cold, wet, and wind makes Iceland's winter particularly harsh.

But Rannveig embodies an Icelandic appreciation of the winter in its windy, frosty glory. Each of the scents in Fischersund is inspired by a family memory, and the perfume ingredients are local to the island. One scent, on a table covered in spongy moss, caught my attention.

"This is called *útilykt*," Rannveig explained. Útilykt is a special Icelandic word: translated directly, it means "out-smell." It's the scent that clings to your clothes and hair after returning inside from outdoors.

I was charmed. People who live in cold places often relish this particular smell. In *Moominland Midwinter* by the Finnish author Tove Jansson, one of Jansson's beloved Moomins—fictional creatures reminiscent of marshmallowy hippopotamuses—wakes up during his hibernation and ventures outside alone. Encountering snow for the first time, the Moomin detects "a more serious smell than any he had met before, and slightly frightening. But it made him wide awake and greatly interested." This smell is so beguiling that people across the Nordics, from Svalbard to Reykjavík, not only dry their clothes outdoors, but also hang their duvets outside in an attempt to bring that iconic, fresh smell into bed. Every Sunday, unless it's pouring, Rannveig airs her family's comforters outside. "I have to," she tells me, "or else my mother . . ." She made a noise and a face that indicated she'd be in dire trouble if she failed to conduct this ritual.*

In theory, útilykt can apply to many scents throughout the year. But there's nothing quite like that wintery crispness. Cold weather slows down molecules in the air, making it harder to detect odors, which is why winter air often smells so clean. One study looked at smells in nature across seasons, and "fresh" was the most common descriptor of winter woods. And, at least for the perfumers of Fischersund, útilykt is undeniably a winter smell. Rannveig explained that each scent has an accompanying poem. She sprayed me with perfume and recited while I closed my eyes and inhaled deeply:

---

*Smell isn't the only reason to air out your laundry in winter: if you're lucky enough to live somewhere with very cold winters, you can literally freeze-dry your laundry outside. Through sublimation—in which solid, frozen water evaporates directly into a gas—wet things freeze and then dry quickly and beautifully in subfreezing temperatures. This is also the science behind freeze-dried food!

Headwind in every direction

Drifting snow creeping under coat collars

Snow beads on wooly mittens

Berry colored tongue and head resting on a pillow of moss

Lawn mower in a distant garden

An undressed Christmas tree blowing down the sidewalk
in the sea breeze

Frosted windows, weather forecast
and the car heater on full blast.

The scent transported me so spot-on that it bottled an Arctic freshness I thought impossible to capture. In Iceland, and at Fischersund, not only is the smell of winter celebrated enough to have its own name, but it's so treasured that the family perfumers spent countless hours tinkering with herbs, oils, and essences to bring forth the scent memory of winter.

Even the last line of the poem, which evokes the uncomfortable sensation of huddling in a frigid car waiting for it to thaw, has been requisitioned into a lovely memory. "Because it's such a common experience," Rannveig said. She described this familiar feeling: bundled in her car in the morning in the freezing cold, gripping her coffee mug, shoulders hunched, waiting for the car to warm and the windshield ice to melt. But she described it with a kind of cheerfulness. I pointed out that it seems like a fundamentally disagreeable experience, and yet the perfumery has incorporated that moment into the scent, heightening it to something quintessential about enjoying the air of winter.

She gave me a lighthearted retort: "What are you gonna do? Are you gonna bitch about it? You can't bitch about it. This is

your life, for seven months of the year. You just have to roman-
ticize it."

THE POWER OF LANGUAGE

Rannveig's refusal to bitch about the season is unusual: people
all over the world love to hate on winter weather.

From Fairbanks to Kyoto, people make small talk about the
weather. This conversational habit comes from an urge to affil-
iate: the weather outside unites us. Discussing the rain, heat, or
cold is a way of connecting. Trash-talking winter weather might
be the season's most popular sport, and we seem to do it every-
where: with our colleagues in the office, with the cashier at the
grocery store, with our parents on the phone. We complain
about the weather in garbled speech with our mouth full of
sharp pointy things at the dentist, and moan about the cold to
no one in particular on the bus. Even those who discuss the
weather at a professional level seem to enjoy winter-bashing.
Listen to the way weather forecasters talk about winter—there's
a lot of "hunker down," "it's a cold one," and "stay inside."

Every fall, I see a slew of *New Yorker* cartoons about how
terrible winter is. One has a person walking into a snowstorm,
first in a T-shirt, and then in more and more layers until they're
bundled up. Above them are labeled the seven stages of grief,
from denial to acceptance—comparing the arrival of winter to
the loss of a loved one. Another favorite shows two people walk-
ing in the snow, with the caption "I've blocked all Instagram
pictures from California." Once you start noticing this winter
whining, you'll see it everywhere. Like taking the red pill and

awakening from the matrix, if you open your eyes to winter bias, negative winter mindsets appear around every corner. In many places, winter-complaining is an ingrained part of the culture. I've heard it called a national pastime in the UK and Ireland. When it seems like everyone around us is bemoaning the season, it's no wonder many people unconsciously adopt a winter-is-dreadful mindset.

This winter-bashing creates—and reinforces—our mindset about winter. Words are powerful, and saying something out loud makes it real. Our words direct our and others' attention, and we saw in the last chapter how merely attending to something shapes our experience. When we repeat something over and over—whether that's complaining about winter weather or criticizing ourselves—we etch the lines of our reality deeper with each repetition. The language we use shapes how we understand and perceive the world around us.

LERA BORODITSKY IS A COGNITIVE scientist at the University of California San Diego who researches the quirks of language that influence us. Her work is revealing how our words shape what we see at a fundamental level. In English, for example, the colors red and light red have two different names: red and pink. But "blue" can encompass both dark blue and light blue. In Russian, however, different shades of blue are considered different colors: *goluboy* for light blue and *siniy* for dark blue. Because there are separate words for these two colors, differentiating them comes more innately and intuitively: Russian speakers are significantly faster at distinguishing between light and dark blue. The language we use informs what we notice and absorb about our surroundings. Traditional Sami directions were based on relation to the coast: the Sami word *davvi* refers to "toward the coast," and *lulli* means "away from the coast." But depending on where you are, *davvi* might be north or it might be west; *lulli* could be south but it could also be east. To give directions, those using these traditional Sami words would have to be aware of where the coastline is, informing their understanding of their location on a moment-to-moment basis and requiring coastal positioning to be top of mind.

And our language influences how we conceptualize our very selves. Hebrew, for example, is a highly gendered language: even the word "you" differs when you are speaking to a man or a woman. On the opposite end of the spectrum is Finnish, which has no gender markings in nouns or even personal pronouns (in Finnish, the word *hän* can mean either "he," "she," singular "they," or "it"). Consequentially, research shows that Hebrew-speaking children learn their *own* gender a year earlier than Finnish children. And countries that speak more gendered languages (languages where even the nouns are gendered either male or female) tend to have greater gender inequality than countries with less gendered languages (either languages like English, which gender pronouns but not nouns, or languages like Finnish, which lack even gendered pronouns). Boroditsky sums it up thusly: "Learning to speak these languages requires something more than just learning vocabulary: it requires paying attention to the right things in the world so that you have the correct information to include in what you say."

Language also shapes, and reflects, our values. I think often of the Yiddish word *machatunim*: your kid's in-laws. These are the parents of your child's spouse. Because Yiddish has a special word for this (as does Spanish, *consuegros*, for co-fathers-in-law, and *consuegras*, for co-mothers-in-law), they are considered members of your extended family. The word reflects this special connection and underscores its importance in the Jewish (and Spanish) communities: The people I know who still use this word are those who are especially close with, and cherish, this relationship between in-laws.

The causality of the language-cognition relationship goes both ways: how we think influences how we speak, but research is piling up to support the idea that how we speak influences our thoughts. As Boroditsky writes, "Changing how people talk changes how they think." By deliberately shifting the words we use, we can change our mindsets: in one study, cancer patients who were shown videos of researchers, doctors, and cancer survivors describing the cancer journey as manageable or even an opportunity to make positive life changes were less bothered by physical symptoms, engaged in more adaptive coping mechanisms, and had reduced distress and symptoms during treatment. In another randomized controlled study I was part of at Stanford, describing minor, not-dangerous side effects of treatment for life-threatening food allergies as a positive sign that the treatment was working led to significantly reduced patient worry when they had symptoms, decreased symptoms as treatment progressed, and an increased biomarker of treatment efficacy.

So making small talk by complaining about the weather isn't as harmless as it might seem. Think about how powerful it would be if we did the opposite: if we used our language to celebrate winter. If, instead of telling us to "stay inside" because "it's gonna be a cold one," the weather forecasters told us to "get ready for a cozy weekend." Imagine if, instead of hearing your colleagues come into the office talking about how wet and nasty it is out, they commented on the smell of the rain. This is the power of having words like the Danish hygge ("cozy contentment") or the Norwegian practice of calling an at-home Friday night *Fredag kos* ("Friday cozy")—labeling winter pleasures helps them feel more real and gives them more substance. We can use our language to continuously and consciously shape our experience, which influences not only our mindsets, but the mindsets of the people around us. In speaking lovingly about winter, we can shape how the season feels.

THREE WINTERS

One of the ways our language about winter fails us is by collapsing a three-to-seven month season into a single word: "winter." Like using the word "blue" for a wide range of shades, calling the entire season "winter" trains us to view it as a singular entity. But people who have lived alongside winter for thousands of years think—and talk—about the season differently. Taking inspiration from the Sami, we can start viewing winter not as one long, unchanging time of year, but as a season composed of dynamic parts.

The Sami are the Indigenous people of Northern Europe (and are, in fact, the only Indigenous Europeans recognized by the European Union). Historically, the Sami moved freely throughout the Arctic region of Sápmi—what is now Norway, Sweden, Finland, and Russia—before borders drawn without their consultation erected invisible barriers on the routes they used for reindeer herding, fishing, and their nomadic lifestyle. As longtime stewards of Europe's Arctic, the Sami were, and are, intimately familiar with the landscape, nature, and changing of the seasons. Their views on Nordic nature, and winter in particular, demonstrate a level of nuance made possible via close observation of the natural world. Today, most of the world either splits the year into two seasons (rainy and dry seasons in tropical climates) or four seasons (winter, spring, summer, and fall in more temperate locations). Even places that have very short springs and falls, like the Arctic, still tend to break the year into four seasons, in spite of winter's dominance. But traditionally, the Sami had eight seasons: in addition to winter, spring, summer, and fall, the Sami have four bridge seasons: spring-summer, autumn-summer, autumn-winter, and spring-winter. Rather than dates on the calendar, these seasons were heralded by events in nature; in Lapland, early winter might be marked by the arrival of the white-throated dippers, the shortening of the days, and the waters of Lake Inari freezing over. Late winter might begin when the snow buntings and whooper swans arrive; they are the first migrating birds to return north to nest. The timing of each season might vary from year to year with the behavior of animals or the temperature.

Seasonal understanding also depended on the traditional subsistence livelihoods of the Sami. Because much of the Sami community relied on reindeer husbandry, the year turned around the reindeer life cycle. The new year began when calves were born, and other periods of the year were marked by the rutting season, the roundup season, and the season for slaughter. For those whose families relied on fishing, the conditions of the ice dictated the yearly rhythm: in the fall and spring, as Lake Inari is freezing over and melting, there are lulls in the calendar, times for rest between fishing and ice fishing seasons. These ways of marking the year are still observed by many present-day Sami whose livelihoods involve fishing or reindeer husbandry.

Taija Aikio works at Siida, the Sami museum in Inari, Sápmi; is Inari Sami; and told me that these seasonal classifications are still used in the Sami community today, particularly the spring-winter designation. In Inari, which experiences the Polar Night for a month each winter, true winter is considered the time of year when the sun doesn't rise. Taija told me that they start talking about *giđđadálvi*, or "spring-winter" in Sami,* usually beginning at the end of February or early March. "It's still very much winter, because it's cold, there's a lot of snow still. But the sun is out." The return of direct daylight heralds a season on the cusp. Giđđadálvi is a time for a special kind of snow in Inari: "In the winter the snow is very fluffy and airy, and then when the sun comes out it sort of melts the top layer, and then it freezes. So it's very hard and you can walk on top of it and ski," she said. This "snow crust" season is the best time of year for skiing. As the conditions of the natural world change, so does the way people interact with it, ushering in new phases of winter.

MOST OF THE NORTHERN HEMISPHERE uses the astronomical seasons to delineate the year, meaning that each season starts on the solstice or equinox.† In the astronomical designation most frequently used in the US, winter starts on December 21, long after we've started getting into the holiday spirit. Starting on the solstice means that winter begins as the days get lighter, rather

---

*Note that there are several different Sami languages that vary by region, and so the words for "spring-winter" may differ; the northern Sami word and spelling are used here.
†There are some exceptions. For example, meteorologists and climatologists often use the meteorological definition of the seasons, in which the seasons begin on the first day of the month that includes the solstice or equinox: this makes the first day of winter December 1, and the first day of spring March 1. And in Ireland, people often refer to the Celtic or Irish calendar, in which winter starts on November 1 and spring begins on February 1.

than being centered around the darkest time of the year. Likewise, winter ends on March 21: late for Georgia and California, but early for Maine or Michigan.

It wasn't until I learned about the eight seasons of the Sami that I questioned the way we split our year into four equal seasons. I understand the need to have a shared calendar, a common framework to communicate across locations. In the US, this challenge is complicated by a large country that includes Montana and Texas, Alaska and Hawaii, Minnesota and Louisiana. But the urge to reduce the natural world to what can be predictably scheduled further divorces us from a seasonal way of living.

Taking inspiration from the Sami and other ancient cultures around the world who organize the year around nature,* I started thinking about conceptualizing winter differently. What if we had a more colloquial language for describing winter's phases? One that, like the Sami seasons, could adapt flexibly to our environment, weather, and temperature from year to year?

In parts of the US, winter can easily be five months, spanning far beyond the official three months it's allotted on the calendar. In Lapland, winter often lasts more than half the year. In Ireland, they say winter lasts eight months. Splitting winter in three distinct phases, as the Sami do with autumn-winter, winter, and spring-winter, draws our attention to the season's evolution and influences our expectations and behavior. Autumn-winter, or early winter, just after the end of daylight saving time, is about slowing down and reacquainting ourselves with activities that

---

*My other favorite example is the Japanese 72 micro-seasons calendar, which originated in the sixth century and was used alongside the lunar calendar until 1872, when Japan adopted the Gregorian calendar. It includes very specific seasons, such as "North wind blows the leaves from the trees (November 27–December 1)"; "Ice thickens on streams (January 25–29)"; and "Hibernating insects surface (March 6–10)."

shine in the dark. Spring-winter, or late winter, however, is more about reemerging from our chrysalises, welcoming back the sun, and looking forward to longer days. Reducing both of these times of year to "winter" fails to highlight winter's patterns: how the days get darker and then lighter again, how nature slowly falls asleep and then quietly wakes back up. Many people feel frustrated at the end of winter, when they're mentally ready for spring—when warm days and flower buds might tease us—but winter still lingers. Splitting winter into three can help us anticipate, and talk about, the length of winter while attuning ourselves to the shifting seasons and changing daylight. It may also help us appreciate the in-between weeks that are neither full winter nor full spring.

Another benefit of a nonofficial, non-calendar-based conceptualization of winter is the ability to adapt flexibly across climates. My designation of winter's sub-seasons growing up in New Jersey would be very different from someone else's living in Santa Fe, Billings, or Miami. Perhaps you live somewhere, like the Sami, dictated by snow. But perhaps your winter markers have more to do with changes in daylight, rain, or fog. Perhaps you mark the seasons by last harvests and first plantings in your garden; by the times of year that galoshes are required or not; by whether or not the sun streams through your kitchen window.

Imagine splitting winter, wherever you live, into early winter, midwinter, and late winter. As someone raised in the four seasons of the northeastern US, I think of early winter as the period when the darkness is oncoming, from the time the clocks change in late October or early November until mid-December. This is when winter is still new and exciting, and getting to wear a fluffy sweater feels like a special event. The days are getting darker, and the ability to eat dinner by candlelight is novel again.

For me, midwinter begins in mid-December when the holiday season is ramping up, and goes until late January, comprising the winter holidays. This is the heart of winter, when the days are at their shortest and I most need to turn inward. It includes the solstice and the New Year, and feels like a time for contemplation and rest.

And then comes late winter, or spring-winter, or what I think of affectionately as "still winter," as in the time of year that everyone kind of forgets is . . . still winter. Late winter starts at the end of January and continues until spring arrives, which in any given year might be early March or mid-April, depending on temperature, precipitation, and whether or not the groundhog sees his shadow. The days are lengthening, and I can start to feel the sun, but it can still be cold, and the combination of fresh winter air and sunlight can be lovely. I'm also starting to see physical signs of spring—little buds on the trees, plants poking their way out of hard earth—and the increasing daylight is preparing me to reemerge as well. Like Taija told me, this can be a particularly handy season to separate out: at a time of year when many are growing tired of winter, giving this season a special designation can help us notice and appreciate the lengthening daylight bringing us closer to spring.

Giving winter three sub-names facilitates appreciation of the changing, dynamic nature of winter and allows us to ritualize each inter-winter period, leaning into the specific comforts and pleasures of each sub-season. Early winter is for winding down and putting on my winter skin, luxuriating in sleeping more. Midwinter is the time of holiday frenzy, rituals, and taking a pause: when candles burn nearly all day, and I celebrate the turning of the year and stay in my pajamas for a week between Christmas and New Year's. Late winter is the time for welcoming back the sun, when it becomes easier to get outside because either the snow is at its best or the weather is getting warmer, when I observe the earth's new growth and revel in yoga by candlelight because I know soon the days will be long and full of activity again.

Because our language influences how we think and feel, giving things a name makes them real and sets our expectations. Learning from those who have been winter experts for thousands of years, like the Sami, can help us understand and appreciate the dynamic rhythm of winter, and can better prepare us for its beginning, middle, and tail end.

SAYING IS BELIEVING

Words are so powerful that psychologists have an intervention technique called saying is believing. This strategy is relatively simple: if you want to get someone to believe something, get them to say it. If I wanted to use this technique in a study on wintertime mindset, I might ask you to read a few articles about how people in Tromsø tend to have more adaptive wintertime mindsets and what behaviors support this mindset, and then write a letter to an imaginary winter skeptic, highlighting the benefit of cultivating a more positive wintertime mindset and how it can impact your experience of the season. Research shows that this technique is effective in helping change people's mindsets. It has been used frequently in growth mindset interventions: Students who are actually the target of the intervention are asked to read an article about how intelligence can grow with effort and then write a letter to a younger student or give advice to a friend who is struggling in school, focusing on how you can get smarter through your actions and sharing personal stories of times that this was true for them. In essence, this approach gets people to "internalize the ideas by endorsing them to someone else." It forces these participants to think about the intervention message and put things into their own words, using their own experiences. In doing so, participants see how the desired message is relevant and true in their own lives.

Getting people to say something in their own words changes how they think about it. Explaining a mindset to someone else requires us to combine our knowledge and experiences with new information. It forces us to stop and think: How is this true? What evidence do I, personally, have that supports this viewpoint?

You can conduct your own personal saying-is-believing intervention on yourself. What if you were tasked with helping a friend who dreads winter cultivate a more positive wintertime mindset? What would you say to them? How would you make the case that winter is wonderful? You can answer these questions and then turn the argument inward, making the case through your daily language that winter is full of opportunity.

FALSE NARRATIVES

Just as our helpful mindsets can create our reality, our unhelpful mindsets become self-fulfilling. Sometimes, negative stories around winter are so pervasive that they trick us into thinking that winter is colder and gloomier than it actually is, discouraging us from looking at the world with fresh eyes and taking in: How cold is it really? We create false narratives about winter, and these narratives become a greater barrier to winter enjoyment than actual winter conditions.

This is something that former Edmonton city councilor Ben Henderson found himself up against. Ben spearheaded the effort to transform Edmonton, Canada, into a "Winter City," which we'll explore in greater detail in chapter 9. Amidst the many challenges he faced, one of the most intractable was a false narrative about what winter in Edmonton is actually like. "The thing we really fought against, and still do, is this myth that it's -40°F for six months of the year," he told me. "We have sheltered ourselves from winter because we imagine it all being like that."

Edmonton is quite cold, and can be quite windy. As a result, many citizens of Edmonton held a pervasive belief that the winter was an endless string of dangerously cold days. But if you look at the numbers, that's not the case. The coldest month in Edmonton is usually January, with an average winter temperature of 14°F. Fourteen degrees is proper cold, but it's certainly nowhere near -40°F; with windchill, it could be uncomfortable, but on a sunny day, with the right clothing, it could be positively pleasant. And that's just the average of the coldest month: some days are colder, but there are also plenty of warmer days. The idea that Edmonton has a six-month winter with temperatures in the negative double digits is more myth than fact.

"The critical thing is not imagining winter based on its worst days, which is what we tend to do. We would never do that in summer, right? We just wouldn't," Henderson said to me. These kinds of misconceptions likely stick *because* they are so extreme: there's a high cost to being wrong on the coldest of days.

If you go out when it is -40°F and you're improperly dressed, or try to stay outside for any significant period of time, there are severe consequences, and you'll remember how unpleasant that experience was. And what's known as the Peak-End Rule in psychology suggests that people judge and remember experiences based on how they felt at the "peak," or most extreme and intense point, and at the end of the experience. So these extreme—and usually rare—instances can become our default memory of what winter is like, even when evidence suggests that's not usually the case.

Edmonton isn't the only place with false narratives about winter weather. London seems to suffer from the same. Lauren Heathcote, a colleague of mine from Stanford who moved back home and is now a professor at King's College London, noticed this herself. She was worried about how the London winters, with their endless chilly drizzle, would affect her after having grown accustomed to northern California sunshine. But upon returning to London, she found herself surprised to face more sunny days than rainy ones. Yet the narrative remained: "England: supposed to be rainy, all the time. England rains all the time," she said to me from her university office, where sunlight streamed through the window on a February afternoon. "It's barely rained since I moved. I could probably count on my two hands how many times it's been a rainy day. And I've been here over a year now." At this point in our conversation, Lauren started to get worked up: a combination of flabbergasted and frustrated at how persistent this narrative is. "People don't notice. Every day, I will wake up and it's sunny. People do not notice that. People are so biased." Lauren bikes to work every day, and she says that in the year she's lived in London, she's been caught in the rain on her bike about five times. "But if it rains one day in a month, people will be like 'Raining again!'"

Visiting London, I experienced this myself: on a day when I spent the morning walking around for several hours, enjoying the crisp November weather and even a bit of sunshine, it rained in the afternoon. Sitting in a pub, the bartender remarked, "What a rainy day!" It seems that any amount of rain is enough to designate a rainy day in our minds—even if the rain is accompanied by equal amounts of sun.

But by using our language selectively, we can direct our attention to what is actually before us; we can gradually overturn these false narratives. When our words adjust to reflect what's truly in front of us, we practice seeing things as they are. Where else in your life might you have deeply entrenched stories that are no longer useful? Where else are the myths of yourself, your family, your workplace, or your community creating friction? How can overturning some of these narratives get you closer to both the winter—and the life—you want to experience?

Our negative wintertime mindsets reinforce themselves: when we complain about the rain aloud, we draw our attention, and everyone else's, to it. We attend selectively to "bad" winter weather, and tell ourselves that's what it's like all the time, refusing to notice—or mention—exceptions to these narratives.

But it doesn't have to be this way.

BE A WINTERTIME MINDSET AMBASSADOR

In my wintertime mindset workshops, I end by challenging audiences to become Wintertime Mindset Ambassadors. After

two hours of learning about wintertime mindset, I ask everyone
to commit to making winter-positive small talk to spread a more
appreciative view of the season. In practice, this means comment-
ing on what you like about winter rather than what you hate:
observing, aloud, how nice it can be to run outdoors without
overheating, or how the darkness encourages snuggly evenings
spent reading on the couch. Rather than bemoaning what's un-
pleasant about the season, highlight the benefits: how delicious
your morning cup of coffee tastes after coming in from the cold,
how cozy it is to work at a desk while it's rainy and blustery out-
side. Talk about the winter-specific activities you're looking for-
ward to: "I'm going to make a big pot of soup this weekend," "I
get to wear my favorite coat now," "I love the Christmas lights
around town." On a crisp winter morning, comment, "What a
gorgeous day" or "It's so nice out."

Almost inevitably, you will encounter winter-bashing when
you try this. Responding can be simple. At a café in Tromsø, I
heard one woman joke to another: "I need to escape the dark-
ness." "I like it!" her companion responded cheerfully. The goal
is not to discount or ignore someone else's experience, but in-
stead to provide a gentle counter-perspective. When all else
fails, sometimes being direct is useful: sharing your own winter-
time mindset journey by saying "I'm trying to focus on enjoying
winter this year" helps others understand your intentions.

This might feel kind of hokey at first—we're so used to com-
plaining that trying to be positive can feel forced. But it gets
easier—and more natural—over time. If this feels inauthentic
or contrived, consider that an indication of how much you stand
to benefit from changing your language about winter. If we feel
silly pointing out how the cold makes it extra pleasurable to

come inside to a warm space, or how the wan light of winter slants beautifully through the trees, it may be a sign that we've really internalized the normative winter-bashing around us.

Even if the words initially feel a little false, using language to deliberately manifest a winter-is-wonderful mindset is a powerful practice. This isn't just a strategy for helping spread the gospel of positive wintertime mindset. While Wintertime Mindset Ambassadors chip away at the prevailing rhetoric that winter is something to constantly hate on, engaging in winter-positive small talk serves as an act of self-conviction. As a strategy, I think "fake it 'til you make it" is tragically underrated. It's often thought to be an inauthentic approach for those who lack the chops to really feel it or do it, but I see it differently: it's a way to close the gap between where you are and where you'd like to be. It's espousing the mindset you're going for before it comes easily. It's a way of trying on a new outlook, seeing how it feels. Like breaking in a new pair of shoes, using words to create your reality requires trusting in the process until your inner feelings match your outer words.

Saying what we appreciate about winter—what we enjoy about the weather or what cozy activities we're leaning into or what aspects of the season we're looking forward to—strengthens our belief in winter's wonder. When we do this repeatedly—to partners, kids, friends, colleagues, baristas—we start to convince not only ourselves but those around us. As a Wintertime Mindset Ambassador, you can be part of changing the culture: word by word, sentence by sentence, these small comments weaken the pervasive negative view of the season. Cultural change happens one conversation at a time.

◆

THE WORLD RESPONDS differently to someone who is open, look-
ing for wonder, and noticing the good than it does to someone
who is closed-off, finding the flaws in any situation, and com-
plaining. Our words direct our attention which, as we learned
in chapter 3, profoundly shapes our experience. Saying some-
thing out loud gives it power—to ourselves, and to others. After
practicing this in winter, we can start trying this out in other
areas of our lives.

See how changing your language transforms your experience
of the season; observe how finding nice things to say focuses
your attention differently, and how speaking something aloud
helps you notice it more in the future. As you work on your win-
ter words, you might start asking yourself: How would your life
be different if you committed to speaking more positively about
other things? How would your attitude change if you spoke lov-
ingly of yourself, your appearance, your body, or your abilities?
How might your relationships change if you refused to bad-
mouth your partner, your parents, your friends? How might you
experience your home, job, or community differently if you con-
stantly made chitchat about things you appreciate in your house,
your work, your town? How can we navigate the real challenges
we face with ourselves, in our relationships, or when it gets cold
and dark in a way that doesn't involve relentless criticism? Our
words direct our and others' attention: What if we took that
power seriously and vowed to start directing attention where we
actually wanted it to go?

This doesn't mean closing our eyes to reality or refusing to
acknowledge problems. There's room for healthy venting, for

lighthearted kvetching, and for talking through concerns with friends, family, and therapists. There's room for noticing when there are issues that require our time and attention or when a job or living situation no longer meets our needs. But we often default to downplaying our enjoyment. Instead, we can vow to use our complaints strategically and discerningly. We can acknowledge that there is a time and place for airing grievances while habitually speaking about the people in our lives and the world around us with an eye toward appreciation. Try it for a day or a week and see how things change. Does it make you feel different? Does it change the way people respond to you? Does it influence your mood or your energy? Take note of what you feel when you use your language deliberately.

Experiment with winter-celebrating small talk and using your language to strengthen your positive wintertime mindset. Enlist family members or friends to your cause, gently reminding each other to speak the winter you want into existence and compassionately holding each other accountable for inevitable slipups. Notice when people around you are winter-bashing, and see how many times a day you can conduct your own saying-is-believing intervention on yourself. Work winter appreciation into as many conversations as you can. Be a Wintertime Mindset Ambassador, spreading the good word far and wide. Then observe the impact your language has on your view of winter, mood, and enjoyment of the season. You might just be surprised at how influential your words are.

WINTER PRACTICE:
TALKING UP THE SEASON

- **Be a Wintertime Mindset Ambassador:** For the next week, make winter-positive small talk with one person each day. Make your observations specific: "I love the crackle of the ice on the sidewalk"; "The rain smells so clean." Commenting on indoor coziness is also allowed. Saying "It feels so good in here" upon entering somewhere warm has a completely different effect than "It's so gross out." If you encounter winter-bashing, try affirming while rebutting: "Yes, but I love soup season"; "Yes, it has been freezing, but I love using my fireplace at this time of year." How does trying to make authentic, winter-positive chitchat change your experience of the season?

- **Make your own seasonal calendar:** Sit down and divide the winter into at least parts. What designates early, middle, and late winter for you where you live? How will you know when each mini-season has arrived? If you want, you can even make your own five- to seven-day micro-seasons for a more elaborate calendar: "We drink the first hot chocolate," "We shop for Christmas presents," "We celebrate Grandma's birthday." This is a great activity to do with kids!

- **Conduct your own saying-is-believing intervention:** Share what you've learned from this book so far with a friend or family member who struggles with winter, making as specific and compelling of a case as you can.

- **Enlist a buddy:** Ask a friend to be your partner in winter appreciation. Each day, text each other a seasonal highlight: one thing you enjoyed about the winter weather, or something that the cold or darkness facilitated for you that day.

Part Two

Make It
Special

5.

IN THE MOOD

W HEN I RETURNED TO TROMSØ, I was euphoric. I hadn't been there in seven years; the familiar smell of the soap in the airport bathrooms and the sight of snowy, pointy mountains whose outlines I remembered like old friends made me giddy to be back in my northern home.

This was a research trip, and there were interviews and writing in my favorite library spots and discussing mindsets, winter, and happiness vs. meaning with Joar. But in between was Tromsø playtime: film festival screenings with old friends, reindeer hot dogs from Raketten, the tiny kiosk in the town center, and riding the cable car to look down at the twinkling island with stars in my eyes. I sipped coffee while snow crystals swirled outside and marveled at how the polar light was even bluer than I remembered. The city was cold: the thermometer's mercury hovered around freezing, and it precipitated—both rain and snow—most days. But Tromsø still emanated warmth. As I walked around, bundled in wool from head to toe, the amber glow of streetlights reflected off of wet pavement. Indoors, toasty bars and restaurants with dimmed sconces and tapers on tables encouraged lingering. Outside the city center, candles or lamps in the windows of wooden houses bathed snow-covered eaves in gold, transforming neighborhoods into gingerbread villages.

It's a thing of wonder, to be back in a beloved place with fresh eyes, to revisit somewhere that shaped you with more knowledge of where that unknown road led. Every familiar corner of campus, every street I still knew how to navigate, every favorite coffee shop washed me in nostalgia. Rob and I—now married—started dating while I lived in Tromsø (he in Baltimore), when he was the only person I could confess my initial loneliness to. Being back in the city with him now, with so much hindsight and gratitude, filled me with awe. Tromsø's winter was the ideal backdrop for feeling all my feelings. The darkness lured me inward. The city's many cozy cafés—Vervet, Smørtorget, Kaffebønna, and Risø—provided me with steaming beverages, comfy chairs, and candlelight by which to reflect. I walked alongside my thoughts through snow and rain on slick streets and let myself get lost in reverie in the library, looking over the fjord at the towering mountain of Tromsdalstinden. The long nights made space for contemplation: feelings too intense to be looked at in broad daylight crept out of my head and curled by my feet in the evening shadows.

Tromsø invites this kind of reverie. Norwegian culture has a quiet softness to it: trekking through the woods in silence, spending a cabin weekend surrounded by loved ones but buried in separate books, hearing the *shhhh, shhhh* of skis on snow: it's a place where companionable wordlessness thrives. In winter, especially, it feels as if places are designed to facilitate intimacy and introspection, all snug nooks and low lighting. Hygge has even been defined as "socializing for introverts." Winter can come as a relief after the high-energy extraversion of summer: a time when people are expected—and allowed—to seek calm. Scandinavians chase peaceful, cozy feelings all winter long, making the season uniquely magical.

SERENITY NOW

These peaceful, cozy feelings are what psychologists refer to as "low-arousal positive emotions." Affective scientists categorize emotions as positive or negative (what feels good or bad) and by how "arousing" they are. Arousal is a physiological state, and it's not always sexual; it includes your heart beating faster, butterflies in your stomach, and feeling highly alert. High-arousal positive emotions, like excitement and joy, are stimulating and energetic. In contrast, low-arousal positive emotions, like contentment and serenity, are calming and tranquil.

It's not objectively better to experience high-arousal positive feelings than low-arousal ones, or vice versa. But there is evidence that, on an individual and cultural basis, people tend to prefer one class over the other. Americans and Canadians generally value high-arousal positive emotions. When researchers asked different groups of students to describe their ideal state, a representative European American student wrote, *"I just want to be happy. Normally for me that means I would be doing something exciting . . . I just like excitement."* But contrary to Americans, East Asians (for example, in China, Hong Kong, Taiwan, and Japan) tend to value low-arousal positive emotions most highly. When asked the same question, a Hong Kong Chinese student wrote a typical response: *"My ideal state is to be quiet, serene, happy, and positive."* Both students expressed a desire for happiness, but they defined happiness differently: for some, happiness means excitement, while for others, it means serenity. This cultural difference in preference has been observed within the US as well: Asian Americans, on average, value low-arousal positive emotions more than European Americans.

This preference—this value—is both individual and cultural. It's why the most socially desirable answer to the question "How are you doing?" in the US is "Great!" and why enthusiasm is often viewed as synonymous with dedication and commitment in an American context. It's why ideal American job candidates often convey *excitement* and *passion* about the work. And it's why popular children's birthday party activities in the US (and UK) are often exciting: pool parties, roller-skating, laser tag.

Like mindsets, these valuations don't come out of nowhere. Our emotional preferences are shaped by our families, our peers, our communities, and the media. Together, these key influencers inform what we desire and how we feel we should act. Is it better to come across as excited or as cool and collected? Do we want to feel giddy and enthusiastic or calm and serene?

Jeanne Tsai, a psychology professor at Stanford University, has pioneered work on "ideal affect"—how people ideally want to feel and how this varies across cultures. Tsai and her colleagues investigate how the media reflects and perpetuates a hierarchy of emotional states, with high-arousal positive emotions being perceived as best in the US and Canada, and low-arousal positive emotions taking top spot in places like Taiwan and China. Since many of these preferences emerge at a young age, Tsai and her colleagues have used their academic expertise to study children's books. "We looked at best-selling storybooks in the United States as well as in Taiwan, and we coded the emotional content of those storybooks," Tsai explained. "Particularly, we looked at the emotional expressions of the characters in those storybooks." In the US, stories like *Where the Wild Things Are* have characters—like Max—bounding along as part of wild rumpuses. "We found that in American storybooks, best-selling storybooks, the characters show more of these open, toothy, what we call these 'excitement smiles,' whereas in the Taiwanese best-selling storybooks, more of these characters showed these closed, smaller, what we call 'calm smiles.'" Bigger smiles suggest more high-arousal positive emotions, and American storybook characters smile more broadly than their Taiwanese counterparts. American characters are also more likely to be engaging in high-arousal activities, like running and jumping, than Taiwanese characters. Tsai and her colleagues also studied smiles in other media. In the US, best-selling women's magazines are more likely to feature cover women smiling broadly; in China, the women sport calm, close-lipped smiles. Looking at the official pictures of politicians, business leaders, and academics, those in the US are six times more likely to be seen smiling widely than their Chinese counterparts.

"So the idea here is that illustrators and publicists and advertisers choose images that reflect the cultural ideal. And then we, as consumers of those images, see thousands and thousands of those images on a daily basis, and begin to internalize those ideals. We internalize them without even being aware of it, and then we reproduce them," Tsai said.

These emotional-state valuations influence our choices and behaviors. How we spend our money, where we vacation, what activities we pursue for exercise, and what we think of as a fun weekend are informed by our desire for higher- or lower-arousal feelings. Research shows that these values even influence our mindsets about aging: as our ability to engage in highly stimulating physical activity declines, do we view that with dread or can we think of calm and peaceful activities to look forward to? And when others match our ideal affect—when they display the emotions we value most—we're more likely to judge them favorably. Our ideal affect can shape how we perceive others, how much we enjoy daily activities, and whether winter's calm feels boring or peaceful.

I OFTEN WONDER if the Western preference for high-arousal positive emotions is one of the reasons we don't enjoy winter more. If summer is more associated with running and romping, messy outdoor play, and BBQs, maybe winter's low-arousal pleasures make the season seem boring. Winter certainly provides opportunities for high-arousal activities—skiing, playing ice hockey, snowball fights, jumping in puddles, cold-water swims. Yet the season lends itself especially to calming activities: quiet winter walks, sinking into the bath, intimate dinner parties, candlelit movie nights, reading, baking, and crafting.* Perhaps the per-

---

*And many high-arousal winter activities aren't regularly accessible to most. For example, skiing, hockey, and ice-skating are location- and weather-dependent and can be expensive. Popular lower-arousal activities, in contrast, are more broadly accessible.

ceived dearth of exciting activities contributes to a bias against winter, particularly in the US.

Research hasn't yet looked at which emotions are preferred in Scandinavia, but I suspect these cultures might fall in between American and East Asian sentiments. Finland is often ranked as the "happiest country on Earth." But visiting Finland, you're unlikely to observe outward, obvious signs of this happiness. Finns don't usually display the broad, toothy grins of Americans and might even describe themselves as gloomy or moody: Finland is home to the greatest proportion of death metal bands on Earth. What's described as "happiness" can really be thought of as a kind of contentment: not a jumping-for-joy giddiness, but a strong, solid sense of well-being, enabled by Finland's robust social safety nets, which give people security and stability.* Part of Finland's success in world happiness rankings may be due to a definition of happiness that is more low arousal than high arousal: a quiet, grounded satisfaction with the overall state of one's life.

Acknowledging and embracing low-arousal positive emotions can be an entry point to increasing winter enjoyment. We can purposely see winter as a time of year to lean into these emotions. Rather than feeling bored or stifled by quieter activities, we can thank winter for making space for the serene. If "for everything, there is a season," winter can be the season of low-arousal positivity: of calm, cozy, relaxation, quiet intimacy, and connecting deeply—with others, with ourselves, and with our interests. Here lies an avenue for changing our mindsets that

---

*Similarly, *lagom* is an important Swedish concept and cultural value: the idea of a balanced state that is "just right"—not too much and not too little; finding contentment in satisfaction.

can expand our sense of happiness at any time of year: even when we don't feel like jumping for joy, we can connect to a wide variety of ways to feel good. During quieter, slower seasons, we can lean on our low-arousal positive emotions to nourish and sustain us. By enjoying a greater range of positive emotions, we can find more ways to feel happy, and find happiness in more situations.

AND THERE'S NO better place to start than with the emotion at the heart of Scandinavia's love affair with winter: hygge.

BIG LIGHT OFF

Copenhagen in January involved a lot of pallid, low-lying clouds and rain that oscillated between mist and downpour. Rob and I were out to a casual dinner when I started reflecting on the differences between Danish restaurants and the establishments we'd been to in the US the week before: celebratory, special occasion places. But the ambiance of those lovely restaurants at home and the restaurant in Copenhagen was worlds apart. I slowly asked Rob: "Am I . . . crazy? Or can you feel a difference?"

"It's not even close," he replied.

THE RESTAURANT we were at in Copenhagen was ordinary, nothing lavish or exclusive. And yet the vibes were immaculate. Soft lamps hung over the tables, providing diffuse light that allowed us to read the menu but wasn't harsh. When we arrived, we hung our coats next to our table on real coatracks—rather than smushing them behind us in a booth or hanging them wetly on the backs of our chairs. Candles adorned every table—not tea lights in little glass cups, but big, fat pillar candles with meaty flames. The restaurant's warmth melted the chill from my bones and washed away the memory of the cold, damp walk there, relaxing my body without effort.

It's not that there aren't cozy restaurants throughout the US. There are thousands of warm dining establishments with good lighting, leather booths, checkered tablecloths, and coatrooms. But coziness is not the default atmosphere in much of the US: many places remain chilly in winter and have harsh overhead lights. Real candles are treasures often reserved for fancy—and expensive—eateries. The epiphany I had in that Copenhagen restaurant is that at least some aspects of hygge are almost trivially replicable, and many places could easily be made cozier. Turn off overhead lights and make the lighting soft and low. Put candles on every table. Make it warm enough that being inside allows people to recover from the cold. Give people somewhere to hang their jackets.

These simple acts add up. Soft lighting takes advantage of the darkness, giving the indoors a quiet quality that can't be replicated when it's bright and sunny, turning long winter nights into an asset. Proper heating promotes physiological relaxation—our muscles hold tension when they're cold—and allows us to bounce back from being outside, which makes it easier to get out in the first place. And a place to hang coats facilitates dressing appropriately for the weather. I think of how many times in the US—growing up in New Jersey, visiting Chicago, even out to dinner in foggy San Francisco—when it felt like, in the winter, I just couldn't get warm. Even in restaurants, I'd often leave my coat on.

Culture is the difference between what is done here and there and what is done everywhere. A few cozy restaurants stand alone; when most establishments are cozy, you get a cozy culture. When everywhere is cozy, it's easier to enjoy the dark days of winter. The Nordics' trademark coziness is part of what enables people throughout Norway, Finland, Denmark, and Sweden to embrace the season. In this part of the world, people look forward to the opportunities for hygge that winter brings and see it as a special emotion to luxuriate in during the darkest times of the year. It's a balm for long nights and a way to recover from the fast pace of spring, summer, and fall. Leaning into winter's coziness is also a chance to cultivate our appreciation and enjoyment of low-arousal positive emotions like calm and contentment.

PERHAPS NO INGREDIENT in the physical surroundings is more important to inducing a sense of coziness and cultivating hygge than light.

Interior designers, Scandinavians, and the cozy-obsessed all have an understanding and appreciation of good lighting. Soft lighting is the difference between fighting *against* winter darkness (trying to banish it, mentally and physically, by flooding our homes with bright, overhead lights) and working *with* winter darkness by inviting it in, allowing it to gather softly in corners and under tables, and complementing it with diffuse, amber light. Paradoxically, brighter lights in winter can make us feel more tired: the contrast of indoor flood lights and outdoor blackness is taxing, whereas soft lighting feels restful.

Candles invite intimacy and relaxation. The average Dane burns 3.5 kilograms of candles a year, with almost 60 percent of Danes lighting candles daily. The ubiquitous nature of candles in Denmark—particularly iconic pillar candles—makes coziness a commonplace part of everyday life. In the US, hygge spots must be sought out like hidden gems, and candles are reserved for special occasions. In Denmark, the cozy vibe is the default: an inexhaustive list of places I saw open-flame candles in Copenhagen included casual and fine-dining restaurants, coffee shops, lanterns on the sidewalk, a grocery store window, and a hair salon.

Scandinavians in general and Danes in particular are choosy about quality of light. Warm light has reddish undertones (like the sun and fire) and feels more natural. Cool light has blue undertones and feels artificial (like the lights in hospitals and the blue lights of phones and computer screens). The warmer a light, the more natural it feels. It's also easier on our eyes (hence current problems caused by too much exposure to blue light via our screens, and why bright overhead lights can make us feel tired in winter). Being thoughtful about light creates a pleasant atmosphere: while colder light can help with concentration and can be good for workplaces, light in relaxing spaces should be warm.

Since living in Norway, I've become obsessed with what I call Big Light Off: turning off large overhead lights in favor of only twinkly lights, candles, and soft lamps. Big Light Off is time for reading, resting, and snuggling. Big Light Off allows for conversation, secret-sharing, and whispers, and helps me wind down at the end of the day and get ready for sleep*; research suggests that exposure to even normal living-room lights before bed suppresses the release of melatonin, so Big Light Off time can help you fall asleep faster. It fast-tracks intimacy and makes space for vulnerability, changing the feel of gatherings completely. I've been known to enter parties and stealthily turn off overhead lights and switch on lamps to achieve the perfect Big Light Off vibe. If someone tries to turn on a Big Light during Big Light Off time, I will hiss at them like a raccoon caught in an alleyway. If you banished all overhead lighting—all Big Lights—from your home this winter and used only Little Lights, you'd be 90 percent cozier, guaranteed.

Scandinavians naturally observe Big Light Off during the many hours of winter night. I've seen this in homes throughout Norway, Finland, and Denmark, and from outside as well. It's common to see lights or lit candles in the windows of Nordic homes, which often have outlets in the ceilings above windows for hanging lamps. These lights are a boon for both those on the outside looking in and those who look out from indoors and see a glow against the blackness of the night. Window lights make outdoor winter walks feel warmer and more communal, brightening neighborhoods and city streets for everyone.† It's a shame that in most places, Christmas lights are expected to come down in early January, during the darkest part of the year, when we need luminosity and comfort the most. In Edmonton, Christ-

---

*Implementing evening Big Light Off time can also be a good strategy for disconnecting from screens before bed, which can improve sleep quality, helping reduce winter lethargy.
†If you're concerned about energy prices or sustainability, warm-toned LED lights use very little energy and achieve the same effect.

mas lights have been rebranded as "Winter Lights," and people are now encouraged to leave them up all season long. Enthusiasts leave theirs shining until the spring equinox at the end of March.

HYGGE HAS BECOME an around-the-world sensation, a Scandinavian export as well-known as Ikea or Lego. It's encouraging that people are eager to embrace coziness and ready to hear strategies for making dark days feel comforting. But I can't help but feel that part of hygge's massive success is its marketability. Countless advertising campaigns promise that *this* blanket, *this* candle, *this* lamp, *this* living room furniture, *this* tea will bring you the coziness you're craving. Part of hygge's spread around the world is driven by companies seeing dollar signs. In this interpretation, it's something to be purchased. A curated aesthetic that can—and must—be bought.

The stuff can help—soft blankets, peaceful lighting, and fuzzy slippers all facilitate serenity. Physical objects influence our mental states, which is why many people feel calmer and better able to think in organized spaces, we relax in the presence of soft lighting, and gathering around fire helps us speak more vulnerably. There are lots of wonderful things that can help a space feel cozy; I'm particularly attached to my chunky, purple, weighted blanket and my Mr. Coffee coffee warmer, and I insist on having a shaggy rug at my bedside so I can get up without stepping on the cold floor. But focusing solely on trappings of coziness distorts the concept, making the aesthetic of hygge the goal. The idea of a quick fix, in the form of stuff, is an appealing solution to the problem of winter woe. It's easier to buy a few scented candles than to fundamentally change our relationship with darkness. But the feeling of hygge is profound and cannot be credited to material things alone. Chunky sweaters and hot chocolate are neither necessary nor sufficient in creating coziness.

Hygge, and the Norwegian counterpart *koselig*, is an internal state more than an aesthetic.* It's a feeling of contentment, and a gentle peacefulness. It's the vibe between Christmas and New Year's (now sometimes referred to as "Twixtmas"), when you lie around with your loved ones, eating cookies and getting confused about what day of the week it is. It's coming home on a Friday night after the end of a long week, with no plans ahead, no rushing, nowhere to go, when you can kick off your shoes and take off your hard pants and snuggle on the couch. It's the feeling of a snow day we remember from childhood: a disruption of the normal, a new possibility, being home in a storm, hearing the wind whip and watching the rain lash the windows while knowing you're safely cocooned indoors.

We don't need fancy stuff to feel hygge. With the right mindset and intention, any space can be made hygge; without such intention and emotion, no amount of fuzzy blankets and candles can make a gathering feel cozy. In Norway, calling something koselig is a profound compliment, and not only can dinner parties and nights reading in front of the fire be koselig, but so can hikes, ski trips, school days, and even meetings. I once attended a small conference on the science of meditation in Tromsø, filled with warm people and good conversation, and I overheard one of the participants tell the conference organizer,

---

*Meik Wiking, the author of *The Little Book of Hygge*, makes this point as well—it's often a misinterpretation, or willful ignorance, of his writing that reduces hygge to a commercial aesthetic.

my friend Ida, that it was a really koselig conference. Ida was thrilled.

As you cultivate your appreciation of low-arousal positive emotions and lean into winter's coziness, remember that the things are not the hygge. Fostering small moments of peacefulness and connection, intimate conversation, and quiet contentment are far more essential and impactful than the latest soft-toned Scandinavian home decor.

HYGGE AROUND THE GLOBE

Scandinavia sometimes seems to have the monopoly on coziness, but hygge is just one flavor, and there is coziness to be found all over the world, if only we look for it.

In Vienna, coffeehouses serve hot drinks and sweets as diners idle away afternoons sheltered from the cold. The buildings themselves are often stately and gorgeous: marble countertops and wood paneling, high ceilings and gold table lamps. Waiters and waitresses wear crisp uniforms with formal shirts and black jackets. Coffee is served on a silver tray with a small glass of water. Everything is done just so, yet the formality is in service of a restaurant that is not stuffy but comfortable and relaxed, where everyone seems at ease. While Viennese coffeehouses are popular year-round, in the winter they take on a special resonance as refuges. To have a place enticing you to leave your house, that doesn't rush you, where you can read or think or talk for hours is the embodiment of hygge. It goes beyond the commodification of coziness. Their enduring impact is as public spaces for private thought and conversation; places that are of the world and in the world, yet invite solitude or intimacy. At Café Tirolerhof, a waiter whose grumpy face belied his warm demeanor chided us gently against impatience: thinking he hadn't seen or heard us the first time we asked for the check, we flagged his attention and asked again. "Relax," he admonished playfully. "Sit, enjoy, take your time. Give me a minute"; this was despite a line of patrons out the door waiting for tables. At Café Schwarzenberg, rather than the standard description of the restaurant's founding, the menu provides a philosophical overview of the importance of such a place: "A cozy atmosphere has no bounds, and you can surrender yourself completely while having a cup of coffee." The Viennese have perfected the art of taking something mundane—our daily cup of coffee—and turning it into a small, miraculous ritual.

In Japan, cramped restaurants and *izakayas* create cozy, steamy environments for sipping hot sake. At home, families gather around *kotatsu*: a low table with a heater underneath, over which a blanket is draped, creating a nest that chases away the chill and a hub for eating, doing homework, and connecting. In the Netherlands, wood-paneled, candlelit, and overly toasty "brown bars" ooze coziness, and people huddle for hours drinking beer and playing cards as rain falls over the canals outside. In the Outer Hebrides, whiskey is sipped around wood-burning stoves with roaring fires, a striking combination that warms you inside and out.

Scandinavia doesn't even have a monopoly on elevated, untranslatable words for coziness. The Dutch word closest to hygge is *gezellig*, which is more of a cozy conviviality. There's an important social component to gezellig: it's about not just physical coziness, but feeling comfortable and content with friends, with good conversation and good energy.* In Germany, land of Christmas markets, *gemütlichkeit* is "a feeling of warmth, friendliness, and good cheer." Throughout Scotland and Ireland, the Gaelic word *cèilidh* captures a cultural value of cozy, communal gatherings: essential year-round, but especially when winter winds howl. Many cold, damp, gray countries have special words and concepts that capture feelings of coziness.

THE UK IS TRADITIONALLY REGARDED—by locals and foreigners alike—as having a particularly gloomy winter. But my view is that the UK has a cozy culture for which it is rarely recognized. Lauren Heathcote, while telling me more about the fears she had moving from San Francisco to London, revealed that she has come to appreciate English winter culture more since returning home. "Moving to London, the winter and the dark was a big thing. And your research has been back of my mind," she told me. Her familiarity with wintertime mindset inspired her to look at London's winter differently. She described the UK's pub culture as a beautiful British institution of coziness: pub-goers nurse mugs of mulled wine while dogs roam, curling in front of the fire or under tables at the feet of patrons. Golden light emanates from windows as you walk down the road. The British might not have a mega-marketable word for it, but the coziness is there, waiting to be observed. "I always pay attention to that," Lauren tells me. "And really notice that and see there's a very sort of conscious effort to use light and open fires. And every high street has five or six pubs on it, minimum, and they'll

---

*Gezellig is even cited as a reason many Dutch women prefer to give birth at home rather than in a hospital: it's cozier and more intimate.

often have fires, they'll have candles on every table. And so that feels really special and lovely." Add to the UK's pub culture big Sunday roasts for dinner, all-day tea drinking, and specialty in producing hearty, steaming meat and veggie pies, and it's hard to see how the UK isn't hailed the world over as a hygge winter destination.

British coziness can be a paradox: even amidst behaviors, decor, and atmospheres that are undeniably cozy, it doesn't seem to be a very explicit part of the vernacular like it is in Scandinavia. "People do it, we do it. But there isn't the discussion around it," Lauren reflected. As Lauren experienced when she moved back to London, our mindsets can help us reap the rewards of cozy stuff and hygge environments. But without the mindset, the presence of these cozy comforts can go overlooked and underappreciated.

With a positive wintertime mindset, however, coziness can transform mundane activities into seasonal indulgences. Watching TV or a movie by candlelight, with a mug of something warm, becomes a chance to feel peaceful. In Norway, they call this kind of at-home lounging on Friday evening "Fredag kos": Friday cozy. Many of us might spend Friday evenings unwinding on the couch. But the difference between "What are you doing tonight?" "Oh nothing, just staying in," and "What are you doing tonight?" "Fredag kos" is as vast as the difference between "frozen H2O" and "snowflake." The benefits of having a special word go beyond the literal translation: by naming it, hygge is elevated as an important part of Danish culture and a treasured winter joy.

To feel more of these warm and fuzzy winter emotions, we can turn to our own cultures. To me, there's nothing more hygge than a Friday night Shabbat dinner—saying goodbye to the workweek, lighting candles, eating a special meal, and relaxing with family and friends. It's something I look forward to, and I don't need to pretend to be Danish to access it. I can make my own family traditions into a cozy practice that takes on a special winter flavor, with chicken slow-roasted over root vegetables, dark red wine, and apple cake and tea for dessert. What parts of your culture might not be branded as cozy but actually are? Where can you make your own cozy rituals, borrowing inspiration from parts of the world that excel in this area while adapting them to your climate, your country, and your life? By valuing the coziness around you and finding moments to add a little extra koselig, you'll transform winter into a season of quiet contentment. Because our mindsets don't just influence how we see winter: they influence what we feel during the season too.

SEEKING AWE

Becky stood next to me on the viewing platform. Our breath fogged in front of us and planks of smooth wood stretched beneath our feet, designed to blend in to the scenery around us. Our mittened hands gripped the iron railing. Ahead stretched the Bergsfjord, a calm watery outlet that gives way to the snowy Bergsbotten mountain range, with its distinctive U-shaped dip between peaks, a study in contrasts as the jagged points of the mountains smooth into gentle curves. The lights of a village twinkled far below, golden against the freezing night.

But Becky and I weren't taking in the scenic vista that brings road trippers from all over the world and is a highlight on the

Senja *nasjonale turistveger,* or Norwegian Scenic Routes. On this night in January 2015, when she came to visit me in Tromsø, our eyes were glued to the sky.

Above us, the midnight darkness was beaten back by the glow of the aurora borealis. Not only greens, but pinks and purples striped the sky. This aurora was particularly intense: vertical streaks of light looked like curtains blowing in the wind, undulating like eels, moving as if alive. The northern lights are translucent, and through green and purple shimmers stars glowed, pinpricks of stagnant light, backdrop to the watercolor fireworks. My nose burned with cold although my body was full of heat and wonder. The intensity of it was physical, and I found myself running up and down the wooden beams, needing to get the energy out, until I was scolded by a photographer for shaking her camera. (Later, I learned that the northern lights can only be photographed with long-exposure camera shots, which require absolute stillness in order to come out clearly, and I felt guilty for my jolting enthusiasm.) Becky and I held hands, twin necks crinking to the heavens, and I overflowed with gratitude for every experience, every breath, every footstep that led me to this, allowing me to bear witness to something so wondrous with someone I love so much. What I was feeling was awe.

AWE ARISES WHEN something takes our breath away in wonder. At the beach, watching the waves crash; standing in a forest, marveling at giant redwoods or sky-high pine trees; meeting a baby for the first time, cooing over fingernails that seem too tiny to be real: these moments are, quite literally, awe-some.

Awe is one of our most profound and potent emotions—though it's one we may think about the least. The study of awe is relatively young: modern scientists have been researching it for a few decades, far less time than they've spent on emotions like happiness, sadness, or anger. Psychologists who study awe say it falls "somewhere between an emotion and an altered state of consciousness" and that it has two key qualities. First, awe involves perceptions of vastness. In surveys, researchers measure this by asking people to agree or disagree with statements like "I felt that I was in the presence of something grand." This sensation of vastness can be physical (looking at the ocean, the stars, or a mountainscape), conceptual (encountering an earth-shattering idea or meeting a charismatic leader like the Dalai Lama) or emotional (witnessing the birth of a child or hearing a symphony play a stunning piece of music). The vastness is out of the ordinary, so it shakes up our everyday reality, which leads to the second aspect of awe: the need to accommodate this vastness mentally. Awe-inspiring experiences challenge our everyday perceptions, requiring us to update our mental models. Researchers measure this component of awe with statements like "I struggled to take in all that I was experiencing at once." That's why awe-full experiences often elicit newfound perspectives: things that seemed hugely important may suddenly appear less so compared with watching a new life come into the world, looking into the infinite night sky, or the triumph of a great piece of music.

WHEN WE LOOK at winter with a sense of wonder, it can be a season full of awe. The clean whiteness of fresh snow, the movement of fog and rain, the twinkly lights of Christmas trees and ornate shop displays can all invoke a sense of amazement. In addition to intensifying our appreciation of calm and cozy feelings, we can use winter as a chance to strengthen our capability for awe.

Virginia Sturm, a professor at the University of California, San Francisco, led the first study to test whether people can deliberately cultivate awe in daily life. In this study, people in their sixties, seventies, and eighties were asked to take a weekly outdoor walk for at least fifteen minutes. One group was randomly assigned to just walk. The other group was assigned to take *awe* walks. These participants were told to "tap into your childlike sense of wonder" and to "approach what you see with fresh eyes." They were encouraged to seek out new places, because "you're more likely to feel awe in a novel environment where the sights and sounds are unexpected and unfamiliar to you," but also told that "there's nothing wrong with revisiting your favorite spots if you find that they consistently fill you with awe."

Over eight weeks, the awe-walkers reported greater joy and experienced greater prosocial positive emotions. These benefits went beyond the time participants spent walking. "I was surprised that the awe walks had what we call a spillover effect," Sturm explained. "It wasn't just during the walk that people reported not only more awe, but other positive emotions." Those who took awe walks, compared with those who took normal outdoor walks, reported more of the emotions that foster connection and help us build relationships even when they weren't walking. They also reported larger decreases in daily distress over time. Awe, Sturm told me, "sets us up to deal with stressors more effectively, and gives us more space to respond without having a full blown negative emotional reaction." Just fifteen minutes of awe-walking a week for two months heightened joy and weakened distress.

This joy was visible: participants were asked to take selfies during their walks. The research team then coded participants' smile intensity in those pictures. "We were really surprised to see, over time, people's smiles got bigger when they were taking the awe walks." The research team traced silhouettes of each person in their selfies and computed the number of pixels in the person's face versus the background. Over eight weeks of awe-walking, participants' faces shrank relative to their scenic backgrounds. Sturm and other researchers refer to this as displaying a "small sense of self." This isn't a bad thing: if you've ever felt tiny in comparison with the hugeness of the ocean, the tallness of trees, or the bravery of someone fighting for justice, you've experienced this small sense of self. Awe puts ourselves—and our problems—in perspective.

Research shows that awe helps us feel more life satisfaction, more connected to humanity and the world, and less bogged down and annoyed by day-to-day concerns. Awe is associated with reduced symptoms of post-traumatic stress disorder (in both military veterans and young people from underserved communities), feeling happier on a moment-by-moment basis, and reduced daily distress. Experiencing awe might even make you nicer: the emotion is associated with greater generosity and prosociality (in lab experiments, this included helping people more, cooperating more, sharing more, and sacrificing more for others), less narcissism, and decreased aggression.

According to Sturm, our mindsets can help us feel more awe. "I am really a proponent of not just the walk, but the mindset." She brought up what's referred to in psychology as the "upward spiral of well-being": "where, when you have positive emotions, that begets other positive emotions and makes it more likely that you'll feel more. In that spirit, we thought awe might perform in a similar way, where a little awe would help you feel more awe." Sturm highlighted how the benefits of awe walks sneak up on you. "Really, you're just like, 'Oh, I'm appreciating this leaf,'" she says. "And then the downstream effect is, maybe I'm a little nicer. But it wasn't deliberate or effortful."

Internally, positive awe experiences have been linked to increased arousal of the parasympathetic nervous system, which is associated with feel-good states, including social connection, feeling calm, and positive emotions. "When we feel awe," Sturm explains, "our heart rate is slower, our breathing is slower and deeper, and our heart rate is more variable. And all of these things are good in terms of not only promoting this quiet, peaceful internal state, but also helping us to recover from stress and negative emotions." After being primed to feel awe, people report lower stress levels and exhibit decreased sympathetic nervous system arousal (the system that kicks us into high gear, or fight-or-flight mode) when talking about daily stressors. In our brains, awe reduces activity in the default mode network—a region associated with mind-wandering (feeling distracted and disengaged from the present moment) and self-reflective thought (feeling self-conscious and focusing only on ourselves). These neural findings indicate that awe can induce unselfconscious present-moment awareness. And out of all the positive emotions, awe is the strongest predictor of lowered levels of IL-6, a chemical messenger often produced by damaged tissue cells that triggers inflammation and—when overactive—can lead to chronic illness and susceptibility to sickness. So feeling awe isn't just healing for our minds—it can have positive effects on our bodies as well.

◆

HOW CAN WE get more awe in our daily lives? It would be great if we could all see the northern lights when the sun sets, spend hours each day taking in sweeping city skylines, or immerse ourselves in the forest on our lunch break. If you do any of these regularly, you have a fast-track to awe. But what if we don't live in the mountains or the forest? What if we don't have easy access to stunning nature or beautiful cities? The awe-walk study, like the Noticing Nature Intervention, shows us that it's less what we look at than how we see it. We don't have to wait for awe to wash over us. In the awe-walk study, people in the awe-walk group were able to feel more awe *on purpose.* They became better at noticing awe-inspiring scenes or small objects of wonder. This suggests it's possible to purposely increase our awe by harnessing our attention. By adopting the perspective that tiny miracles are all around, we can strengthen our ability to feel awe.

Awe may be a particularly useful antidote to some of our winter woes. By increasing feelings of connection and decreasing distress, awe can uplift gloomy moods and weaken feelings of loneliness or isolation. Awe can soothe the winter blues, counteracting some of the staleness we feel when winter seems to drag. The intensity of winter storms, the vastness of a night sky full of stars, the resilience of life that pokes through frozen ground: all can invoke feelings of awe. By shaking up our everyday conceptions, awe can help us see the season with fresh eyes. Sensitizing our awareness to awe when the trees are bare and the grasses dormant makes it more likely that we'll notice the wonderful, magical, and delightful at any time of year. A reliable mood-booster, meaning-maker, and perspective-giver, awe can be a potent ally during the winters of our lives: times of hardship, grief, stress, or struggle. Intentionally seeking awe is a practice that can set off your own personal upward spiral of positive emotions when you need them most.

MAKE YOUR TIME outdoors this winter count double by leveraging the benefits of awe. First, set the awe-walk intention. (Not every walk has to be an awe walk, so choose deliberately). Put your phone on do not disturb (or on airplane mode, or leave it at home) to facilitate being present. Keep a casual, easy pace—you notice more when you slow down. Consider walking somewhere new, since novelty cultivates awe. Places with beautiful nature are especially good: shores near water (ocean, lake, or river), clear nights when you can see the stars, anywhere at sunrise or sunset, tree-lined trails. Put one foot in front of the other and activate your awe-eyes. Look at your surroundings with a fresh perspective: views, nature, objects, even other people. Keep a lookout for small wonders: a flash of red robin against white snow, new buds sprouting on bare branches, an interesting frost pattern, the reflection of lights on rain-slicked streets. Try to find the vastness in what you're observing, whether it's an expansive vista or the delicate veins of a leaf. Think about what it takes for you to observe what you're seeing: the magical combination of sun, light, and soil that makes plants; the millennia of heat and wind that form rocks; the incredible human collaboration that builds cities. Not every awe walk has to have a life-changing revelation, but if you find yourself marveling at the improbable miracle of your own existence, lean into it.

And then, when it's over, allow yourself to move on. Maybe that means returning to child- or elder-care tasks, maybe it means heading out to wait tables or stock groceries, maybe it means returning to a full inbox for an afternoon of email slogging. The beauty and benefit of an awe walk is that, while it can remove us from the day-to-day, it still remains accessible. It's right outside our door, any time we want it.

TO REALLY *FEEL* WINTER, we can lean into our low-arousal positive emotions, intentionally cultivating an appreciation for feeling calm, cozy, and content. Use your physical surroundings—particularly low lights and candles—to create a serene atmosphere. Notice how the darkness is an opportunity for peacefulness that can be hard to find in bright daylight. Draw from your own history, culture, and traditions to create moments of hygge. Practice finding awe, especially outdoors. See how acknowledging winter as a season for a more subtle, subdued kind of pleasure gives you permission to find well-being in everyday moments of peace. And observe how the mindset you adopt impacts your feelings. Embracing winter as a season of awe, calm, and hygge can strengthen your ability to feel these emotions year-round.

WINTER PRACTICE:
SETTING THE MOOD

- **Lean into LAP:** What are your favorite low-arousal positive activities? The ones that make you feel calm, content, and at ease? Puzzling, knitting, taking baths, baking, reading, playing calm video games, slow walks, meditating, and painting can all be ways to cultivate low-arousal positive emotions. Over the next week, pick one or two activities that feel peaceful and relaxing and try to enjoy them at least once a day. How does it feel to proactively pursue peace? Where else can you find quiet contentment this winter?

- **Big Light Off:** Set up your space with small lamps, twinkly lights, and candles to facilitate Big Light Off (thrift stores often have many lamps on offer). Each evening, declare it "Big Light Off," and turn off all large overhead lights. How does changing the light in your home impact how you feel? How does it impact your sleep?

- **Cultivate cultural coziness:** Drawing inspiration from Scandinavia and hygge, what cultural traditions did you grow up with that make you feel cozy? These might be Shabbat dinners, Sunday roasts, particular comfort foods from your childhood, or warming drinks. Look at some of your favorite winter foods and activities from when you were young and see if there are any traditions you can draw on from your own culture to help you feel cozy this winter.

- **Take an awe walk:** Go on a walk with an eye for awe. Put your phone away, walk slowly, and look at your surroundings with fresh eyes. What do you see? What does awe feel like for you? How does taking an awe walk influence the rest of your day?

6.

NIGHTS, LIGHTS,
AND RITES

OUTSIDE, it was proper dreich (adjective, Scottish: dreary; bleak [especially of weather]), typical of early February on the Isle of Lewis, in the Outer Hebrides, off the coast of Scotland. We traveled to the Western Isles to experience a winter with less ice and snow and more wind and rain. The Isle of Lewis did not disappoint. The day's weather alternated between driving rain, drizzle, and magnificent sunbeams shining through the clouds onto the grassy, treeless hills of "the rock," as my host Jon Macleod affectionately calls the island. Wind was the only constant, which oscillated between breeze and gust outside Grinneabhat, the former school turned café, hostel, and cultural organization in the tiny village of Bragar. Grinneabhat's inviting café space, with its friendly wood-burning stove and view of the loch, had been transformed for the evening, its tables pushed into a large U-shape and adorned with red roses, for Burns Night.

Rob and I were elevated to guests-of-honor status, seated at the head table. We watched, wide-eyed and giggling, as the kilted bagpiper, bedecked in knee-high green socks and red-faced from piping, slowly entered the room. The thirty or so attendees—village members young and old—rose and clapped to the primal wail echoing from the high ceilings. Behind the bagpiper, one of the chefs reverently carried the star of the show: the haggis. The atmosphere was playful, welcoming, and infectious. The evening held the air of ceremony with the trappings of formality—fancy dress, celebratory food, rapt attention—yet didn't take itself too seriously.

In Scotland, Burns suppers celebrate beloved national poet Robert Burns. The gatherings are usually on his birthday, January 25, in the heart of winter, although this one had been organized for our visit in early February. Burns nights follow a formula, starting with the piping-in of the haggis, the humble yet revered food of Scotland, which Burns described as the "Great Chieftain o' the Puddin-race!" A savory pudding of sheep's organs minced with spices, cooked inside the animal's stomach, the large, balloon-like sausage filled with ground meat appeared particularly comical held aloft and solitary on a white plate.

We had been briefed on the order of events, so I was able to—mostly—contain my amusement when a young man in his early twenties stood up and began reciting a poem to the haggis. "Address to a Haggis" is one of Burns's most well-known and most cherished poems, in which he adoringly and humorously describes the sausage, expounding on its importance in Scottish life. While other cultures may turn up their nose at such lowly fare, of those who are "haggis-fed," Burns wrote, "the trembling earth resounds his tread." Reciting this poem in front of a crowd is no easy feat; it's filled with eighteenth-century Scots phrasing, which makes the performance akin to reciting Shakespearean English. At one point, props were used, as the speaker referenced a blade and dramatically stabbed the haggis, spilling its innards, and the room erupted in applause.

After the jokes and toasts died down, the haggis was served on a bed of mashed potatoes and roasted vegetables; it had an earthy, warming flavor, rich in umami.

That evening—the food, the drinks, the bagpipes, the japes, but most of all the conviviality and community—was exemplary of Scottish cèilidh culture. Cèilidh originally referred to a specific type of event, with folk music, dancing, and storytelling, but the word—particularly on the Isle of Lewis—now encompasses a wider variety of communal gatherings. Grinneabhat's three functions are listed in large letters on the building's facade: *leabaidh* (next to a stick figure asleep in bed), *cafaidh* (next to a steaming mug), and cèilidh (next to three stick figures with their arms around each other). While cèilidh isn't reserved for winter alone, cèilidh culture is essential for surviving the season on the Isle of Lewis, which can be particularly harsh: dark and gloomy, accompanied not by snow, but by frigid, sleeting rain and raging gales. The previous winter, Jon told me, the wind monitor on the island snapped at 130 miles per hour. In the Outer Hebrides, he said, winter is "the thing that makes or breaks you." People visit the islands in summer and see an idyllic natural wonderland. Dreaming of communing with nature and living amongst the elements, they move onto the Isle of Lewis, only to later discover they can't make it through the dark months. Cèilidh culture takes on urgency in winter, when find-ing community is crucial to thriving.

My foray into life on the island was shepherded by Jon, a multimedia artist who speaks about the Isle of Lewis and its history the way someone can only when they are in love with a singular place. He told us about the island's landscape, history, and ghost stories; showed us the peat he burns in his fireplace, which he harvested from a bog in his yard; shared the Gaelic names for traditions, plants, and the weather. He gave us a true taste of cèilidh culture: despite the island's gorgeous landscape, filled with muted, purply-brown shrubbery and the ever-changing, roiling gray and navy and sage green sea, my most magical experiences were those when I was embraced by the community. Being in on the joke at Burns night; visiting An Lanntair, the arts center in Stornoway and chatting with the locals about island weather; spending the evening at Jon's house, drinking tea by the fire with him and his friend, artist and archaeologist Anne Campbell, crying with laughter listening to her dog, Ben, howl along to his favorite Celtic song. The closeness I encountered filled the long nights and stormy days. An older gentleman I met on the beach told me that on the island, winter is a time to "gather round, tell stories, make music, and pass the bottle."

Winter invites ritual gatherings. Burns nights, holiday tradi-tions, Sunday suppers: all help us find closeness. Winter rituals imbue the season with meaning, joy, and comfort. They roman-ticize winter and make it special. By cultivating and embracing winter traditions, we give ourselves something to hold on to, to keep us tethered to ourselves and each other through the darkest days of the year.

HELLO DARKNESS, MY OLD FRIEND

Winter on the Isle of Lewis, Jon explained, "is like being in a submarine. It's almost a countdown into darkness, you can't believe you're going down and down and down into this darkness, and just when you think you can't go any darker, it starts to get light again."

Darkness is one of the season's biggest challenges. Especially in places with milder winters, where there's no snow to reflect light and brighten the landscape, short days and relentless clouds can make the season feel interminable. Yet darkness is also winter's most reliable feature. The cold can be capricious and the snow elusive, and, as climate change heats the planet, both cold and snow are becoming rarer. But even places with relatively warm winters—San Diego, Florida, Spain, and Sydney—are still significantly darker in winter than summer. We can always count on the winter solstice to be the darkest day of the year.

The long nights of winter are a source of many complaints: about the difficulty of getting up in the morning, of leaving work under the night sky, or of how dreary it feels to go weeks without seeing the sun. Early evening darkness can feel like an impediment to socializing, exercising, or pursuing weeknight leisure. Yet the subtle and delicious joys of darkness beckon to those willing to see it another way. The darkness invites intimacy and coziness, enabling candlelit dinners. It invites rest, allowing for early bedtimes and late mornings. It invites us to gather round, becoming a backdrop for pulling each other close and telling stories.

The darkness also invites rituals: from the small act of walking through the house and turning on lamps to Hanukkah, Diwali, St. Lucia's Day, and other festivals of light to romantic dinners and Christmas-themed pajama parties, long nights unlock a world of activities that feel discordant with bright, sunny days. Rather than pushing against the darkness, ask yourself: What is better in the dark? All sorts of pastimes—from family-friendly to family-making—benefit from the cover of darkness. Movie nights. Bonfires. Star gazing. Even activities that lend themselves to sunshine can be done in the dark, where they take on a more contemplative, gentle quality: evening walks where sounds become more noticeable and shadows create fascinating patterns; yoga, stretching, dancing—moving our body in low lighting connects us with our breath, with our muscles and bones; bathing and showering in darkness or by candlelight gives us a break from sensory overload and days full of screens.

Darkness calls to poets, writers, musicians, artists, and crafters. In an article for *The Guardian* titled "Why I Adore the Night," author Jeanette Winterson writes about how moonlit hours allow a different kind of thinking to emerge: "I have my best ideas at dawn or at nightfall, but not if I switch on the lights—then I start thinking about projects, deadlines, demands, and the shadows and shapes of the house become objects, not suggestions, things that need to be done, not a background to thought." Winterson's observation is supported by science: one study found that both thinking about darkness and actual dim lighting increased creativity. Darkness increased people's efficiency in dreaming up creative answers and the number of unique solutions they proposed. According to this research, darkness makes people feel free, loosening our usual constraints and encouraging us to take risks: perfect conditions for artistic pursuits. It can be hard to bare our vulnerabilities and deep feelings in the glaring light of day; we admit more—to ourselves and others—under the safety of shadows.

Darkness is not merely the absence of light: it is the presence of something else entirely. Embracing darkness recasts a source of winter woe into a time of magic and possibility. No other strategy embodies the spirit of shifting your wintertime mindset as completely as finding joy in the darkness: faced with something we have no power over, we can push back and complain, or we can collaborate with the night to transform darkness from oppressive gloom to cozy wonder. Learning to work with the darkness, rather than against it, is a micropractice in finding the possibilities amidst any challenging or unpleasant situation beyond our control. And fighting it is ultimately futile: darkness falls whether we wish it to or not. Cecilia Blomdahl, a photographer who lives in two months of full night every winter on Svalbard, says, "It's going to be there no matter what, so try to find the magic in it."

THE DARKNESS PROVIDES another advantage: it gives us the opportunity to spend the season gathering around fire.

BY THE FIRESIDE

The Isle of Lewis is the most elemental place I've ever traveled. There, you can feel the interplay of earth, water, air, and fire keenly. The earth rises and falls, the peat bogs suck at your boots. The lochs ripple and the waves of the Atlantic, which have traveled unobstructed for thousands of miles, crash against the shore. The wind blows. And, in homes and cafés, fires burn. For thousands of years, until as late as the 1960s, people in the Hebrides lived in "blackhouses"—long, stone structures with pitched, thatched roofs weighed down with rocks and netting to prevent them from blowing off in high-speed winds. In winter, the animals joined the families living inside, protecting them from the elements and contributing their warmth to the house. At the center of it all was the fire. Lit in the middle of the large, open living space, the lack of a chimney made it less of a hearth fire and more of a bonfire; smoke rose above head-height before drifting through the porous roof, where it served as a natural insecticide, killing pests that might otherwise live there. Each summer, the smoke-infused thatch was peeled away and placed in the fields as nutrient-rich fertilizer, and a new roof was constructed. At the preserved Blackhouse in the village of Arnol, a sign, written in both Gaelic and English, reads: "The peat fire was the centre of family life, and was never allowed to go out."

Jon told us that the exception to this strict rule was on New Year's Day, when all village fires except for one would be extinguished, plunging the community into darkness. Then the villagers would come together around the singular remaining fire to welcome the new year. After gathering, they'd light torches from the central fire and carry the flames back to their homes, reigniting their hearths. One life-giving flame became many, burning throughout the village, linking the homes and people to start the new year.

ON THE ISLE OF LEWIS, everything still shuts down on Sundays: a community-wide sabbath. During the very off-season of early

February, we were the only guests at Grinneabhat, the hostel/café/community center for the villages of Bragar and Arnol. We were told to make ourselves at home in the café, where Burns supper was held, and which turned into our private living room. Emptied of its usual customers and staff and the sounds and smells of the café, the room had the feel of a school building (which it was, from 1878 to 2012) after-hours: a liminal mix of peaceful and eerie.

Yet the room had a small wood-burning stove, and Tina, the Grinneabhat manager, started a fire for us. Despite upturned chairs and empty tables, Rob and I gravitated to the café, just us two. The fire gave us something to huddle around, and felt like having a pet in the room, our little companion. The flames changed the atmosphere, transforming what might have been a slightly sad, creepy experience into something snug and enchanting. A fire in the hearth keeps us company, gives us something to tend to, and relaxes us: one study found that merely watching a video of fire with sound in a darkened room significantly lowered participants' blood pressure. Being near fire is an activity by itself. It makes sitting around in a group feel easier and more natural by providing a focal point, somewhere to place your attention, allowing lulls in the conversation to feel peaceful and safe rather than stilted and awkward. I often put on a show "in the background," but having a fire takes the place of ambient TV-watching: it provides the light, noise, and companionship of TV while leaving more room for thinking, breathing, and reading. Winterson describes this phenomenon: "When all the lights are on, people tend to talk about what they are doing—their outer lives. Sitting round in candlelight or firelight, people start to talk about how they are feeling—their inner lives." Sitting fireside creates camaraderie, facilitating connection with ourselves and others as if by enchantment.

FIRES—IN THEIR MAGIC, their sacredness, and their life-giving necessity—invite ritual. Lighting candles; striking flint on stone; creating towering pyramids of tinder and setting them aflame: all are opportunities for intention and meaning, for bringing ourselves into the present and pausing with gratitude.

Opichi Commanda is an expert in fire rituals. An Indigenous firekeeper living about two hours north of Toronto, Opichi is a member of the Anishinaabe tribes of the Great Lakes region, which spans present-day Canada and the US. Between classes at her teachers college, Opichi spends her days in a tipi, fireside, where she starts and tends both social fires, which bring people together to chat and relax, and sacred fires, which are used in ceremonies of celebration and mourning.

Opichi told me that she's become "a more grounded person just being around fire all the time." In the Anishinaabe and other Indigenous traditions, "fire is essentially a vessel to the spirit world, to speak with our ancestors," Opichi said. The fire is considered a doorway to a spiritual realm, in which ancestors can hear the prayers and conversation of the living, connecting those on Earth to those who have come before. Firekeeping helps Opichi feel close to her ancestors and speak to loved ones she's never met through the medicinal herbs, intentions, and thoughts she puts into her fires.

The rituals of firekeeping involve both the actions performed and the mindset and intention of the firekeeper, and every step is imbued with purpose. Opichi begins fires by cleaning the space, because "a clean physical space is a clean mind." Before every fire, she smudges herself—an Indigenous practice of burning sacred herbs, such as white sage, and bathing in the smoke—for grounding. She arranges the *semaa* (tobacco) with her left hand—the hand closest to her heart. "If you hold tobacco, it's absorbing whatever you're thinking," Opichi told me. She uses tobacco to send her intention into the fire. She invites desired spirits and concentrates on what she is asking of the fire, whether it be a social fire to connect people, a sacred fire to heal or commemorate, or a working fire to clear brush. She thinks good thoughts to infuse the fire with positive energy as she strikes flint against steel to create sparks. During the first ten minutes of a fire, while new and delicate, she supports it with kind words and good intentions.

Opichi told me that fire responds to those around it. "I've spoken around a sacred fire before, and I've said something, and the fire has started crackling like crazy," Opichi recounted, "and I knew at that minute that I wasn't monitoring my thoughts as well as I should." When tending to a fire, Opichi emphasizes intention and attention. "People are picking up the energy of that fire," she told me. "You have to mind your thoughts and prayers and language around a sacred fire," she explained. The fire absorbs and then transmits the energy of those who care for it and the people around it. "If you have a firekeeper who's in a bad mood lighting this fire, then everyone who is there is going to be in a bad mood."

There is something sacred about gathering around any fire. We use fire to herald special moments: in Judaism, candles are lit at sundown to begin holy days; we blow out birthday candles to make wishes and celebrate turning one year older; bonfires mark festival days. The simple act of being around fire, as it becomes more of a luxury and less of a necessity in our modern world, is its own kind of celebration. Treating it as a sacred time—whether over a candlelit dinner or gathered around a hearth—is an opportunity to bring mindful attention to long winter nights.

WHILE OPICHI IS CLEAR that "putting some wood on your fire at home does not make you a firekeeper," she also provides instruction for how Indigenous teachings can inspire more meaningful fires for everyone. She advises using natural materials like birch bark rather than artificial fire starters, paper, or cardboard, to make the fire more connected to the earth. Starting your fire with good intentions helps it carry positive energy to embrace you in warmth and comfort. And watching your language around fire—treating it as a living friend, an honored visitor—can elevate the impact of your fire on your mood and your well-being.

If you don't have a fireplace at home, a cluster of candles can provide a similar focal point, and even a candle can be reminiscent of a sacred fire. After a winter solstice celebration, Opichi decided she wanted to shift from relying mostly on artificial light to using more candlelight at home. Her mentor told her, "It might not be this massive bonfire, but a fire on a candle is still a fire." Even when lighting a few candles at home, Opichi uses her firekeeper's approach to elevate the experience: "I think of it as a sacred fire, I mind my thoughts around it, and it keeps me really centered."

Others who spend a lot of time with fire echo Opichi's ideas. Ida, who studies mindfulness at the University of Tromsø, finds lighting candles at home to be grounding. She says, "The rituals

NIGHTS, LIGHTS, AND RITES *167*

of lighting candles may become valuable mindful moments, an opportunity to pause for a while." Gathering around fire is even part of the school day in Norway: the students in Ida's daughter's third-grade class were asked at least twice a month to bring a log of wood to school in their backpacks. The class would then spend part of the day outside—rain or shine—around a bonfire built from these communally contributed logs, grilling fish cakes and hot dogs and roasting marshmallows. Perhaps these fires carried with them the intention of each of the children, the love and care of parents dutifully placing logs of wood in brightly colored backpacks before the school day began. Like Opichi's social fires in the tipi, these bonfires invite a gathering, a sharing, and a coming together, in the heat and the light.

WHAT MAKES A RITUAL?

In *The Power of Ritual: Turning Everyday Activities into Soulful Practices*, Casper ter Kuile quotes activist and minister Kathleen McTigue in defining rituals as having three necessary components: intention, attention, and repetition. Intention requires us to ask, "What are we inviting into this moment?" Attention requires us to ask, "Are we fully present as we perform this action?" And repetition requires us to ask, "When can we come back to this practice again and again?"

We all perform regular actions that are not rituals: we have routines, like heading to work, and we have habits, like brushing our teeth. But rituals have a larger purpose than the action reveals. Lighting candles so you can see after the sun sets isn't necessarily a ritual, but it can easily become one when the focus is to mark a transition in the day and celebrate darkness. Rituals imbue the ordinary with meaning. They can turn the mundane into the holy, the everyday into the special. They help mark the passing of time and provide comfort. They invite mindfulness: the very act of a ritual requires our attention to be real.

Elevating the ordinary into ritual requires nothing more than a shift in mindset, and engaging in rituals can also help us cultivate desired mindsets. Our mindsets influence our behavior and inspire action, and our actions reinforce our mindsets. When we view darkness as a part of winter to be treasured, we are more likely to dim the lights, light candles, and invite the night to envelop us in a cozy, quiet atmosphere. Simultaneously, the very act of luxuriating in candlelight and letting in the darkness reinforces our positive mindsets about winter, reminding us that even darkness can be a delight.

Ali Crum says that mindsets are "thermostats, not light switches." While moments of insight can inspire us to adopt new mindsets, and a-ha moments can help strengthen those mindsets, changing our mindset is not one-and-done. It is not as simple as flipping a switch that then remains "on" indefinitely. Rather, like thermostats, we might set our mindsets to a certain temperature, but that thermostat is then constantly readjusting, reacting to the ambient climate: making the room cooler when it gets too hot, and hotter when it gets too cold. We adjust the thermostat regularly: making it cooler before bed or warmer when we wake up, turning it up or down depending on the weather. Similarly, our mindsets require regular check-ins, and cultivating more useful mindsets is an ongoing practice: our external conditions and internal states can make adopting desired mindsets more or less effortful. Getting in the habit of checking

in with our mindsets helps us cultivate them over time. Rituals—
actions undertaken repeatedly, with intention and attention—
can serve as reminders, pinging us to notice our mindset. Rituals
deepen the grooves on which our mindsets run, making it easier
for us to inhabit desired mindsets at specific times.

I FIND IT HELPFUL to think of rituals in terms of their timescales.
We might engage in smaller, daily rituals: journaling before bed,
enjoying our coffee while looking out the window, lighting a
candle when it gets dark. We can engage in more midsize ritu-
als at slightly longer timescales: weekly sabbaths, from work or
technology; Sunday dinners; monthly date nights. And there are
rituals we practice yearly: observing the winter solstice, celebrat-
ing the New Year, religious or family holidays. If you're trying
to add more winter rituals into your life, start with one ritual at
each timescale. Maybe this year you add in a new annual ritual:
a fancy, sit-down dinner, or a casual potluck, or a night of wine
and painting; a Christmas day sauna or swim in the ocean; a
solstice tea swap or ode-to-the-moon writing night. For midsize
rituals, you can find—or start—a recurring monthly activity:
pasta making, knitting nights, jam sessions, Mario Kart tourna-
ments. I met a woman in Saskatoon, Canada, who built an igloo
in her backyard each winter and invited her friends over to sit in
the igloo, drink hot chocolate, and read poetry to each other.
On the most bite-size, consistent scale, what tiny rituals or
micromoments can you invite into your winter days? I look for-
ward to lighting a candle on my desk when the sun sets as it gets
darker. Winter sunset can be a particularly good time for a
small daily ritual: making a sunset tea tray, with a hot drink and
a little treat, pairs something often seen as negative (the early

darkness) with something delightful to reclaim sunset as a time for pleasure. You can tailor your rituals to your needs: Are you craving more winter connection, introspection, outdoor time, or creativity? When it comes to rituals, try not to overthink it. Start small and let things grow organically, seeing how they evolve. Bring a bit more intention and attention to your existing practices, elevating them for the season. Do what feels good, aim for consistency over perfection, and see how it goes.

Ter Kuile also writes that rituals provide connection at four levels: with ourselves, with each other, with nature, and with the transcendent. This gives us another framework for conceptualizing rituals. What rituals of yours are private, and bring you closer to yourself? Perhaps journaling, taking baths, meditating, or going on solo walks. Which ones help you gather and connect to others? Hosting dinners, game nights, or book clubs; taking shared breaks and vacations; making cookies and decorating trees. What rituals bring you closer to nature? Not just those that we enjoy outdoors—winter walks and New Year's Day polar bear plunges—but also those that connect us to nature's rhythms: lighting candles at sunset, solstice bonfires, drinking hot chocolate on the first snowy day. At every level, these rituals have the potential to connect us to the transcendent: to our heritage and culture, to feelings of awe, to a higher power, and to the great miracle of existing.

HOLIDAY RITUALS

When asked to imagine winter joy, many people think of baking Christmas cookies and decorating the tree, making dumplings,

watching holiday movies, lighting Hanukkah candles and eat-
ing latkes. In the Northern Hemisphere, winter is synonymous
with the holiday season. The weeks leading up to Christmas
and New Year's can be a time of stress, but also of fun, anticipa-
tion, and tradition: the careful selecting of gifts, the rearranging
and decorating of the house, the cooking, the special music, the
nostalgic movies. Whether you celebrate Christmas or Hanukkah
or Yule or the solstice or nothing at all, the winter holidays
have permeated American culture—and many other cultures—
thoroughly. And there's lots of nondenominational, trans-
religious things to enjoy about this time of year: seeing towns
and cities lit up with twinkly lights, drinking mulled wine, and
visiting holiday markets for warming foods and special trinkets.

These holidays provide a natural axis around which to build
ritual: many people, like my sister-in-law, spend the time from
Thanksgiving to Christmas covered in flour and smelling like
vanilla, making cookies to gift to friends, family, coworkers,
and mail carriers. My aunt Karen spends weeks decorating her
log cabin, meticulously replacing dish towels and shower cur-
tains and night-lights with their Santa-themed counterparts and
devoting hours to dipping pretzels and marshmallows in choco-
late. Cecilia Blomdahl told me that the dark days of the Polar
Night make the holiday season especially magical on Svalbard,
where she hosts an annual evening for making gingerbread
houses and watches Hallmark movies near daily: "I've made the
season into this little dream world, where I do everything that I
love, and I do it each year, no questions asked."

We each have a chance to make the season into our own per-
sonalized dream worlds, drawing from our backgrounds and
traditions to do so. My friend from the Stanford psychology

department, Gregg Muragishi, grew up as a fourth-generation Japanese American in Los Angeles. LA might not be the most wintery place, but his family still marked the shorter, colder days with shabu-shabu—Japanese hot pot. Gregg brought this tradition to San Francisco, where we'd help him chop mountains of vegetables and make dipping sauces so we could spend an evening fishing dumplings and mushrooms out of boiling pots of kombu-infused broth as the room filled with steam. My roommates and I in California drew from a combination of Jewish upbringing and bartending experience to create our own winter tradition: an annual Vodkas and Latkes party, for which we spent weeks infusing vodka with ginger and cinnamon and peeling, chopping, shredding, and frying potatoes (our record is 693 handmade latkes).

My favorite holiday ritual comes from Iceland, where the season leading up to Christmas is the *Jólabókaflóð*: the Christmas book flood. Reading is very popular in the Nordics, and especially so in Iceland, where books are the most popular Christmas gifts. To prepare, the nation's publishers release a slew of titles in early winter, even sending out a special catalog. This season culminates in a maximally cozy Christmas Eve where people exchange books and then spend the evening reading and drinking hot chocolate, a tradition Becky and I co-opted during a particularly relaxing Christmas spent at her cabin in the redwoods.

HOWEVER YOU CELEBRATE and observe the winter holidays, your traditions likely span more than the one or two days of the holidays themselves: they bleed into a holiday *season*—for some, the most wonderful time of the year. The actual holiday days may be all you hoped for: enchanting and heartwarming, restful, a container for core memories. But sometimes they're just fine, or even disappointing. Yet a holiday season—with movies you watch every year, time spent shopping, cooking, or baking, and seasonal missives to loved ones—can span weeks and is often the part of winter people enjoy most. The rituals and traditions of November and December holidays give structure and meaning to dark days.

While there's plenty that we can't easily bring with us into January and February—visits from loved ones, time off from school and work, a cultural pause and reset—we can look to the holiday season for inspiration about ways to relish winter beyond the new year. By investigating what we enjoy during the holiday season, we can pinpoint strategies for making winter wonderful in January, February, and March. If you love parties and socializing, you can host dinners, organize a book club, or arrange a soup-swap. If you love baking, you can branch out and bake something new, or make Valentine's cookies for family, friends, and coworkers. If it's showing your love through gifts, you can send notes and small care packages to friends or relatives you didn't exchange holiday presents with. If it's the decorations, try refreshing your space with winter decor that's not so holiday-themed (my mother decorates with snowmen so they can be left up well into March), or maybe the long nights of January are a time to hang the art you've been meaning to put up. If you miss the Christmas ambiance, make a cozy playlist filled with soft music for your evening soundtrack or rewatch other comforting, nostalgic movies you haven't seen in a while. And if you enjoy visiting holiday markets, many cities host winter festivals in late January and early February; patronizing these festivals can connect you to community and winter joy.

Noticing what holiday rituals you're drawn to can help you find inspiration that will last after the final plates have been cleared and the wrapping paper has been thrown away.

This was an insight one of my students, Alex, had. In my Stanford Continuing Studies course, Mindsets Matter, I teach my students about wintertime mindset and ask them to practice embracing winter and then reflect on the experience. Here's what Alex wrote:

> *I noted that I have a very positive wintertime mindset before the holidays, but then feel it goes downhill. So for this week I investigated what I did differently then: What was I appreciating, how was I maybe amplifying the coziness, or the joy of the season then that dropped off in January? I found I was no longer relishing a warm drink in the evenings. I had put away my Christmas sweaters, and wasn't watching holiday movies with my husband. So I moved all my comfy regular sweaters to the front of my closet to wear, I bought more hot cocoa and whipped cream and kept that warm beverage train rolling in the evenings. I also specifically recreated the special cozy conditions of watching a fun movie together while it rained outside even though it wasn't a holiday themed movie. All of it made me feel appreciative, cozy and joyful. Being aware of my mindset helped me take specific actionable steps to change it rather than just linger in what I was experiencing and accepting that as the only way it could be.*

You can create winter-specific rituals wherever you live. For maximum impact, focus on finding comfort in the darkness, gathering around fire, and leaning on holiday traditions. Adding more rituals into the season helps us find more connection, meaning, and fun throughout winter; elevating the mundane with our intention, attention, and repetition brings magic to long, dark evenings. Rituals can help us through other challenging times in our lives as well: What do we do when it feels like darkness surrounds us? Defiantly, willfully finding ways to celebrate the everyday trains us to make our own meaning and to marry hardship with jubilation. Creating personal and familial rituals gives us something to lean on in difficult times, allowing us to find routine and comfort no matter the weather. By uplifting ordinary activities into purposeful rituals, we can spin everyday practices into moments of significance, filling our days with wonder in winter and beyond.

WINTER PRACTICE:
RELISHING RITUALS

- **Light it up:** Find a way to add more fire into your life this week. Make use of your fireplace if you have one, set up a candle display, or have an outside bonfire. All add warmth and light to winter days.

- **Experiment with small-, medium-, and larger-effort rituals:** Write down three different rituals you'd like to try, one at each timescale: A small daily ritual (for maximum accessibility, aim for this to take no more than five minutes); a midsize monthly ritual; and a one-time larger ritual. Try implementing these new rituals this winter. How do these rituals change what you notice and feel during the winter months?

- **Take inspiration from the holidays:** Ask yourself what you enjoy most about the holiday season, then brainstorm a non-holiday corollary. Pick a day for that activity in January or February: make Valentine's day cookies or write cards; have a cozy seasonal movie night; host a hot chocolate party. Convert your "holiday spirit" into "winter spirit" to find connection and joy after the holidays are over.

Part Three

Get
Outside

7.

YOU'RE NOT MADE
OF SUGAR

DID NOT WANT to get on my bicycle.

The puttering, sputtering drizzle didn't make a sound on the hood of my raincoat, but soaked me silently. The temperature hovered in the low forties—warm enough that my hesitance made me feel like a wimp. I had been in much colder places recently. But above-freezing rain seeps into your bones, chilling you more effectively than a downfall of snow.

The Amsterdam sky hung low, lifeless in its usual flat, February gray; the only color came from amber streetlights lining the canal. I reminded myself that using my body for transportation was part of what brought me to the Netherlands, an idea that sounded good from a hilly city in California. After seven years in the Golden State, Rob and I moved to Amsterdam, ready for a new adventure and drawn by the city's crooked beauty and fantasies of northern Europe's winter inspiration. Home again in our new city for a few days, I was back to running errands by bike.

Wiping the puddle from my seat, I extracted my ride from the tangle of parked bikes and zipped my coat to my chin. I began pedaling through the city, cranky and stiff, missing Scandinavia's considerably colder but drier winter weather. I knew, in the logical recesses of my brain, that once I started biking, I'd feel better. Somehow, that didn't make it more appealing.

As I whizzed through the city, legs pumping, my heartbeat quickened, my breath deepened, and my core warmed. My Norwegian wool mittens with the little foxes on them kept my fingers warm, and my raincoat kept me dry. My face was covered with a cold mist that, while not exactly pleasant, was bearable. I rode by tilting houses, cramped bars, and glassy canals. I cycled past and alongside other bikers in raincoats and rain pants. As my body heated, my mood lifted. The wind and rain on my face started to feel refreshing. It was annoying to be proven wrong so quickly; my reticence was misplaced. I felt alert and free, flying through Amsterdam, inhaling the winter air. I arrived at my destination in far better spirits than when I departed, with ruddy cheeks and messy hair and a smile on my face.

I've experienced this phenomenon countless times, and yet still struggle to internalize the lesson. When it is cold, dark, or wet, I do not want to go outside. I want to stay snug indoors, warm and dry. But if I overcome my indoor inertia and venture out, it's never as bad as I thought it would be. In fact, I don't know that I've ever regretted such an excursion. Yet no matter how many articles I write, how many workshops I deliver, how many journalists interview me as a winter expert, I find it hard to take my own advice: *Get outside in winter. Don't let the weather stop you. An outdoor excursion almost always feels better than we expect.* Still, a little voice whispers: *You could always take an Uber.*

My winter biking is motivated in no small part by a culture that encourages cycling in all weather. Nothing makes me feel more like an Amsterdammer than a rainy bike commute; an oft-quoted Dutch expression summarizes local attitudes: "You're not made of sugar, you won't melt in the rain." I'm aided by a culture where bike lanes are safe and convenient, rain gear—coats, pants, and boots—is ubiquitous; it's seen as healthy to bike everywhere, year-round; and where everyone has experienced the vigor of arriving to a gathering breathless and soggy. Knowing that my friends will be biking to our meetups and trying to recognize the times I feel better for having cycled encourages me to bike in all but the worst downpours.

MOTIVATING OURSELVES TO GO outside in winter—particularly when it is frigid, gray, or damp—can be one of the season's biggest challenges. Those of us who didn't grow up in winter-loving climes, who don't hail from cultures where dressing properly for winter is the norm, and who never fell in love with winter sports like skiing or ice hockey—myself included—are often hesitant to expose ourselves to the elements. Yet people who thrive during the season invariably find ways to spend time outdoors. Whether skiing, swimming, hiking, or just walking their dog around the neighborhood, being outside is a meaningful part of their winter lives. When I ask Cecilia Blomdahl, a photographer who lives on Svalbard, what she looks forward to in winter, she said she loves hiking in the dark, with only a headlamp for light. When I ask Taija Aikio, who works at the Sami museum in

Inari, about her ideal day during the darkest time of year, she talked about walking outside and then lying on her reindeer skin atop a frozen lake, staring at the stars and looking for constellations. When I asked Rannveig Kristjánsdóttir, the Icelander I met at a perfume shop in Reykjavík, what she loves most about winter, she told me about sinking in to one of the city's geothermal outdoor pools and watching the mist rise around her into the night.

Getting outside in winter is essential. The belief that we can't enjoy ourselves outdoors is largely responsible for the idea that winter is limiting; this perspective makes the world feel out of reach. But this view is erroneous and self-fulfilling. If we remain cooped up, we *will* feel winter's limitations, and our mood will drop, no matter how hygge we make it inside. In places like Tromsø, northern Finland, and Svalbard—all of which have long, dark, cold winters—the idea of staying indoors all season is ludicrous. By taking inspiration from these hyperborean locales, we can overcome our hesitation to getting outdoors in winter. Learning how to get outside more not only helps us enjoy the season, it can teach us lessons about motivation that will serve us long after winter ends.

PUSH AND PULL

Our mindsets influence our motivation. When we think "Winter is dreadful," we expect that being outside in winter weather will be unpleasant. Armed with this mindset (conscious or unconscious), we can't help but focus on our frozen fingers and toes, our running nose, or our constant shivering. This leads us toward "avoidance motivation": a desire to avoid the pain of exposure to the cold, wet, and dark. It pushes us away from spending time outside. The decision to stay indoors and avoid winter is a reasonable response to this perspective.

But when we adopt the mindset that "winter is wonderful," we expect that being outside in winter will be delightful, and we notice when going outside in winter includes the fun of playing in the snow, the pleasing sound of rainfall, or the invigoration of fresh air. We associate spending time outdoors in winter with feeling alert and rejuvenated. This leads us toward "approach motivation": a desire to maximize the pleasure of cold-weather excursions. It pulls us to spend time outside. We expect that facing the elements will boost our mood, and that we will return home heartier and happier than when we left, ready to enjoy indoor warmth more for having been outside.

AMONG MANY PSYCHOLOGICAL STRATEGIES for increasing motivation, a basic principle involves reducing our avoidance motivation and increasing our approach motivation. By removing barriers to getting outside in winter—particularly unhelpful beliefs that discourage us from going outside—we can increase our willingness to embark on outdoor excursions. Likewise, if we can increase the appeal of going outside in winter—by noticing the gratification to be found outdoors—we can make it more likely that we'll actually *want* to spend more time in the season's open air.

REDUCING AVOIDANCE

The desire to stay inside in winter often arises from several unhelpful beliefs:

1. You can't go outside in bad weather.
2. Going outside in the winter will be unpleasant.
3. Being outside in the cold is unhealthy.

These beliefs reflect a conscious or unconscious mindset that winter is dreadful and limiting and reinforce the idea that winter is a time when you can't do much. To help us get outside, we can examine where these beliefs come from and whether they are true.

Limiting belief #1: You can't go outside in bad weather.

To overturn the idea that you can't go outside in bad weather, simply observe people in places where very cold, long winters are the norm. Northerners who live through extreme winters have no choice but to adapt to the cold. Alice Qannik Glenn was born and raised in Utqiaġvik, Alaska, home of about five thousand residents and the northernmost town in the United States. Growing up, the only time she had a snow day was when it got down to -60°F with windchill, because then it was "so cold that they can't get the school buses running." But throughout winter—in the dark of the Polar Night and temperatures in the -30s—she was outside: walking to school, building mini-igloos for her dog, and doing donuts on a sled tied to the back of a snowmobile. "People know that, if you just stay inside all winter, considering how long it is, you'll go crazy. So you have to go out-side. It doesn't stop your life just because it's cold outside."

Those living in Utqiaġvik, Tromsø, Svalbard, Inari, and else-where with harsh winters know that "bad" weather—when it's cold, sleety, or snowy—isn't a reason to stay indoors. Rather, it's those who live at middle latitudes, who experience slightly more temperate winters, who often believe we can't, or shouldn't, go outside when the sun sets, the temperature drops, or the rain falls. People at these latitudes aren't forced to adapt to intense winter conditions. At the same time, living in a cli-mate with less extreme winters (like London, New York, Berlin, or Tokyo) can make it more likely we *will* be uncomfortable outside: when having proper winter gear isn't a matter of life or death, people are more likely to dress inappropriately for the season.*

Enjoying ourselves al fresco requires equipping ourselves for winter weather. In places with harsher winters, children learn to dress for the season from a young age. There's a famous Scandi-navian saying: "There's no such thing as bad weather, only bad clothing." (In Norwegian, it rhymes: *Det finnes ikke dårlig vær, bare dårlig klær.*) This isn't just practical advice: physically pre-paring to go outdoors by layering appropriately is a way of set-ting realistic expectations while engaging with winter as it actually is. This kind of acceptance and initiative reflects an adaptive wintertime mindset, one that works with the chal-lenges of the season to ensure comfort.

---

*And while colder winter weather may be, paradoxically, more comfortable than slightly warmer, wetter weather, even the coldest locations have shoulder seasons full of chilly rain, and people in these places still go outside during these times of year.

◆

TO DRESS FOR WINTER, wool blends are the most effective fabrics for keeping you both warm and dry (high-quality, soft, thin woolen undergarments are commonly available and affordably priced all over Scandinavia; I'm still waiting for the rest of the world to catch up). Experts (and Norwegians) recommend a moisture-wicking, woolen base layer to draw sweat away from the body (cotton stays damp for hours); a fluffy middle layer to trap body heat; and an outer, waterproof shell to shield against rain, snow, and gale. Don't forget your legs: one lesson I've learned repeatedly is that if your legs are cold, you will feel cold. Cecilia also turned me on to a tip: in addition to thick wool socks, she advises getting winter boots one size too big, which allows the air around your toes to heat up, keeping them warm. Add mittens, a hat, and a scarf, and you'll be toasty all winter long.

Scandinavians also take winter safety seriously. Headlamps help people see in the dark, and people of all ages wear shoe spikes (sometimes called microspikes or cleats), rubber webs studded with metal prongs that can be stretched and secured to the bottom of your shoes. I don't think I could have survived the uphill trek to the bus stop from my apartment in Tromsø without them; if you live somewhere with icy, slippery sidewalks, adding ice spikes to your winter wardrobe can help you walk outside safely and confidently. And in Tromsø, everyone wears light-reflective clothing to ensure safety when walking, jogging, or biking in darkness: kids wear reflective vests to school, and the University of Tromsø handed out free reflective zipper-pulls to international students who might be unaccustomed to ensuring that our winter gear is high-visibility.

◆

AS I WAS WRITING THIS BOOK, my aunt Donna—an active woman in her seventies who lives in Philadelphia—went on a much-awaited trip to Antarctica at my uncle's behest. Aunt Donna is often cold and was worried she wouldn't enjoy herself if she was freezing. To prepare, she invested in merino wool clothing, wore many layers, and donned the heavy-duty suits provided to tourists who visit Antarctica. During a trip filled with icebergs, glaciers, and penguins, she hardly felt cold.

But when she returned to Philadelphia, she wrote me an email: "Well, I have to admit that I've been freezing since returning from Antarctica." She found herself back where it was 40° warmer, yet feeling colder than when she was near the South Pole. "The problem, I quickly realized: I'm not dressing for winter!" At home in Philadelphia, putting thought and effort into dressing warmly each day seemed unnecessary. Yet it turned out to be utterly essential to her winter comfort.

I often find that extra layers are even more necessary in cities with milder winters. Arctic cities are built with winter in mind, and indoor facilities are usually well-insulated and cozily warm no matter the temperature. But some places where winter brings temperatures in the 20s to 40s (Fahrenheit) also experience hotter summers, and thus may be draftier in the winter. Layering up means staying warm both outdoors in the elements and indoors in places that are poorly heated.

THE RIGHT CLOTHING is also critical in locations that aren't cold enough for snow but still get chilly rain. Climates with cold, damp winters may be even more challenging than places that are far darker and more frigid. When I traveled in the Arctic—in

northern Norway and in Finnish Lapland—I regularly encoun-
tered temperatures in the single digits Fahrenheit. Yet the only
time I heard people complain was when it got too warm. There
was a special revulsion reserved for temperatures just above
freezing. Part of it was the wrongness of the weather for the
season—now a more regular occurrence due to the changing
climate. But people were also reacting to the fact that nippy, wet
weather is especially uncomfortable.

But every winter climate has its pros and cons. Places blessed
with snow are brighter when it's dark out and have more oppor-
tunities for winter recreation like skiing, snowmobiling, and
ice-skating, but also tend to have darker, shorter days and lon-
ger winters. Places with a lot of chilly rain don't have as much
access to winter sports, but endless shoveling is not required and
winters are often shorter. Places with mountains for skiing and
scenery have beauty and recreation but highly variable weather
that is difficult to prepare for. Some places get a lot of sun, but
also a lot of wind. Others get very little sun, but the clouds insu-
late, making it warmer. Nowhere is perfect, but nowhere is per-
fectly terrible either. The conditions of any location are improved
by dressing for the weather you have.

Limiting belief #2: Going outside in the winter will be unpleasant.

We often expect that going outside in winter will be painful. We
think we will feel cold, damp, or stiff. We anticipate our toes
freezing and our nose running.

Winter's cold can, of course, feel unpleasant. But we often
assume it will be colder, wetter, or darker than it is. One reason
our expectations can mislead us is due to what psychologists

call "affective forecasting errors." Affective forecasting is a fancy way of saying "how we think we're going to feel," and humans are notoriously bad at it. To understand this discrepancy, psychologists ask people how they think they'll feel in hypothetical situations, and then follow up to see how people actually feel when those situations come to pass. We're usually fairly decent at knowing whether we'll be happy or sad if something happens, but beyond that our imagination fails. We think good things will make us happier than they do, and that bad things will make us sadder, and we think both happy and sad emotions will endure longer than they do in reality. In one study, college students thought they'd be happier than they actually were if they got to live in the best dorms, and thought they'd be unhappier than they ended up being if assigned to the worst dorms. In another, untenured college professors overestimated how upset they would be five years after being denied tenure. And both men and women inaccurately predicted how upset they'd be after a breakup: they tended to think they'd be utterly heartbroken, when in reality they were merely sad.

Affective forecasting errors can discourage us from getting outside in winter. Being cozy and warm indoors makes the weather seem especially daunting. Looking out from inside, our eyes are not adjusted to the night, and the dark appears foreboding. Intermittent precipitation appears to be a nonstop downfall. Without time to acclimate, the initial temperature outside feels icy. But when we venture out, it's often not as bad as it looked. Ida says that going outside in winter is an opportunity to be "mindful about what actually *is* before us, instead of only deeming the situation 'too cold to be considered anything but a painful lack of Celsius degrees.'" And research suggests that people substantially underestimate how much of a mood boost a walk in nature will provide.

This is a secret known to people who live in the far north: when dressed appropriately, going outside in the winter is rarely as unpleasant as we expect. Cecilia, who ventures out regularly in Svalbard's completely sunless Polar Night, pointed this out to me: "When you sit inside and you look through those windows and it's dark, you feel trapped. But when you go out there and you realize you're under the sky of stars, you see a completely different world, it's probably a lot quieter, and you see the city life. There's so much beauty when you go outside in the darkness. It will feel liberating."

WHEN WE'RE MOVING, it can be warmer than we expect: my sister-in-law, a distance runner in New York, looks forward to her winter runs, when the crisp air compels her to keep moving and she doesn't come home drenched in sweat. This is something you have to experience yourself to internalize. I first met Anthony Taylor while recording a podcast together for The Great Northern, a winter arts and culture festival in the Twin Cities of Minneapolis and St. Paul, Minnesota. An outdoor activist and community development innovator, Anthony connects communities of color, including immigrant communities, to outdoor activities in the Twin Cities. Many of these immigrants come from warm countries in South America or Africa and are unused to Minnesota's cold. To help them see the possibilities in winter, Anthony told me about one of his strategies: "What I do is I trick someone into an outdoor activity with the right jacket, with the right amount of activity, so that they experience themselves overheating outdoors. It is such a mind-blowing activity for someone to be out on a day they perceived as too cold to go out and find themselves unzipping a jacket or taking off gloves." He helps people learn through their own experience that what they thought would be painfully frigid can be positively roasty, permanently altering their understanding of the cold.

Affective forecasting errors occur in the rain as well. On the Isle of Lewis, I was chatting with someone about the weather who remarked, "You're sitting inside, looking out the window and thinking 'I really don't want to go out there!'" Anne Campbell quipped back: "And then you go out and you realize—it's actually not so bad!" Anne told me that despite the island's reputation for miserable winter weather, there are actually very few days where it's so rainy you can't be out at all. Anne used to work with tourists on the Isle of Harris. Those who travel by car, she said, asked, "When's it going to stop raining?" and complained about the precipitation putting a damper on their travel plans. But those who walked or came by bike remarked, "It's great weather!" Being outside in the elements transforms them from burden to boon.

IN ADDITION TO *OVERESTIMATING* how uncomfortable it will be, we often *underestimate* the pleasure to be found in ventures outside. I've seen this winter-outdoors-affective-forecasting-error many times, not only in myself, but also in my students. When they step outside initially, many people think their predictions have come true: they are freezing and uncomfortable!* But as

---

*If this happens to you frequently, try bundling up to go outside and then doing a few jumping jacks before heading out the door. The cold will feel like a relief.

people spend more time outside, especially walking or moving, their bodies warm. Their moods begin to lift. The air around them turns from frigid to crisp, not through an objective change in weather but due to a shift in perspective. People are surprised—shocked, even—by how pleasant it can be outside when it's shivery, damp, and dark. Once you experience this yourself, it becomes easier to motivate yourself next time. In my Stanford course Mindsets Matter, I assign students to go on an outdoor winter excursion. One of my students, Hardik, experienced how one venture led to another:

> It was obvious to me that I had to try running for 3 miles early in the morning to experience the wintertime mindset. On Saturday February 6th, the thought of leaving my 73°F room and embracing the 35°F air gave me shudders. But I did take your advice of layering up and convinced myself that it would be a way to reconnect with the old days while I was studying in Pennsylvania or traveling through Switzerland. On the run, every single bone of my body cursed me for the cold air. My glasses stayed foggy throughout and my fingers kept digging into my sleeves trying to avoid the experience. I just kept running and then started enjoying it. The trail was mostly empty, the sun was just rising and it felt blissful. I forgot all about the cold and was happy that the sun rays weren't as strong and that my body was cool throughout the run. It was a surprise. I went for two more runs in the week, with each one less difficult to begin than the previous. It was a realization that I never gave myself permission to enjoy the cold. I'm hoping to use this positive energy to get over some other fixed mindsets that I have in my life related to my career and relationships.

Here, not only did Hardik's experience lead to repeat runs, it also transcended wintertime mindset. Ida put it this way: "Although it can be a bit of a strain to get out, when you first are outside, with good clothing, it always feels better than you thought it would, less windy, less cold than it looked from inside. Instead, you feel refreshed, you feel maybe a little bit robust and vital, and feel the benefits of being in contact with the elements, the rhythms of life and death, with nature, which might also help us put things in our life into perspective."

Limiting belief #3: Going outside in the cold is unhealthy.

"Don't stay outside too long, you'll catch a cold!" "You'll get sick playing outside in this weather!" I grew up hearing this kind of refrain. Where I was raised in the US, it's a common folk belief that being outside in the cold makes us sick, that we can *catch* a cold by *being* cold. This myth likely started because cold and flu viruses are more common in colder months. But this belief is not evidence-based.

When I moved to Norway, I was surprised to discover that they hold the opposite view. Throughout Scandinavia, people see the cold as healthy—especially for children. Kids have recess outside, dressed appropriately, in all but the most extreme and dangerous conditions. In Tromsø, I saw kids on the playground, wearing reflective vests for visibility, in the middle of the Polar Night, in below-freezing temperatures, in rain, and most certainly in snow. I've stood at a bus stop in Tromsø on a 20°F day, listening to shrieks of delight as children slid down icy hills on saucer-sleds.

Where I grew up, recess was regularly canceled and substi-
tuted for indoor movie-watching when the weather was consid-
ered too cold, wet, or snowy. "If you take your kids inside
because the weather isn't perfect, what is that teaching them?"
Cecilia asked me. She said that in her childhood in Sweden,
"We're out in any weather learning that you can have fun in the
rain. That's when you go jump in puddles. You have to be out-
side playing in the snow." She told me about how all year they
waited for the first snow, because then the kids would go out-
side and roll around in it, naked: "It was pure excitement."

Keeping kids inside in bad weather ensures they will be antsy
without a chance to run around and burn off excess energy. It
also *increases* the chance of illness: when students are cooped
up without fresh air, seasonal illnesses travel from kid to kid
and are brought home to parents and siblings.

In the Nordics, the belief that cold air is healthy extends to
tiny babies, who nap outdoors all winter. In Iceland, Rannveig
told me that when she was a baby, she "napped every day out-
side for two hours." In Copenhagen and Stockholm, daycare
centers hold nap time in neat rows of open-air bassinets on the
sidewalk, and parents leave babies snoozing outside while they
meet friends for coffee. In Finland, babies as young as two weeks
old nap outside. At home, parents put little ones in prams for
nap time in the garden, dressed snugly in woolen onesies, jack-
ets, and hats, wrapped in down-filled sleeping bags, and laid in
fur-lined strollers. Only their eyes, noses, and mouths are left ex-
posed. Parents believe being snuggled up in the cold helps them
sleep more soundly, and that fresh air is good for their lungs and
immune systems. Research suggests they might be right: one

study found that babies took longer naps when they slept out-
doors in winter temperatures ranging from -17 to 41°F.

The idea of leaving your baby outside—especially in a public
place—might sound strange, or even neglectful. The safety of
Nordic countries makes this open-air sleeping possible. A Dan-
ish woman was once arrested for leaving her baby to nap outside
a café in New York City, despite this being perfectly normal
parenting in Denmark. But even if you don't live in a place where
you can leave your baby outside, a winter walk in a pram or
stroller might help them slumber more soundly. These practices
show us how variable perspectives on cold and health are. The
idea that the cold makes us sick isn't an evidence-based fact or
even a universal belief: it's a particular mindset about the im-
pact of cold on our bodies, and one that it might be time to
overturn in favor of more updated, nuanced ways of thinking.

LIKE OUR BROADER mindsets about the season, the beliefs that we
can't go outside in bad weather, that going outside in winter is
unpleasant, and that the cold is unhealthy might feel like facts:
maybe we grew up hearing these ideas from family members or
people in our community, or we personally experienced feeling
shivery and uncomfortable outside in winter. Few people enjoy
the feeling of being freezing cold, but you don't have to in order
to find pleasure outdoors. When we've fortified ourselves ap-
propriately, armed with the right clothing and mindset, we can
go outside in any weather, and, in doing so, find that perhaps
winter isn't as limiting as we thought.

INCREASING APPROACH

We can also find ways to amplify the pull of the outdoors. By increasing the appeal of outdoor activities in winter, we increase the likelihood that we'll *want* to spend leisure time enjoying the season's fresh air and nature.

NORWEGIANS HAVE A GUIDING PRINCIPLE that motivates them to spend time outdoors year-round: *friluftsliv*. Coined by the Norwegian playwright Henrik Ibsen in 1859, friluftstliv, directly translated, means "open air life." But friluftsliv may best be understood as finding freedom in an open-air life. In Norway, friluftsliv is a cultural identity, a shared value that influences daily life in profound ways. Children are introduced to nature, taught to navigate independently outdoors, and encouraged to practice friluftsliv starting at a young age; exposure to friluftstliv is prevalent in schools throughout Norway. This cultural ideal makes spending time in nature, in all seasons, an ingrained part of everyday life.

Helga Løvoll is a professor in friluftsliv at Volda University College in Norway. She fell in love with winter nature as a child: when she was eight years old, her favorite activity was skiing in the forest—sometimes with a friend, but often by herself. Løvoll told me that the most important aspect of friluftsliv, for her, is "the mental part of having a break from everyday life, and kind of getting closer to my more authentic self." Friluftsliv is about communing with nature and with yourself, and about unburdening oneself from anything but being present. It's about disconnecting from the day-to-day in order to connect with something older, wilder, and larger.

To practice friluftsliv, follow several key principles: 1) experience nature, broadly defined; 2) rely on your own body for movement and transportation (you can drive to an outdoor place, but the activity doesn't begin until you get out of the car); 3) participate in nature holistically and with all of your senses; 4) engage in outdoor activity without competition (hockey games are fun, but not frilufstliv); and 5) respect nature in your actions. Løvoll says that having the right knowledge also facilitates friluftsliv. Wearing the proper clothing or knowing how to set up a campsite to block the wind creates the comfort necessary to find ease in nature. But what friluftsliv looks and feels like varies from person to person. In their book on Norwegian friluftsliv, the professors of sports science and pedagogy Annette Hofmann, Carsten Gade Rolland, Kolbjørn Rafoss, and Herbert Zoglowek summarize it thusly: "This definition covers all activities carried out in the open if—and this is the determining factor—they are undertaken with the right attitude." When it comes to friluftsliv, the specifics—what outdoor activity we do, where we do it, and with whom—matter much less than our mindset. We can bring the friluftsliv approach to walking the dog, drinking beer (in Norwegian, *utepils* means "outdoor beer"), or bird-watching as much as we can to skiing, backpacking, and climbing mountains. Løvoll echoes this flexibility. Friluftsliv "can happen everywhere," she said to me. "It's about awareness, attention to details, and attention to our surroundings." In Løvoll's view, even a short time with this attention outdoors can provide a "break from everyday life."

This nonrigidity invites us to find our own forms of friluft-sliv. We can practice friluftsliv in the way that speaks to us, fits into our lives, and accommodates the climates and landscapes in which we spend time outdoors. It doesn't have to be compli-cated. As Ida puts it, "Put enough clothes on so that you won't become wet or freeze and go out! Go to the nearest spot around you that you like: in a park, at the harbor, along a river through the city, in the woods, at the top of a roof where you get a good view. Take it in! Feel the temperature, the wind, the air. Smell! See! And—importantly—bring hot coffee in your thermos!"

TAKING INSPIRATION FROM the Norwegian practice of friluftsliv, we can strive to incorporate time outdoors into our daily life, regardless of weather or season. Three especially useful strate-gies can help:

1. Focus on short-term rewards.
2. Practice wise self-compassion to notice patterns.
3. Leverage social support.

These strategies all draw on the science of motivation to pro-pel us out of our winter burrows and into the great outdoors, and help us cultivate the mindset that winter is wonderful by connecting us to more opportunities for winter recreation.

Strategy #1: Focus on short-term rewards.

We often try to motivate ourselves—and others—by emphasiz-ing the benefits of a behavior. Look at efforts to help people engage in healthy habits, like exercising more, eating more vegetables, or quitting smoking. Most of these well-intentioned attempts to convince people focus on how these activities will make us healthier or help us live longer.

We all want to be healthier and live longer, but these are long-term rewards. Trying to get someone to do something *today* for the promise of a future benefit lacks the oomph of immediate gratification. Having to make a real and present sacrifice—like skipping dessert or going to the gym instead of relaxing at home—for a distant benefit often feels like giving up something for nothing. Yet well-meaning parents, teachers, and experts constantly tout such far-off rewards to motivate healthy behaviors here and now.

Kaitlin Woolley is an expert in the science of goals: how we achieve them and when and why our efforts fail. Her research finds that rather than focusing on long-term benefits (like health), we should focus on immediate rewards. Instead of thinking about how it's "good for us" to go outside, her research suggests it's more effective to think about how donning our winter gear and heading out for a walk will feel good *now*. In one study, Woolley asked people at the gym to choose either their most enjoyable workout or the workout that they felt was most important for their health goals. These exercisers were unaware that one of Woolley's research assistants was observing them. When asked, most everyone in the study—90 percent of them—said they go to the gym primarily for long-term health benefits, and there was no difference between the groups in what workouts they actually chose. But the gym-goers who picked activities they enjoyed completed an average of eleven more reps than those who picked workouts they thought were best for their health. Woolley found the same results when she looked at healthy eating. When participants in a lab experiment were

asked to choose between the carrots they found the healthiest
and those they thought were tastiest, the people who chose car-
rots for the immediate reward—taste—ate 50 percent more
than those who ate for health.

IF I MOTIVATE myself to go outside on a cold, rainy day by telling
myself that I "should" go because it's "good for me," I'm focus-
ing on long-term rewards, which usually succeeds only in mak-
ing the activity feel like a chore. But when I remind myself that
going outside will feel good *now*, that afterward I'll feel more
alert and refreshed, better able to focus on my other daily tasks,
and more patient with my partner, dog, and myself—that's a
more compelling reason to get out the door.

How can we transform what might be a long-term goal—
spending more time outside in the winter to improve our health
and well-being—into a short-term reward? First, we can make
the activity itself more enjoyable: we can bundle up so we're com-
fortable. I have several overly large, thick coats that make me
feel like I'm wrapped in a stylish blanket as I head outside. We
can pack a warm thermos of something nice. We can choose a
favorite activity—walking or skating or skiing or bird-watching.
We can ask a friend to join us, making it a special outing. We
can listen to music or a podcast or an audiobook. We can think
about how a winter walk will make returning to our cozy homes
feel more pleasurable, allowing us to spend the rest of the eve-
ning on the couch, accomplished and relaxed.

Focusing on short-term rewards is also about making things
fun. When we treat healthful behaviors as punishments, the
odds that we'll stick with them are low. Exercise doesn't have to
be running on a treadmill—it can be dancing, roller-skating, or

biking. Healthy eating doesn't have to be a dry salad—it can be vegetable-laden curry or cinnamon-baked apples. Leveraging these short-term rewards can help us translate our good intentions into beneficial behaviors beyond winter. Often, our attempts at self-improvement feel punitive; we try to berate ourselves into healthful habits. Instead, we can make the things we know we *should* do feel like things we *want* to do. Going outside in winter doesn't have to be a chore; it can be a chance for mindful alone time, a gathering with friends, an awe walk, an opportunity to notice the way nature changes throughout the season. Jon Macleod told me about the games they'd play in the gusts of the Isle of Lewis: running at superhuman speeds with the wind at your back; going to a hilltop and jumping into the gale to see how far backward you'd be thrust; making "wind cockerels" by sticking feathers into a potato and watching it spin and fly. Playing in winter weather can help us reconnect to the way we experienced the season as children, as a time of thrilling mess and frigid fantasy.

Then there is the reward of coming in from the cold: returning to warmth, putting on the kettle, changing from boots into slippers. Time outdoors enables the singular delight of having *been out*, so now you can fully *stay in*. This too is part of getting outside in winter: the opportunity to return somewhere warm and welcoming, and to fully luxuriate in leaving the cold behind.

Strategy #2: Practice wise self-compassion to notice patterns.

Sometimes the best way to motivate ourselves to get outside is to practice self-compassion.

The word "self-compassion" might conjure images of spa days and bubble baths, taking it easy and being patient with ourselves. These can be forms of self-compassion, and I love a good bubble bath. But there are other kinds of self-compassion too.

Another kind of self-compassion is sometimes called wise or fierce self-compassion. As a complement to accepting ourself exactly as we are, wise self-compassion is about looking carefully inward to recognize when our behaviors bolster or reduce our well-being. Sometimes, dealing with our inner selves is like parenting a child: treating a child with compassion doesn't mean giving them whatever they want, or letting them do whatever they want. If a child never wants to take a bath, the compassionate response is not to let them remain filthy, but to try to communicate the necessity of bathing, or to help them make bath time more fun.

I first learned about wise self-compassion while studying at the College for Higher Tibetan Studies in Dharamsala, India, as part of Emory University's Mind-Body Sciences summer abroad program. Living in the foothills of the Himalayas, meditating in the Tibetan prayer hall every morning at six a.m., I was immersed in the culture and theory of Tibetan Buddhist contemplative science. There, I encountered instruction not only on how to practice self-acceptance, but also how to look inward, with a loving eye, to ask myself where and how my behaviors might be causing my own suffering. These teachings encouraged me to look at which of my patterns were contributing to my unhappiness, and then to resolve—compassionately—to interrupt those patterns.

When I moved to Tromsø a few years later, I brought this perspective with me. I started to notice how, during the cold days of the Polar Night, I was reluctant to go outside and preferred to stay home, languid and horizontal, whenever possible. But on days that I had to go out, to get to the university or meet friends, I bundled up and braved the weather and, as a result, felt more awake, more vital, and more cheerful.

Even now, I look outside on brisk, soggy, windy days, and my body and mind tell me to stay indoors. Wise self-compassion is recognizing this pattern and realizing that my desire to stay indoors is misleading. And so motivating—sometimes forcing—myself to go out in the cold is wise self-compassion, where the kindest thing I can do for myself is get up, put on my leggings and boots and coat and hat and mittens, and step out the door.

We can motivate ourselves by tuning in to these patterns. How do we feel on days that we stay indoors? How do we feel on days when we venture out? There's room for both: indulgent, restorative couch days and active adventure days. But if we find ourselves out of balance, noticing which activities *actually* make us feel good and which activities we only *think*—perhaps mistakenly—will make us feel good can be a powerful tool for encouraging us to take a walk.

GOING OUTSIDE IN WINTER—and examining how we feel as a result—is an exercise in understanding our patterns of motivation. Are there times when what we're drawn to only makes us feel worse in the long term? Are there times when the things we don't want to do actually provide a significant boost? Do we revert to unhealthy coping mechanisms when we're feeling down? What behaviors—physical, mental, or social—help us feel stronger, happier, and more alive? Understanding our patterns can give us insight about what to lean on in difficult times. When

I'm feeling stressed and overwhelmed, I feel like I don't have time to exercise, go for a walk, or meet up with friends. But the activities that I'm quick to dismiss in busy times are the same ones that help me stay calm when the responsibilities piling up feel like they're pulling me under. It's only through recognizing my own unhelpful tendencies that I've learned to ignore the voice in my head telling me I have no time to work out when I'm under deadline, and to remind myself that prioritizing movement and fresh air makes me more efficient and effective. Every time I return home calmer and more vibrant from a venture into the cold, I understand myself and my patterns a little bit more.

This kind of wise self-compassion also gives me a sense of accomplishment. Part of winter's appeal is the fact that it's *not* as easy as going outside on a day when it's 70°F and sunny. Instead, I'm giving myself a chance to do something that feels a little difficult and to overcome a challenge. And if I was able to do that, what else can I do?

Strategy #3: Leverage social support.

Inviting a friend to join you is one of the most effective motivational techniques: the social accountability of another person relying on you makes it harder to cancel plans, and the addition of a buddy can make any outdoor winter activity more fun.

Being with a friend in nature can even make difficulties seem easier. In a study so memorable it inspired Becky's first tattoo, research participants were walked to the base of a hill and saddled with a heavy backpack. These participants were then asked to estimate the hill's incline. Some participants did this alone, but others were accompanied by a friend (who wasn't allowed to weigh in on the assignment). Participants with a friend estimated that the hill was significantly less steep than participants who made the estimate alone. The comfort of having a friend nearby made the hill before them seem gentler and more surmountable. And among participants who had a friend with them, the longer the pair had been friends, the less steep participants rated the hill. Having a friend with us can make the world appear less challenging. While no one's tested it yet, maybe having a friend with us makes the world appear brighter in darkness or feel warmer in the cold.

There's something especially bonding about doing things together outdoors in the winter. Anthony Taylor, who likes to help Minnesotan immigrants overheat, is also the founder of Melanin in Motion, an organization that connects black, Indigenous, and people of color (BIPOC) residents in the Twin Cities to outdoor activities and opportunities. In this role, Taylor teaches fat biking, snowboarding, and skiing to kids, teenagers, and families, inspiring a love of the outdoors and appreciation of winter sports in communities that have been historically excluded from these activities. Writing for The Great Northern blog, Anthony noticed a peculiar pattern while evaluating the impact of Melanin in Motion. Some families in the program began with summer activities while others started with winter sports. Families who started in the winter were twice as likely to return the following year as families who started in the summer, and four times as likely to return for a third year. "Winter experiences forged deeper connections between people," Anthony wrote. "Navigating cold temperatures together and experiencing the unique environmental opportunities winter provides created a greater experience of adventure and growth, shared success, and camaraderie."

Anthony isn't the only one to observe this. Jane Hurly studies the experience and meaning of leisure with recent Canadian immigrants. Her research brought her to the Long Lake Outdoor Centre in Alberta, where she spent the weekend with seventy refugees who came to the Centre to camp and participate in activities such as snowshoeing, skiing, and ice fishing for the first time. For these refugees, Canada's winters were an unfamiliar and daunting part of acclimating to their new homes. Many arrived for the camping experience uncertain and hesitant. But over the weekend—supported by Alberta Parks' staff—a nurturing and adventurous community formed. The campers found themselves trying new activities and making friends. Nicole, a thirty-six-year-old immigrant from the Democratic Republic of the Congo and a single mother of three, was inspired by watching the people around her walk on a frozen lake and snowshoe for the first time. In her thesis, Hurly shares Nicole's reflection that upon returning home, she felt more connected to Canada. She said her winter camping experience "helped me to be part of the country and enjoy it, and settle in it." Hurly's research found that this camping experience helped many of these refugees feel more comfortable in their new climate and facilitated integration into their new homes.

EMBRACING THE COLD together can help us create memories with loved ones. One of my students described a particularly memorable outing with her family during the early days of the COVID-19 pandemic:

I planned a special outing for my parents and aunt who have been housebound during the pandemic. Their vaccine day had arrived and everyone was anxious about the process. To celebrate the occasion, we picked up a delicious lunch afterward and drove to the beach. Unable to walk on the sand, we parked where we could see the water and hear the waves. Listening to the seagulls and hearing the waves even on a dreary, overcast day was delightful. It made a simple takeout lunch a very special time with my parents and aunt. It felt wonderful to be such a positive influence and provide them with something different from their current homebound routine.

Being proactive and creating an activity that made everyone happy made me realize what profound influence we have in our own lives. Even in the baby steps. Small incremental changes make lasting impacts. Simply feeling the wind with the windows down transported them to walking along the beach. Nobody even seemed to notice it was cool, overcast, and dreary outside. Prior to this, I would have never gone to the beach on a drizzly, rainy day. What a memory we would have missed.

Helga Løvoll shared how being outdoors with others, removed from the concerns of day-to-day life, makes you "feel more connected to the people you are with." Løvoll has experienced this not only as a researcher of friluftsliv, but also in her personal life. When you're together in nature, free from distractions, "the topics you're talking about shift, so they're more questioning of meaning, and life, in a larger perspective." The intimacy of being outside in nature, of walking and talking, invites people to share more openly and vulnerably than they normally would.

Inviting friends or family members to join us in our winter excursions can motivate us to spend more time outdoors, and our time outdoors with loved ones can deepen our connections. Every shared observation of nature's beauty, shared experience of feeling the cold brush against our faces, and shared thermos of hot chocolate brings us closer together.

WISE MOTIVATION

We can also practice winter wisdom. Certain weather is harder to embrace, or more dangerous, than others. The goal of this chapter is not to get you outside when it's -35°F and dangerously cold, to take a stroll when it's pouring, or to go hiking in an icy, slippery windstorm. Rather, the goal is to expand your sense of what weather it's possible to enjoy and to help you overcome barriers and tap into motivation to spend more time outdoors this winter. And when you have no choice but to brave the elements—to get to work or school, to walk your dog or shovel your driveway—to help you have a better experience. Winter wisdom is making the most of what's in front of you, whether that's enjoying a rainy day, or—if conditions are truly unsuitable for outdoor activities—luxuriating in the feeling of staying indoors and watching the weather from a distance.

Experimenting with different strategies for getting outside in winter can teach us lessons about our motivation and how it works. Bundling up and facing the cold gives us an opportunity to learn more about ourselves and our patterns, to notice what our desires are pulling us toward and what they're pushing us away from—and when these desires enhance or undermine our well-being. We can use winter's challenge to conduct little experiments: How do I feel after compelling myself to get outside, perhaps despite initial reticence? How does inviting a friend along change my experience? Were my expectations about how it would feel outside—my affective forecasting—correct or inaccurate? These daily or weekly practices give us greater insight and more tools for motivating ourselves year-round. We can begin to see when our affective forecasting is working against us, and learn to calibrate our expectations while also remaining open to how things actually are. We can allow ourselves to be surprised and to overturn our preconceptions. We can tap into motivation that is fun and social rather than punishing or forceful. And most of all, we can gain a better appreciation for our ability to confront darkness, cold, and wet, and to not just survive these trials, but to enjoy them.

The magical mixture of fresh air, contact with the elements, and movement are natural antidepressants, counterbalances to dark and dreary days and times of strife and struggle. By getting outside, you can unlock a new world of winter's opportunities. Along the way, you might just find yourself embracing an open-air life.

WINTER PRACTICE:
GETTING OUTSIDE

- **Winter-proof yourself:** This week, experiment with really dressing for the weather and go outside in the worst weather you can (safely) experiment with. Pile on extra layers, put on a waterproof coat and shoes, and see if you can get so warm you need to take off a layer or unzip your coat. How does it feel to go outside dressed for the weather? Does it feel different than your usual excursions? Bonus points if you go outside while it's actively raining or snowing.

- **Practice friluftsliv:** Over the next week, commit to fifteen extra minutes outside per day: drinking coffee on your porch, taking a walk, or riding your bike. How does adding a few minutes of outdoor time to your day impact your mood and energy?

- **Phone a friend:** Invite a friend for an outdoor activity: a walk, hike, bike, or bonfire. After the activity, debrief: What did you notice? How did it feel? How does going outside change the experience of socializing?

- **Reclaim a summer love:** Think of a summer activity you enjoy that can be safely reclaimed in the winter: beachcombing, a favorite hike, even having a picnic are all possible with the right clothing and a thermos full of coffee. Try your summer activity in winter and see how it feels.

- **Expectations vs. reality:** Go on a winter walk. Before you leave, think about how you expect it to feel. Then during and after the experience, check in with how you're actually feeling. Did your expectations match reality?

8.

SINK, SWEAT, OR SWIM

ROB AND I FLEW from Amsterdam to Tokyo, eager to experi-
ence Japan's mountainous regions, where winters can bring
meters of snow, and the country's famous *onsen* culture. We
traveled to Kaminoyama Onsen, in Yamagata prefecture, drawn
by its reputation as a hot-spring city with many traditional onsen
hotels—a popular tourist destination within Japan, but one that
foreigners are less likely to visit. On our second night, our pres-
ence at a local barbeque restaurant was so surprising that other
diners stopped to ask why we were there. Rob and I were eating
soft-serve ice cream* outside the restaurant with our feet in an
ashiyu, one of the town's communal hot-spring footbaths, as we
tried to explain my research to some curious locals through a
translator app.

Now we were at Arimakan ryokan, one of the country's
3,000 onsen establishments that harness the nation's 25,000 nat-
ural hot springs to fill tubs, Jacuzzis, and baths with geothermal

---

*It's never too cold for ice cream.

water. For thirty minutes, we had the private rooftop onsen to ourselves. A wide, shallow basin steamed into the evening air. The compact rooftop patio was bordered by a delicately land-scaped Japanese garden, sparse with vegetation at the tail end of winter. Orb lamps dotted the periphery, and a small pagoda rose over the bath's shallow end. Beyond the rooftop, village lights shone on the mountains of Kaminoyama.

The night was black and cold, but the patio was bathed in golden light. As we eased into the steaming waters, it began to snow. Flakes drifted down, melted by the heat rising from the bath before they could hit the water. Goosebumps appeared on my arms. My bottom half was relaxingly warm, submerged in the hot spring. My top half was refreshingly cold, face and shoulders kissed by snowflakes. The contrast in temperatures, the crisp air, the evening darkness, and the chilled wetness of snow combined in a peaceful haze. I sat in the misty waters watching the snow fall, listening to the quiet of the night.

After our late-night soak, we made our way back to our hotel room, forgoing our Western-style beds to burrow into the futon nests rolled out on the tatami floor. The hot-water bathing had simultaneously relaxed my muscles and exhausted my system: I sank into a deep and easy sleep.

THE BENEFITS OF BATHING

Japan may be the most bath-obsessed nation on the planet. A national survey found that in winter, 70 percent of people in Japan bathe daily; another study found that 93 percent of Japanese people living in Japan take baths. Bathing in Japan is so popular that research studying the health benefits of bath-taking often have to split participants into two groups: high-frequency bathers who take at least one bath a day, and less-frequent bathers who bathe less than seven times a week (one study that split participants thusly found that two thirds of participants were in the high-frequency group). At Arimakan ryokan, women sat on plastic stools under taps around the periphery of the bath room, washing their hair, scrubbing their bodies, and brushing their teeth before entering the communal tubs. In Japan, you scrub yourself *before* entering the tub, so you are clean when you begin your soak. People in Japan take baths to warm their bodies, recover from fatigue, relax, and improve sleep.

In her 1946 book *The Chrysanthemum and the Sword*, cultural anthropologist Ruth Benedict called the Japanese bath "one of the best loved minor pleasures of the body." "For the poorest rice farmer and the meanest servant," she wrote, "just as much as for the rich aristocrat, the daily soak in superlatively heated water is a part of the routine of every late afternoon." This nationwide pastime likely evolved due to the country's abundant mineral-rich, naturally occurring hot springs, which bubble up from the islands' volcanoes and have made hot water accessible to the masses for more than three thousand years. Additionally, Japan's houses are made to withstand brutally hot and humid summers, so, in winter, the cold seeps right in. Daily bathing helps people warm up, particularly before bed. I experienced this firsthand when I stayed at a rural farmhouse in Yamagata; rooms in the house were warmed by space heaters, and late-night trips to the bathroom were frigid affairs. Our evening excursions to the local onsen were a relief, and a chance to thoroughly scorch myself before sleep. Some say you're not done in the onsen until you reach *yudedako*, which literally translates to "boiled octopus," the blissful, mind-clearing state of being fully cooked by the water.

MODERN RESEARCH CORROBORATES centuries of cultural practice: hot-water bathing has numerous health benefits. Most of this research is done in Japan, where the bathing fanaticism provides ideal, naturally occurring conditions for study, as people can be divided into groups based on how frequently, how long, and at what temperature they bathe, and whether they do so at home or in public baths. Visiting a naturally fed hot-spring onsen weekly, as compared with monthly, was associated with significantly decreased risk of all underlying disease in a study of more than 1,200 elderly Japanese. Another study of almost 900 participants found that those who bathed in hot water at least five times a week scored significantly lower on an index of atherosclerosis, a buildup of plaque that thickens arteries and puts people at risk of heart attack and stroke. A secondary study of 150 of these participants tracked for a year found that more frequent bathing was associated with decreased level of B-type natriuretic peptide, a hormone change indicating effective heart function. Bathing more often was associated with increased cardiovascular functioning and decreased risk of heart failure, heart attack, and stroke in elderly Japanese patients, supporting other research that found that hot-water immersion is healthful and protective for patients with heart failure. Daily bathing is also associated with better hemoglobin A1C control in patients with diabetes.*

---

*Even as it provides these healthful benefits, hot-water immersion is not without risks: drowning while soaking in a bathtub is the most common cause of accidental home death in Japan, and is most common among the elderly. Experts suggest mitigating this

The research also supports another common practice: taking a hot bath to relax before bed in the evening. Numerous studies suggest that a 10- to 30-minute bath, 30 to 120 minutes before bedtime, improves sleep, especially in winter. Nighttime bathing is associated with better sleep quality and efficiency; decreased "sleep onset latency," or how long it takes you to doze off; and reduced nighttime blood pressure. And if you don't have a bathtub, a shower helps too. A broader meta-analysis of "water-based passive body heating" found that as little as ten minutes in a hot shower or bath one to two hours before bedtime improves these sleep metrics. Other research finds that even a hot footbath can help you snooze more soundly. Nighttime bathing improves slumber because increasing your body temperature substantially sends your body a message to cool down, triggering internal temperature down-regulation, which stimulates the release of melatonin. This is also why it's good to sleep in chilly rooms: cooler body temperatures are associated with non-REM sleep, the deepest level of sleep. Hot baths before bed improve sleep for insomnia sufferers and can reduce depression symptoms. One study found that people who took baths more frequently were less likely to be depressed three years later, an effect that was especially strong for bathing in winter.

JAPAN IS ONE of many cultures with a long history of communal bathing; Russian baths, Turkish and Moroccan hammams, and Korean spas are all distinct, with their own histories and traditions. And Iceland is well-known for its public pools and

---

risk by heating dressing rooms or bathrooms thoroughly, so that the shock of entering the hot water is lower and likelihood of fainting reduced.

lagoons, fed by geothermal water. Icelander Rannveig Krist-jánsdóttir's most beloved winter tradition is going to the pools after dinner. "You go and you can't see anything because it's all foggy from the steam. And then you take a shower, and at the pool you put on your pajamas straightaway and then just zip your coat over them, and then you go home and you're already in your pajamas and all ready for bed!"

Like Japan, Iceland is rich in natural, geothermally heated water. Public pools are a national treasure, and Icelanders of all ages soak regularly. While in Iceland, I visited a typical pool, Sundhöllin, on a Saturday night in early February. There, I saw how the pools are a winter refuge with my own eyes. I stopped in on the city's "pool night," when normal entry fees were waived for the evening. The place was packed. I heard a mix of languages and saw a diverse group of people: old men sitting quietly, women with swim caps, groups of twentysomethings flirting with each other. Even at ten o'clock at night there were families, and children splashed around, lying on their stomachs in the shallow kids' pools. In addition to children's swim facilities, the shower room had a baby bathtub and baby seat. Other amenities support regular visits: well-equipped showers, vanity tables with hair dryers, and, my favorite contraption, a metal bin that you shove your suit into that vibrates violently to shake off excess water, allowing you to take your bathing suit with you for the rest of your day.

ICELAND WAS ALSO where I had my first communal bathing experience years ago, on vacation with friends in my midtwenties. We opted to visit a local pool, forgoing the crowded, expensive, and infinitely photogenic Blue Lagoon for what we deemed a more authentic (and affordable) experience. But my main memories aren't of the warmth of the hot tubs or the heat of the sauna. Instead, I remember the trepidation, fascination, and relief of the women's locker room. I was unused to stripping naked in front of many other women—the closest I had gotten was in high school gym class, where changing was done furtively, or at gyms, where the self-consciousness combines with a strange competitiveness and it seems like everyone is fitter than you. But in the Icelandic locker room, I was surrounded by women of all ages in a greater variety of shapes and sizes than I'd ever seen, walking around unabashedly in the nude, joking with friends, and helping children get dressed. In a moment of twenty-five-year-old insight, it occurred to me that the only women I saw naked were women in TV and movies—women whose full-time jobs involve strict diets and intense workouts and who have teams of lighting and makeup specialists to airbrush every flaw. Being surrounded by women so comfortable in their own skin evoked an unnameable emotion, a swirl of inspiration and affirmation, a sense of camaraderie, a wondering of how different my relationship to my body might be if I lived in a communal bathing culture such as this. A feature on Iceland's pools in *The New York Times Magazine*, which called the pools "a great leveler," made the same point: Icelandic women in the article talked about the importance of seeing "real women's bodies," and how useful it is for young women to see pregnant women baring all. Here is another way hot-water bathing might boost our mental well-being: shedding our outer layers in a safe space may help us appreciate our own skin a bit more.

◆

HOT BATHS CAN be an indulgent ritual that eases the chill of winter and confers measurable health benefits. But it's not the only way to warm up in winter. For some people in the north, the preferred way to bathe isn't in water—it's in the sauna.

SCHVITZ HAPPENS

"Sauna" is a Finnish word—perhaps Finland's most well-known export, beating out Nokia phones and the iconic, orange-handled Fiskars scissors—and, in Finland, life begins and ends in the sauna. Literally. Traditionally, that's where women gave birth—as saunas were reliably sterile environments accessible to most—and where dead bodies were cleaned and prepared for burial. Kaisa, our host in Ii, told me of a Finnish legend that the earliest settlers to arrive in Finland first built a sauna before building other structures, like houses.

Finland has more than an estimated 3 million saunas for a population of about 5.5 million: that's one sauna for every two people. There, saunas are seen as necessities, not luxuries. For the Finns, having a sauna in your house is somewhat equivalent to having a bathtub in the US. Not *everyone* has one, but a home sauna is quite normal and not reserved only for the wealthy. Apartment buildings have communal saunas, large office buildings have saunas for their workers, and the president and prime minister each have official saunas. When I asked Kaisa if she uses the sauna in her house often, she said, "Not often . . . maybe once a week." When I asked Varpu Wiens, a researcher at the University of Oulu, if she had a sauna in her house, she said, "Of course. I have two."

Finland ranked second in the world for gender equality in 2022. It was the first country to extend the right to vote for all women and men in 1906 and the first country to elect women to parliament in 1907. It is also known as a world leader in education, which is often credited to reforms that focused on equality rather than excellence. The high standard of life in Finland is, in part, a side effect of a nation that has doggedly pursued equality.

The country's sauna culture informs these ideals. A Finnish saying states: "All are created equal, but nowhere more so than in a sauna." A bit of magic happens in these wooden boxes. Sauna bathers are stripped down, literally and figuratively. There is no hierarchy: bosses and employees mingle, parents and children commune, and the wealthiest and most powerful are as naked and sweaty as everyone else. In the sauna, no one is more or less important. Everyone is afforded the same courtesy, and everyone is consulted before the water is poured on the rocks to make *löyly*, the resulting steam. Like gathering around fire, the sauna invites intimacy and conversation. The Swedish Sauna Academy's motto is *In sauna veritas*, or "In sauna, there is truth." In the dark, the heat, and the nude, people open up. Antti told me a story: a man learns that one of his close friends has broken up with his longtime girlfriend. The man is hurt that his friend didn't share this, and broaches the topic, asking why he wasn't told. His friend replies: "Well, we haven't been to sauna together!"

The sauna is a sacred place. "You take a shower to clean your body. You take a sauna to clean your soul," Antti told me. Special occasions are still celebrated there; in the summer, birch leaves are collected during the two weeks they are in season, dried, and saved for the Christmas sauna, when they become tools for gentle flogging, boosting circulation and filling the air with their fresh scent.

The sauna invites a mindful pause in its preparation as well as its use. Most Finns still use—and prefer—traditional, wood-burning saunas, whereby the wooden rooms are heated via a small iron fireplace. This is despite the ease and convenience of more modern, electric versions. In wooden saunas, the fire must be started and logs must be fed continuously to keep the room hot. They can take several hours to warm, but the atmosphere provided by the crackling fire makes it worth it, and tending to the sauna becomes a ritual in itself. Heat is increased both by stoking the flames and by pouring water over the rocks atop the stove; the löyly singes your skin pleasantly as the moisture hits you. During the men's sauna time, Antti showed Rob how to make a sacrifice to the "sauna gnome" by pouring a bit of his beer on the hot rocks, which, once the alcohol burned off, filled the room with the yeasty smell of fresh-baked bread.

IN FINLAND, the sauna has been called the poor man's pharmacy. Emerging research substantiates this sentiment; going to the sauna has an astounding list of health benefits that make me wonder why it isn't prescribed for conditions ranging from in-somnia to hypertension to chronic pain to asthma. In addition to easing stress and promoting relaxation, sauna bathing can improve sleep, skin conditions, and circulation; lower blood pressure, which can prevent or even treat hypertension; improve lung function and reduce pulmonary diseases; reduce pain and increase mobility for patients with rheumatic disease; provide relief for headaches and arthritis; and boost the immune system, making people less susceptible to colds and viruses. Going to the sauna increases interleukin-10, an important cytokine for healing that reduces inflammation and the stiffness of blood vessels, which in turn lowers the risk of developing the arterial plaque that can lead to heart attacks or stroke. Regular sauna bathing lowers cholesterol, increases the body's ability to burn fat for energy, and increases insulin sensitivity, decreasing risk of diabetes. And regular heat exposure makes you a better "sweater"—your body learns to sweat more efficiently, strengthening your natural cooling system.

Like the research on hot-water bathing in Japan, Finland's sauna obsession provides ideal conditions for large-scale, longitudinal studies of the effects of sauna on health. It wouldn't be feasible to randomly assign participants to visit the sauna five times a week for decades, but Finland provides natural conditions for comparing frequent sauna bathers with infrequent ones. The results are remarkable. In a study of more than two thousand men followed for more than twenty years, more frequent trips to the sauna (three to seven times a week, as compared with twice a week or less) were associated with a significantly reduced risk of heart attack, heart disease, and mortality, even after controlling for other health factors like physical activity levels, smoking, and alcohol consumption, as well as demographic variables like socioeconomic status. In another study of more than sixteen hundred men and women followed for more than fifteen years, going to the sauna more frequently—in this case, four to seven times a week compared with once a week—was associated with reduction in stroke risk of more than 60 percent. Other research has found that regular sauna use is associated with an enormously reduced risk (over 65 percent) of Alzheimer's and dementia.

Like exercise, the sauna's heat stresses the cardiovascular system, which strengthens the body over time. Cardiovascularly, going to the sauna looks astonishingly similar to moderate- or high-intensity physical activity like walking. A trip to the sauna may be as beneficial for your heart health as a trip to the gym, which is what reduces sauna bathers' long-term risk for heart attack, heart disease, and stroke. Researchers suggest that sauna bathing may be especially helpful for people who have highly stressful jobs or personal lives, who have little spare time, and who have trouble adhering to exercise and diet recommendations. In other words: everyone.

The astounding health and longevity benefits we see in research about sauna use—conducted most often in Finnish populations—is partially, or even mostly, attributable to the heat exposure. But I've heard experts talk about some of these amazing findings and assume that the *only* important component of the sauna is heat. Yet the sauna is so much more than just a hot box. The sauna is an escape, both physical and mental. It's a time to slow down, pause, and connect: with ourselves, with our bodies, and with each other. The psychological relaxation, the unhurried time away, the social ties strengthened by regular sauna visits: these are all factors that improve health, and it's likely a combination of psychological, physical, and social benefits from the sauna that lead to these gains in health, vitality, and longevity.

WINTER IS THE IDEAL season for indulging in warmth and reaping the mind and body benefits of schvitzing it out in a wooden box or soaking in a steaming tub. But if you can't stand the heat, there is another option that confers similar health improvements. Have you tried immersing yourself in freezing cold water?

GETTING WARM BY GETTING COLD

While back in Tromsø, I reunited with Meghan Bradway, who moved to Tromsø with me as a fellow Fulbright scholar in 2014 and never left; after our year together, she stayed to complete her PhD and is now a research scientist at the Norwegian Centre for E-health Research. As a transplant to Tromsø who has been there close to a decade, I asked her what she thinks helps her most during the Polar Night. Without hesitation, she said it was her weekly jump in the Tromsø harbor as part of a Wednesday morning sauna session with friends and colleagues. Meghan, who struggles with depression and anxiety, talked about how jumping in the frigid fjord waters resets her entire nervous system, helping her more effectively than anything else she's tried, and how she looks forward to that morning each week, leaning on it in hard times and in good.

I also grabbed lunch with Sarah Strand, who completed her Fulbright in Svalbard and stayed on the island for eight more years to research permafrost as part of her PhD. When I asked how she thrived during Svalbard's even more extreme Polar Night—which sees not even a wisp of twilight for two full months—she described her weekly dips, where she'd start the day by stripping naked on the shore and dunking in Svalbard's icy waters.

In Ii, Finland, I asked Antti the same question: What is his most important strategy for feeling good during the prolonged, gray winter? "When you start noticing the darkness is making you depressed," he told me, "you think 'Ah! I haven't been swimming!'"

PEOPLE WHO PRACTICE winter swimming tend to be fanatics about it (I've heard that in the UK, the idea of the winter swimming evangelist is almost cliché). They claim that it refreshes and invigorates them; that it cures their stresses; that it heals their aches and pains; that it makes them feel *warmer* during the winter. I'm somewhat skeptical: for all my love of winter, I hate actually *feeling* cold. My strategies mostly involve cozy indoor delights and dressing appropriately so that even when it's freezing out, I feel snug and toasty. But after encountering winter swimming's popularity in multiple cultures, I can't ignore it as a winter well-being strategy that seems to provide outsized benefits; my friends told me that a minute or two in glacial water bolsters their mood for a week.

I had to try it for myself. My first foray was in Tromsø, where I met Meghan and her colleagues for their weekly six a.m. sauna and dip before work. The sauna, Pust (Norwegian for "breathe"), is a triangular wooden structure made to resemble the racks used to dry cod into *klippfisk*. While sweating in the sauna, you can see through the floor-to-ceiling window over the harbor toward the mainland. In the early-morning polar light, the sky above Tromsdalstinden glowed deep indigo. The lights of fishing boats, mainland homes, and the Tromsø bridge gleamed in golden yellows. The mountains were snow-covered, and the swimming area in front of the harbor was lit from underwater, illuminating the clear, aquamarine depths.

The only thing that dragged me out of bed for this was the

promise of the sauna's warmth, but once I arrived I was confronted with the insanity of immersing myself in an Arctic fjord in January. To even contemplate such a feat, we had to leave the sauna's cocoon and slip and slide on the ice-encrusted platform toward the water. Clad only in my bathing suit, the polar air instantly raised goosebumps all over my body.

Meghan—the pro—jumped straight in, dunking her head and emerging with a shriek. Afraid my body would go into shock, I opted to lower myself into the water via ladder (for beginners, this is a safer approach). At first, I tried not to think too much, but once I entered the water, that wasn't a problem: the cold stole the breath from my lungs and emptied my mind of all thought except the painful pins and needles in my extremities. I treaded water for as long as I could stand—which was about eleven seconds—before climbing the ladder out of the frigid depths and beelining into the sauna. My body tingled as the feeling returned to my fingers and toes; I felt vibrantly awake, more than I had since I'd arrived to Tromsø's Polar Night. And I felt accomplished, tough, like I had conquered something.

Even before I made it back into the sauna, a surprising thought entered my mind: I wanted to do it again.

I WAS HIGH on the feel-good chemicals triggered by cold-water exposure. The intense chill of winter swimming releases endorphins (natural painkillers and mood enhancers also responsible for the runner's high), dopamine (a rewarding neurotransmitter that helps us feel pleasure and is associated with activities like sex and eating delicious food), serotonin (a neurotransmitter that regulates mood, appetite, and sleep), and norepinephrine (a stress hormone that increases energy and mental alertness).

This may be why many people report that cold-water swimming helps alleviate their depression and what makes the practice a reliable strategy for chasing away winter blues. It also explains the allure of an activity that seems crazy until you try it. Antti refers to winter swimming as his "healthy addiction": because of the release of these neurochemicals, winter swimming has a drug-like effect on the brain. Once a highly niche hobby espoused by hardcore outdoor enthusiasts like Wim Hof, the practice has exploded in popularity in recent years, aided by the COVID-19 pandemic, when the need for open-air activities and dopamine hits reached new heights. Alongside this popularity is a surge in scientific research on the effects of cold-water bathing.

Like hot-water and sauna bathing, cold-water swimming is beneficial for a wide variety of ailments, including rheumatism, fibromyalgia, and asthma. Cold-water immersion reduces insulin resistance and increases insulin sensitivity, which makes it protective against diabetes. Short-term cold-water exposure improves the immune system and increases prevalence of leukocytes, or white blood cells; winter swimmers are less susceptible to colds and other infections. Cold-water immersion after exercise enhances recovery, boosting performance during subsequent workouts. It also stimulates blood flow, improving circulation, making it particularly helpful for those who suffer from cold extremities in the winter, as increased circulation helps the body deliver warm blood to fingers and toes.

Most incredibly, research is showing that repeated cold-water exposure transforms our bodies. Recent findings indicate that winter swimming leads to the development of brown adipose tissue, otherwise known as brown fat. The majority of fat in people's bodies is white fat, which stores energy. Brown fat, in contrast, generates energy and is associated with healthful benefits. Brown fat regulates our body temperatures, heating us up when we're cold and cooling us down when we're hot through a process called thermogenesis, which burns calories. This kind of fat regulates our metabolism, maintains body weight, and increases insulin sensitivity. Research finds that people with more brown adipose tissue have lower prevalence of diabetes, coronary artery disease, high blood pressure, and congestive heart failure. Brown fat can even recruit white fat to its cause, turning energy-storing white fat into energy-producing brown fat.

Have you ever noticed that babies don't shiver? For a long time, it was thought that only babies had significant amounts of brown fat: since babies can't shiver, brown fat is necessary to help regulate their body temperatures, particularly when it's cold. Evidence suggested that as babies grew, reserves of brown fat shrunk. But in the 1980s, significant amounts of brown adipose tissue were found in Finnish outdoor workers. This was seen as an anomaly until recent research on cold-water exposure revealed that regular, intense cold exposure increases the prevalence of brown fat. This is how, paradoxically, repeated cold-water exposure helps you feel *warmer* in the winter: by stimulating the production of temperature-regulating brown fat, winter swimming trains your body to heat itself more efficiently.

"SO, TODAY YOU will experience how I survive the winter and the darkness," Antti says to me over coffee and pastries. "Swimming!"

When I went swimming in Tromsø, the promise of sauna warmth offset my fear of the icy water. But in Finland, Antti told me that "if you go directly into the sauna after swimming, you spoil the whole feeling." In my head, I snorted and thought, "Yeah, right." We were to go for a dunk at Ii's swimming spot: a hole cut into the ice in the Iijoki river, kept from freezing over by a pump that circulates water in the twenty-foot-wide swimming patch. There was no sauna, just a heated dressing room. The plan was to walk down the snowy, icy path to the dock, get in, "swim," get out again, walk back to the changing room, and get dressed. There was no promise of warmth on the other side, and I was certain that after our dip, I would be cold all day. The endorphins I experienced in Tromsø were long gone, and truly, I did not want to winter swim without a sauna chaser.

But in the name of research, and to save my pride, I had to. Antti told me that his record for winter swimming is when it's -18°F, so at least this day was a balmy 23°F. I'd borrowed Kaisa's neoprene booties to protect my feet on the walk to the swimming hole; Antti explained that once it gets down to 5°F or so, your feet can freeze to the walkway.

As we walked to the water, me in my two-piece bathing suit with ear warmers on, I briefly considered bailing. But I'd come too far. I followed Antti down the ladder into the frigid water that was, somehow, both colder and warmer than I expected. Nothing could prepare my body for the shocking cold. But as soon as I submerged to my neck, I couldn't feel much of anything. In fact, the anticipation of getting in was far worse than actually being in the water.

The booties helped immensely; in Tromsø, by the time I entered the water my feet were already in pain from walking on the icy platform. In Ii, my feet were fine and only my hands really hurt (the soles of your feet and palms of your hands have high thermal conductance, so wearing booties and keeping your hands out of the water helps tremendously). I was breathing heavily and yelping, but I felt strangely warm treading water, and like I could stay in for a long time. Rob got a nine-second video of me, so I must have been in for a good fifteen seconds.

When I got out, I felt bizarrely fine. The walk back to the changing rooms was far more comfortable than the walk down to the dock had been. My fingers, admittedly, hurt a lot, and opening and closing my hands felt robotic and painful. But my entire body was mostly numb, like I'd been given a full-body shot of novocaine.

Back in the changing trailer, I was mostly dry: the frigid air had evaporated the moisture off me. I was a bit baffled about why I didn't feel colder. My skin was red and splotchy, but tingled pleasantly. The surface of my body felt cool, like a gentle breeze was blowing all over, yet the general sensation was of warmth. As I heated up naturally, without the aid of the sauna, I reluctantly admitted that Antti had a point: it felt nice. The tingling warmth was very pleasant, but I also felt proud, hardy, and adventurous. I've never been much of an athlete or run a marathon; I'm a very slow hiker and always struggled climbing the rope in gym class. But here was a physical challenge I mastered, and I felt an immense sense of accomplishment. Once again, a strange thought entered my mind: maybe we could come back and do it again tomorrow.

MANY PEOPLE INTERESTED in winter swimming want to know: What's the minimum dose needed to gain health benefits? Some research suggests that eleven minutes of cold-water immersion and fifty-seven minutes of sauna per week are ideal to reap the rewards of cold and hot therapy. In Finland, however, Antti's approach to winter swimming was more fluid and intuitive. Rob and I peppered him with questions: How often does he go? How long does he stay in? Antti just shrugged. He said he usually goes two or three times a week, but recently he'd "been a bit lazy," so was only going about once a week. He said that, rather than sticking to a schedule, if he's in tune with himself, he knows when to go. When winter gets him down, he heads to the swimming hole.

Antti's approach provided a commonsense counterpoint to the biohacking perspective I often see regarding winter swimming. The process involves trusting himself and paying attention to his body. In response to our question about how long to stay in—Should we count to ten? Should we try to make it a whole minute?—he told us, "No instructions. Just stay in as long as feels good. However many seconds or minutes feels good." He was also clear that no one *has* to do this. Kaisa, for example, used to winter swim but doesn't anymore. "You have to listen to your body," he explained. "Especially if you have heart problems, then you don't do it. Because it's quite a shock. A good shock, but still a shock!" Evidence—and common sense—supports his approach; like exercise, cold-water swimming and sauna bathing stress the body. While they can improve long-term cardiac functioning in healthy people, those with heart issues should be careful and consult their medical team before diving in.

One component of the experience Antti was adamant about was the walk to and from the swimming hole. He maintained that it's vital to warm your body with the brisk fifteen-minute walk there, and that the walk back was equally necessary for recovering after a dip. "One time I tried driving there," he told us, "and then I was cold the whole day!" Going from your car to the swimming hole means your body hasn't properly warmed up pre-swim, and getting right back into your car after doesn't provide the physical activity needed to get warm again. Coming home and having a nice hot beverage can be a helpful add-on. In Finland, it seemed that the most cutting-edge research was just catching up to their cultural awareness; winter swimming didn't feel like a kooky new health craze, but like old knowledge. It felt like something people don't need a research study to validate, because they have their own life experience right in front of them to tell them everything they need to know.

DO WHAT FEELS GOOD

The best mindsets—those that are the wondrous combination of true, useful, and *welcome*—feel good. Like sinking into a hot bath, they provide relief, because they give us an actionable alternative to the normative ways of seeing things: rather than feeling like our intelligence is fixed and nothing can be done, a growth mindset shows us that we can get smarter through effort. Rather than viewing health challenges—chronic illness, cancer—as catastrophic, our mindsets can help us wring meaning and connection from difficult circumstances. And rather than resigning us to writing off three to six months of the year as limiting and dreadful, they can help us embrace winter and its opportunities. Our mindsets must be grounded in truth and reality, but the most powerful mindsets are those we *want* to hold on to. They help us make meaning out of ambiguity and give us a way forward, toward growth, success, health, connection, or delight.

Often, we view the pursuit of health and well-being as full of necessary unpleasantries. We think we must suffer through the things that are "good for us": bitter vegetables; grueling and time-consuming workouts; the chores of therapy and meditation. This makes these habits hard to stick with; they are activities we feel we *should* do, but not always those we *want* to do. But when we find pleasure in these activities, they become easier to maintain. Eating delicious, fresh, seasonal vegetables is a healthy indulgence; finding an exercise we enjoy—sports or dance or swimming or biking—becomes a hobby we gravitate toward; embracing winter rest and coziness, or venturing outside to find winter wonder, transforms the season into a source of delight. Research—including work from the Stanford Mind & Body Lab—suggests that mindsets can reframe difficult but ultimately worthwhile pursuits, making them more attractive.

The mindsets that healthy activities are unappealing may be particularly American; in the US, there is an unspoken undercurrent that dismisses the easy and pleasurable as unhealthy or health-irrelevant. Taking baths and going to the sauna conjure images of sumptuous spas, time wasted idling in relaxation. Mindsets elsewhere may be better able to reconcile health and pleasure. In Japan, the tastiest food is seasonal and vegetable-laden. In Norway, there is nothing so blissful as a cross-country ski. In Finland, going to the sauna is both health-promoting and relaxing. Like focusing on short-term rewards, adopting mindsets and practices that combine enjoyment, relaxation, and grat-

ification with health and well-being increases the likelihood
that healthful habits will become part of your everyday life, no
matter where you live.

Sauna, hot-water bathing, and winter swimming exemplify
the spectrum of winter feel-good. Hot-water bathing is im-
mensely pleasurable, particularly in winter, as well as health-
promoting. The sauna can be an indulgent way to warm up in
winter: it can also be a schvitzy stressor and test of endurance.
And winter swimming involves a large blast of unpleasantness,
followed by an exhilarating endorphin rush. These are all prac-
tices that can, and often do, feel good in the moment, but their
influence extends beyond the present, cascading into improve-
ments in mood, sleep, and physical comfort. They can change
the rest of your day or your week. You can feel their ripple ef-
fects. They release endorphins and opioids that up-regulate our
ability to feel pleasure, sensitizing us to the good things in life,
and providing an antidote to the emotional flattening—otherwise
known as anhedonia—that is one of the cruelest symptoms of
depression. These practices can also be remarkably accessible. If
you don't have a sauna you can visit, take more baths at home.
If you don't have a frozen lake or river to jump in, a bathtub of
ice water or a basic metal tub, filled and left outside in the win-
ter, work just as well.

Yet their benefits likely come not only from their objective,
physiological effects, but also from our mindsets about them.
The total effect of anything on our health and well-being is a
result of its objective influence and what we think and feel about
it. The mindsets that hot-water bathing, saunas, and cold-water
swimming are enjoyable, healthy winter activities not only makes
us more likely to engage in them, it may increase the magnitude

of their health effects. Through our attention, expectations, emotions, and behaviors, our mindsets can make their benefits more likely: when we see the sauna as relaxing, we're more likely to notice how calm we feel after exiting the heat. If we anticipate mental clarity and a mood boost from winter swimming, self-fulfilling expectations work in our favor.

This is not to say that these activities are always easy: winter swimming requires determination and fortitude, as does sweating it out in the sauna. Yet these can be welcome parts of winter, just as mindsets that feel good can sit alongside feelings like anger and grief. Seeking winter comforts works best when coupled with wise self-compassion and understanding our patterns. There can be moments of doubt and difficulty in cultivating a mindset, even when that mindset feels good. But the most impactful mindsets provide obvious value: they help us rethink our problems, give us tools for achieving our goals, and provide new ways of appreciating the world around us.

If a mindset doesn't help you, reduce your suffering, or bring you closer to who you'd like to be, it's not worth adopting. When we look beyond winter for what other mindsets we might improve, it's perfectly reasonable to focus on the most appealing mindsets. We can take inspiration from Antti and not overthink it. Sometimes, it's okay to just do what feels good: when in doubt, sweat it out; when you're grim, take a swim.

WINTER PRACTICE:
HEATING UP, COOLING DOWN

- **Find a sauna near you:** If you don't live in Finland, chances are you may not have easy access to a sauna. Yet sauna pop-ups are becoming more popular. Investigate whether you can find a sauna where you live: spas may offer sauna sessions with other treatments, and gyms sometimes have saunas and offer day passes for affordable prices. If you have friends who live in apartment complexes with gyms, these complexes sometimes have saunas as well: ask a friend if you can plan a sauna session together. See if it's possible to take a field trip to see what it's like.

- **Bedtime bathing:** Take an evening bath, footbath, or hot shower one to two hours before bed. For extra indulgence, try it by candlelight. Notice if this nighttime body heating has any effect on your sleep.

- **Try a winter swim:** If you live near a river, lake, or beach where you can swim, go for a polar bear plunge—it's better (and safer) with friends, so invite some along. If not, consider setting up a backyard dunk tank for the winter months or do a cold plunge in the bathtub. As Antti says, even without a sauna, heating up naturally afterward "feels wonderful." Notice the physical and emotional sensations you experience before, during, and after your dunk, and don't forget a hot drink when you're done!

9.

CLEARING THE WAY

REUNITED WITH JOAR, my former mentor at the University of Tromsø, in Bardus Bar after eight years apart. In Tromsø's city center, we drank beer by candlelight, sitting on low velvet sofas; at six p.m., night had fallen three hours ago. Seeing Joar again was surreal: since our collaboration, I had moved to California, finished my PhD, moved to Amsterdam, and spoken about our study hundreds of times. Our work together spawned countless news articles, dozens of TV and radio interviews, and the book you're holding in your hands. "Our little study has really taken on a life of its own," I said to him, and we toasted our pilsners.

During our reunion, I got the chance to ask him a question that had been bouncing around in my head for a while. I'm very conscious that I'm an outsider to Norway. I look at Tromsø's winter and culture through my own eyes—perhaps fresh enough to see what locals might take for granted, but tinted by my own history, narrative, and upbringing. I asked him: Is there anything I'm getting wrong? Is there anything I should be sure to mention here?

He thought for a moment, considering carefully. "It's about the right things in the right places," he said. He went on to explain: it's like the hair on your head. On your head is where hair is supposed to be, and we're happy when we have hair there. But a hair in the soup? That's the wrong place. He gestured at the city street outside, with a layer of ice and snow visible. The snow there, he explained, is a nuisance. Not particularly beautiful, and in the way. But the snow in the forest, on the ski trails? A totally different story.

In Tromsø, Joar pointed out, they are adapted for winter. Things don't stop when it snows: the roads are cleared, the buses run, schools and businesses don't shut down. Your winter experience is facilitated. Many negative aspects are alleviated, while the positives are enabled—lighted ski trails, a commute unhindered by snow, easy access to nature. In other words, infrastructure.

I was relieved to hear Joar mention something I've thought about a lot: even as I aim to help people cultivate more positive wintertime mindsets and take individual actions to embrace winter, I know that social and cultural context also matter. How your town, city, state, or country responds to weather and facilitates winter life can make it easier or harder to embrace the season. When thinking about mindset, social psychologists often talk about "seed" and "soil." If the mindset is the seed, then the cultural context—infrastructure included—is the soil. Without seeds, nothing grows, and seeds can grow almost anywhere. But they grow bigger, better, and more easily in the right soil. Infrastructure also shapes cultural mindsets about winter: when winter isn't as much of an inconvenience, when it doesn't prevent you from taking your kids to school or getting groceries, it's

easier to enjoy, individually and collectively. This infrastructure
includes the basics, like plowing roads, insulating buildings
properly, and facilitating outdoor activities. But it can also in-
clude more subtle societal infrastructure: designing cities to
look beautiful in darkness, making public spaces appealing in
the cold, and organizing community events that celebrate the
season.

CELEBRATING WINTER

Winter is a perfect time for community gatherings, and seasonal
celebrations connect us with each other and with a sense of
place. At their best, they take advantage of the cold and dark-
ness to create experiences that might be poorly attended at other
times of year. A musician I met in Minneapolis told me that
winter is his busiest season, when demand for concerts and en-
tertainment soars. As people are drawn indoors, they're more
interested in attending live music. The early sunsets make a
five p.m. concert feel like an evening indulgence. In Fairbanks,
Alaska, the community board at the local café is jam-packed in
wintertime with meetups, events, and gatherings. In summer,
the board is bare as everyone gallivants in the sun and warmth.
And Faclan: Hebridean Book Festival, on the Isle of Lewis, takes
place during Samhain, the Celtic precursor to Halloween, just
after the fall equinox, as the days begin to shorten. Originally,
Faclan was held after the Edinburgh International Book Festival
at the end of August. Roddy Murray, who runs Faclan, told me
this initially seemed like a natural time: literary lovers already

in the area could tag on a trip to the Isle of Lewis and get a two-for-one in their book fairs.

But it didn't work. The crowds from Edinburgh failed to materialize, and the locals on the island—even book lovers—couldn't be coaxed to spend the precious, final days of summer sitting in dark auditoriums listening to authors speak. Why would they spend an evening inside when they could be out picnicking, hiking, tending sheep, or painting the fence? What a waste.

After five years, the book festival moved to the cusp of winter—a landing place that allowed it to bloom into a highlight of the literature and arts scene of the Outer Hebrides.

Winter-focused festivals deliberately, exuberantly, sometimes even defiantly celebrate winter. When Edmonton, Canada, wanted to transform the city's approach to the season, they started with winter festivals. Edmonton was well-known for its summer events—the Shakespeare Festival, the Blues Festival, the Comedy Festival, the Indigenous Peoples Festival, the International Street Performers Festival—but this vibrant, celebratory community culture disappeared for nine months of the year. City leadership set the goal to make the city as known for cold-weather festivals as warm weather ones. This birthed the Silver Skate Festival, a ten-day art, culture, sport, and music festival, and the Flying Canoë Volant Festival, in which racers sit in canoes and whiz down snowy hills to see who can cross the finish line first; this celebration was so successful it eventually caught the attention of Red Bull, who hosted their Crashed Ice event in Edmonton in 2015, with professional racers skating harrowing downhill ice tracks filled with twists, turns, bumps—and yes, many crashes. This also led to Edmonton hosting two Winter Cities Shake-Ups, a conference for urban planners, artists, and entrepreneurs focused on ideas for embracing winter climates in cities across the world. I shared my strategies for cultivating more positive wintertime mindsets for the first time at Edmonton's second Winter Cities Shake-Up in 2017. In between presenting and conference sessions, Becky, who came with me for a winter getaway, and I walked through snow sculptures and mazes, explored outdoor light and color installations, and played "hygge bingo" by visiting the city's coziest downtown establishments.

Winter festivals are an extension of Christmas market season, where people gather to shop for holiday gifts, eat seasonal delicacies, and—if you're in Germany—drink lots of *glühwein*. This hot, mulled wine literally translates to "glow wine," because that's how you feel after you drink it, a combination of tipsy, cozy, and warm. I defy anyone who thinks people aren't willing to spend time outside in winter to visit a Christmas market. Whether in New York, Philadelphia, Chicago, Minneapolis, Denver, Savannah or where they originated throughout Europe—in Germany, Austria, Belgium, and elsewhere—Christmas markets draw crowds. They're an indication that people are hungry for a reason to leave the house and spend an evening outdoors in winter. A promise of community, gathering, and light. Hot drinks, good snacks. A bit of shopping. If we build it, they will come. And while Christmas markets are special—seasonal, festive—their success can be replicated in different forms long after the holidays are over.

Many cities now hold winter festivals at the end of January and beginning of February, during what I think of as the "winter doldrums." This is when the holidays are over and the season is no longer new. It's the middle of winter, with more still to go. Winter festivals enliven this time of year and give people something to look forward to after the post-holiday comedown.

I first experienced this in Tromsø, where, for one week at the end of January, movie theaters, concert halls, performing arts spaces, town squares, and even the sides of buildings are devoted to the Tromsø International Film Festival. The city scurries from venue to venue between screenings, international visitors pore over the film schedule, and children on class trips sit in the town square and watch films outdoors on the "snow screen," often getting snowed on as they enjoy movies while bundled up and wearing reflective safety vests. This is the coldest time of year, when Tromsø gets, at most, a few hours of light a day. Yet people travel from all over to sit in the dark, indoors or out, and watch movies. After the film festival comes Sami Week: celebrated in conjunction with Sami National Day on February 6, the week honors the culture and traditions of the Sami people, a highlight of which is the reindeer race, in which reindeer tear down Tromsø's main street, spurred on by racers on cross-country skis, at speeds of nearly forty miles per hour.*

These festivals show that it's possible to coax people outdoors and create vibrant gatherings in January, February, and March. In Edmonton, the recent focus on winter festivals highlights an eagerness for activities during these post-holiday winter months. From 2012 to 2017, the Flying Canoë Volant Festival increased in attendance from 3,500 to over 40,000 people, and

---

*This is also where I learned that male reindeer shed their antlers each November. Female reindeer, however, don't shed their antlers until their calves are born in the spring—meaning Santa's sleigh is pulled by a team of all-female reindeer.

popularity of the city's winter festivals keeps rising. Likewise, the Hebridean Dark Skies Festival, on the Isle of Lewis, takes advantage of winter's darkness with programs celebrating the night sky, including stargazing events, talks by astronomers, and online workshops like developing your nighttime creativity. The Great Northern, in Minnesota's Twin Cities, keeps growing, with culinary events, ice bars, sauna villages, and immersive art experiences. This festival runs alongside the city's ultra-popular luminary festival at a local lake.

It takes an appreciation of winter, in all its icy glory, to create a winter-centric festival. But it also makes winter a celebratory time. Particularly in January and February, months that can be challenging, these festivals shape our mindsets, rewriting the stories we tell ourselves about winter. They can instill or solidify the belief that "winter is wonderful," giving winter skeptics a fresh perspective and drawing out those who already love the season. They help us see winter differently, through art, music, and conversation. They lure us out of our burrows and show us how much is possible in the winter—whether it's seeing our cities in a new light, admiring snow sculptures, or reminding us how winter's darkness is perfectly suited for movie-watching. A winter festival is a mindset intervention, an immersion and an invitation to celebrate the season.

WINTER FESTIVALS are just one facet of winter culture; to help people view the season as full of opportunity, cities and towns can enact policies that create the conditions for positive wintertime mindsets to grow and flourish.

MAKING A WINTER CITY

"What would it take to make you fall in love with winter?"

This was the question that started a revolution in Edmonton, North America's northernmost city of more than one million people. Ben Henderson, who served as city councilor for fourteen years, dreamed of converting Edmonton's northern climate and long, cold winters from liability to asset. When he was elected in 2007, the predominant view in Edmonton was that winter was a season to suffer through. Henderson realized that an overly negative view of winter was harmful: he attributed Edmonton's challenges attracting top talent to come and work in the city in part to this perspective.

I've heard this economic argument from other city leaders as well. In the Twin Cities of Minneapolis and St. Paul, Minnesota, Eric Dayton is on a mission to "keep the north cold" by promoting a love of winter to inspire climate action and protect the season. He founded The Great Northern festival, a ten-day celebration of art, music, food, films, speakers, and outdoor activities, hoping to reclaim the city's long winters and cold climate as a selling point, sparking the idea that people could move to the Twin Cities not in spite of winter, but because of it.

Henderson saw the same possibility for Edmonton; he imagined a citywide campaign to help people rethink the season as part of what made the city special. His vision birthed the Winter-City strategy: a comprehensive, holistic plan to help Edmontonians embrace winter. He and his colleagues realized that in order to truly transform Edmonton, they'd have to touch every aspect of winter life, from the events people attend, to the infrastructure that makes it easier to get outside and enjoy the season, to the ways businesses operate in wintertime.

The WinterCity team—which included city leaders and a volunteer group that became the WinterCity Think Tank—combined Edmontonians' ideas about what would make them fall in love with winter with urban design expertise and case studies of cities around the world that already embraced winter, including Copenhagen, Oslo, and Oulu. This led to four major pillars of the WinterCity Strategy: Winter Life, Winter Design, Winter Economy, and Winter Story.

WINTER LIFE makes it easier to play outside. The city created Winter Fun Kits, which include portable firepits, kicksleds, and snowshoes that families and communities can rent for picnics or outdoor BBQs; developed and maintained skating trails through the woods, nicknamed IceWays; and funded ski hills to provide lessons and equipment rental to lower-income Edmontonians, focusing on youth, immigrants, and people with disabilities. Winter Life has improved winter transportation for walkers, cyclists, and people who take public transit. Before the WinterCity initiative, there was "no attempt to keep parks open, no attempt to keep trails open" in the winter, Henderson told me. Winter Life changed that, ensuring that parks and trails remain accessible for year-round recreation, even in the snow. The city installed locking ski racks at public transport stations, encouraging people to cross-country ski as part of their daily commute. Bike path maintenance is now given priority, even in the winter, enabling people to bike to work year-round.

City investments inspired individuals to make the season their own: a one-off Winter Bike to Work Day, in which city employees handed out hot chocolate and cookies to commuting cyclists from seven to nine a.m., evolved into a weekly occurrence. One regular member converted his cargo bike into a "barista bike," which he used to make coffee for the group every week.

Winter Design is about designing the city for fun, activity, beauty, and interest, as well as for safety and comfort in darkness and cold. Simon O'Byrne, the WinterCity Think Tank co-chair, wrote, "Winter's long, dark days provide the ideal palette of darkness needed to become a city of light; a place that's known worldwide for brilliant, whimsical night-scaping that playfully illuminates our buildings, public spaces, and infrastructure. We can transform the darkness into something beautiful and fun." This requires a shift in thinking to *always* design with winter in mind. Too often, beautiful outdoor spaces or new buildings are planned to capitalize only on the warm days of spring and summer; before this initiative, the idea that these spaces could become hubs for winter enjoyment was rarely considered.

Henderson told me about a large, central square in the city that was rebuilt with an outdoor café on one side. The square was designed by architects from Seattle, for whom staying out of the rain was top of mind, so they built the patio on the north side of the building, protecting it from the rain—not so much an issue in Edmonton—but also blocking the sun, making it cold and dark during the long winter. As part of the WinterCity strategy, Edmonton began requiring that new construction plans include "four-seasons consideration": designing spaces to capture sunlight and block wind, using light creatively to beautify long nights, leveraging color to contrast winter's gray palette, and installing firepits and warming huts to provide relief from the cold. To do this successfully, designers must really understand Edmonton's climate. Winter Design initiatives have included new lighting of the city's heritage buildings and ice-skating trails, improving public wheelchair accessibility for winter weather, and building pavilions toward the sun and away from the wind. These subtle changes may go unnoticed by many, but they are felt by all: when cities are designed to maximize winter comfort and playfulness, they unlock new ways to enjoy the season.

Winter Economy focuses on enhancing the vibrancy of streets and public places, creating winter festivals, and developing a winter patio culture. Winter festivals became the cornerstone of the city's strategy, providing activities and enthusiasm for the season. These festivals have been especially important for families with young children, who were hungry for things to do in the winter, and with another surprising group: new Canadian immigrants. Henderson told me that immigrants from warm climates especially were "curious about winter. They wanted to know what it was all about; there was this thing they hadn't enjoyed before." These kinds of events are profound in their impact to build—and sustain—energetic and dynamic communities.

Thanks to Winter Economy, winter patios—developed before COVID-19 made them fixtures around the world—were installed to allow patrons to sit al fresco, bundled up and warmed by space heaters or firepits, with blankets on their laps. In Edmonton, now it's possible to dine outdoors at any time of year. I observed a similar phenomenon in Tromsø long before COVID-19: even in midwinter, cafés in Norway had outdoor seating with blankets and heat lamps, and patrons would enjoy open-air coffee or cake* even on cold days. Bringing winter patios to Edmonton was a logistical challenge as much as a mindset one. Patio permits used to run from May 1 to October 1; these and other laws had to be amended. And business owners had to be reminded that even in the summer, on rainy days patios aren't always in use; similarly, winter patios might not be frequented on the coldest days—but it's okay to design spaces to capitalize on mild winter days. A few days where the patio remains empty doesn't make the initiative a failure.

Leaders in Edmonton point out that many of these changes, designed for winter, are useful all year long: outdoor spaces that block wind or buildings illuminated beautifully are attractive in other seasons as well; patios can be enjoyed year-round; ski trails and bike lanes become summer walking and biking routes. Isla Tanaka, head WinterCity planner in Edmonton, summarized it thusly: "If you design for winter first, summer's easy." But if you design without winter in mind, opportunities for cold-weather recreation, connection, and fun will be left unrealized.

BUT HENDERSON and the other leaders knew that the best winter festivals and most creative winter designs alone wouldn't be enough. To convince the residents of Edmonton to take advantage of these new initiatives, they had one thing left to do: change people's mindsets.

A pessimistic perspective of the season was a major barrier. "We were creating our own negativity around it," Henderson told me. People had spent so much time hiding from winter,

---

*Could we call this *friluftscake*?

shying away from it, that they *made* winter miserable. "You got in your car in your connected, heated garage at eight in the morning to drive, it was still dark. And then you went into your underground parking, up there into your hermetically sealed building, then went by a ped-way to have lunch at some mall food court and back again. And then people wondered why they were getting depressed. They were not getting any daylight, they were not getting any fresh air, they weren't going outside at all. And I think winter through that lens seemed much harsher than it actually was," Henderson vented to me.

The fourth and final pillar of the WinterCity strategy is Winter Story. This pillar aims to change the stories Edmontonians tell themselves—and each other—about winter.

The WinterCity strategy was developed by "engaging the entire city in the discussion as much as we could," Henderson said. This ensured that the city's approach truly met the needs of its citizens and gave leadership a head start in changing hearts and minds. "We literally spent six months challenging people to think about what would make them fall in love with winter," Henderson told me. Having so many Edmontonians consider this question forced people to imagine a different relationship with the season. By the time many of these initiatives were implemented, "people had already done the shift in their own minds."

To augment these discussions, the WinterCity team launched social media campaigns inviting people to share what they loved about winter. Marliss Weber, who, along with her partner, Randy, was the social media strategist behind the early WinterCity initiative, said that they were initially met with negativity. "We got consistent comments like 'I hate winter,' 'I'd move if I could,' and 'Winter is boring and cold.'" But it didn't stay that way for long. "It was remarkable how quickly that changed. The following winter, we just didn't see very many negative comments. There was excitement about the change of season. I think people were anxious to embrace some positivity." The team also talked to meteorologists and anchors, recruiting them to speak more positively about winter weather on the local news, and put out a yearly Winter Excitement Guide, highlighting festivals, events, and recreation locations. They enlisted the marketing department of the city's tourism board, who launched a campaign of posters showing people having winter fun in Edmonton with slogans like "Cold? Yes. Dark? Yes. Boring? Never." and "The real fun starts when temperatures drop below zero." Thanks to the WinterCity strategy, Edmonton is emerging as a winter tourism destination, spawning travel articles about the many reasons to visit the city during the coldest months of the year.

Henderson and his colleagues found that people are open to—even eager for—this kind of winter reframe. O'Byrne wrote, "Edmontonians are ready to make the culture shift, no longer viewing winter as something to escape from, but instead as a unique and magical season." It's as if people are just waiting for a reason to get outdoors and embrace winter. "With the idea of making winter exciting, I think there was a kind of hunger there," Henderson told me. His experience aligns with my own: constantly feeling limited by winter is its own kind of exhaustion. The chance to enjoy it is a relief.

THAT DOESN'T MEAN this kind of project is easy or trivial. The initial WinterCity Think Tank was established as a ten-year commitment. While many of these changes were relatively cost-effective compared with the impact and the quality-of-life bene-fits they delivered, the WinterCity strategies require financial investment. Having a champion was key: everyone I spoke with about the initiative mentioned Henderson, his vision, and his leadership. Having someone committed to making it happen and who pushed the city's endeavors to constantly consider a winter lens was essential. Such a wide-ranging enterprise re-quired buy-in from senior staff across departments; without someone pushing it forward, it could have easily fallen apart. And the effort is ongoing, with continued room for growth.

Yet the payoff has already been immense. Edmontonians are enjoying winter more, attending festivals, meeting neighbors, and making memories. They're moving more, recreating more, and are more active. They've reclaimed winter, once a throwaway season, as a time for joy and revelry; what may have been one of the city's biggest drawbacks is now a great source of pride. The city has won multiple awards and become a global leader in winter life and innovation.

Edmonton demonstrates that transformation is possible: even without Viking blood or centuries of city design that prioritize winter comfort, any community can start where they are and build a more winter-friendly, vibrant place to live. Mindsets and culture can be changed deliberately. The city conducted one of the largest and widest-ranging mindset interventions I've en-countered. Edmonton's WinterCity evolution is an example of how culture, community, and infrastructure can change peo-ple's perceptions, chipping away at unhelpful mindsets that may have been formed over decades in favor of more adaptive, more hopeful ways of seeing the world. By focusing on the story—the mindset—*and* the actual conditions in the world—festivals, infrastructure—Edmonton is providing both the seed and the soil for positive wintertime mindsets to take root and flourish.

CLEAR ROADS, FULL HEARTS

After my evening with Joar in Tromsø, the snow flurries gave way to cold rain as the temperature crept above freezing. The night before Rob and I were scheduled to take a weekend trip out of the city, I started fretting. Freezing rain coated the city's streets and sidewalks in a layer of ice. Rather than crunching through snow, we were slipping and sliding and—at least once—falling. I was worried about the roads: Would they be icy? Would it be safe to drive? I'm no stranger to winter driving. I know to pump the brakes to stop, to drive into slides and turns, not to panic.*

Despite this, the freezing rain made me nervous. We'd be driving four hours in northern Norway through rural areas, during the Polar Night when it was bright for only a few hours a day, doing much of the drive on curvy, mountainous roads.

I needn't have worried so much: even as we left Tromsø behind and passed small towns of a few hundred people, the highways were cleared of ice and snow, gravel sprinkled for traction. It was far safer, and easier, navigating the mountain roads of rural northern Norway than I'd experienced driving through snow in many parts of the US. That's the power of infrastructure in a place built for winter: just one day after a freezing

---

*Thanks, Dad.

rainstorm, our path had been plowed. I was reminded that in northern Norway it's not just a can-do attitude that makes it possible to do things in winter weather: this mindset is scaffolded by snowplows and heated sidewalks, physical supports that make the possibilities of winter a reality. When you're still able to travel, adventure, drive, and move safely, it's easier to focus on the opportunities of winter rather than the ways the weather limits you. Mindsets interact with our objective situation: even as our mindsets can offset the negative effects of harsh circumstances, they can't make up for them entirely. If each of us has a range of well-being accessible to us, made possible by our external situation, mindset can shift us along that range, but might not be able to jump us to a new bracket. If, for example, you can't afford to heat your home during winter, mindset alone won't make that difficult reality into a fun experience. Yet given that reality, cultivating a more adaptive mindset—one that inspires you to pile on the blankets, cozy up with a hot-water bottle, and drink cup after cup of piping-hot tea—can make the experience at least somewhat better. Wintertime mindset won't shovel your driveway for you, but it can make shoveling your driveway a lot less unpleasant.

WINTER-FOCUSED INFRASTRUCTURE IS common throughout the Nordics. In Oulu, Finland, the winter biking capital of the world, 950 kilometers of bicycle paths are cleared of snow as a top priority—prioritized even over plowing roads for cars. In a short video about Oulu's bike culture for the BBC, Pekka Tahkola, an urban well-being engineer, explains: "People are sometimes saying that we're 'hardcore,'" he intones to the camera in his high-visibility orange jacket and beanie, referring to people's tendency in Oulu to bike in rain, snow, sleet, and freezing temperatures. "No," he says, "we're just regular wimps who are just blessed with good infrastructure and good maintenance."

Smart infrastructure can also make it safer to navigate winter weather. People—especially women—who enjoy running outdoors in the summer may not feel safe recreating outside in winter darkness; well-lit trails and parks, which draw crowds year-round, can partially address safety concerns. And heated sidewalks make it easier for those with mobility issues to traverse city streets without fear of slipping. Visiting my friend Meghan at her apartment in Tromsø, Rob asked how the sidewalks were kept so clear. "They have heat running under them!" Meghan exclaimed. She explained how the sidewalks around her apartment complex, at the university, and on both sides of the main pedestrian street in the city center all use heat from the industrial waste processing plant, which is pumped under the city to keep sidewalks ice- and snow-free. In Reykjavík, hot water runoff, drawn from the city's geothermal springs and used to heat homes, is diverted to the same effect. Many snowy northern Japanese cities, including Sapporo, have heated sidewalks as well. Even places without geothermal riches can find solutions: cities like Oslo and Helsinki have installed electric elements underneath sidewalks, and government officials state that, over time, this is cheaper than clearing snow and ice. And at least one city in the US has found the same: Holland, Michigan, home to North America's largest snowmelt system, uses an approach similar to the one in Tromsø, relying on waste-heat cooling water from a power plant to melt snow from the streets. The initiative is wildly popular and reduces taxpayer costs by eliminating the need for salting and plowing and reducing frost

damage to sidewalks. Annual maintenance is paid for mostly
from taxes on local businesses, who benefit from the increased
year-round foot traffic. Designing for winter strengthens local
economies by helping people get out in all weather.

AND INFRASTRUCTURE is more than roads. In Ii, Finland, the
winter swimming hole I spent fifteen seconds in with Antti is
maintained, along with the heated changing room, by the mu-
nicipality, for which Antti pays an annual tax of €15. In Inari,
over five hundred kilometers north, Rob and I hiked over a sus-
pension bridge spanning the rapids of the Juutuanjoki river and
found a three-sided *laavu*—a conical Sami structure similar to a
tipi—with a fire burning inside, complete with a pile of dry logs
next to it. It was unspeakably comforting to come across a place
of light and warmth in the middle of the forest after we'd been
hiking for an hour. Saunas, geothermal pools, swimming holes,
ski trails, skating rinks, and warming huts along hiking routes
are all winter infrastructure that—when maintained at a rela-
tively low cost—make it easier to get outside and enjoy the cold.

Indoor design also helps: cozy lighting, coat hooks, good insu-
lation and double entryways to keep cold air from blasting in every
time someone opens the door. Throughout the Nordics, heated
bathroom floors are common: getting up to pee in the night and
stepping out of the shower are infinitely more comfortable when
the soles of your feet are warm. In Japan, a tiny train station in
Yamagata with no Wi-Fi had a heated toilet seat, which made
using the bathroom in the otherwise frigid restroom bearable.

Even the laws can facilitate winter well-being: open-flame
and patio permits can make it easier or harder to light candles
indoors or open restaurant terraces in winter. In Norway—and

other countries including Finland, Sweden, Denmark, and Germany—right-to-roam laws support friluftsliv, protecting unfettered outdoor movement and ensuring that nature remains available and accessible to all citizens, regardless of where they live or what property they hold. In Norway, right-to-roam laws state that anyone is allowed to pass through non-farmland while hiking; on skis, sleds, or snowshoes; or by bike, as long as they do so with thoughtful consideration for the land. Swimming is allowed in all natural bodies of water as long as swimmers maintain a sufficient distance from inhabited dwellings. And anyone is allowed to picnic or camp on all land—regardless of ownership—for up to forty-eight hours, provided they remain at least 150 meters from inhabited dwellings.

Leadership—at the town, city, state, or country level—can facilitate or hinder winter enjoyment. Mindsets help make winter more delightful even in places without great infrastructure, but when our mindsets are supported by the culture around us, it is easier for adaptive mindsets to take hold and grow. At the same time, changing our mindsets about winter and embracing the season can help show lawmakers and other stakeholders that there's demand for the policies and infrastructure that help make winter wonderful—and accessible—for everyone.

CHANGE THE CULTURE, CHANGE YOUR MINDSET

Mindsets are contagious. While we all have mindsets as individuals, our mindsets are formed by the world around us. Some cultures have more positive wintertime mindsets than others.

In Tromsø, my mindset about winter changed organically:
surrounded by people who enjoyed the season, dressed appro-
priately, and loved winter recreation and coziness, I found it
easy to adopt a positive wintertime mindset. My new mindset
was supported by Tromsø's infrastructure, where ski trails are
abundant and well-lit, snowplows clear roads quickly after all
but the most severe blizzards, and high-quality, soft woolen gar-
ments are affordable and easy to find. But it was also supported
in subtle ways by aspects of Tromsø's culture that are easy to
overlook: the way people talk about winter or react to news of a
cold front; how people spend their weekends and holidays—
outdoors, hiking or skiing, or cozy inside by the fire; the avail-
ability of outdoor seating at cafés in winter. It's likely that even
if I hadn't been researching wintertime mindset, my view of
winter would have shifted just by living in Tromsø; the domi-
nant cultural view of winter as something to be enjoyed, not
something to be endured, would have seeped into my psyche.

Some of these mindsets are so ingrained, people might not
even realize they have them. If you ask someone in Tromsø
about their "positive wintertime mindset," they might be con-
fused; to them, lighting candles during the Polar Night and
going cross-country skiing on the weekends might just be what
they do, and not seem particularly profound or indicative of an
extraordinary perspective. It's only in contrast to other ways of
viewing winter that the predominant approach in Tromsø be-
comes apparent; only once I moved to the Arctic did I realize
that my perspective of winter, formed at the Jersey Shore, was
just that—a single, incomplete perspective. One that I could
change.

Even as we are shaped by the culture around us, we also create the culture. What is culture but a group of people and their thoughts, beliefs, and behaviors? Cultural change happens when people change. Mindset change can occur as the result of large-scale intervention, like when Edmonton changed the city's approach to winter. But it can also change slowly, as people shift their perspective. One by one, as individual mindsets change, the effect snowballs (forgive me), eventually shifting the predominant view entirely.

Gandhi is often credited with saying "Be the change you wish to see in the world." But this is a misleading and simplistic paraphrase of what he actually said: "We but mirror the world. All the tendencies present in the outer world are to be found in the world of our body. If we could change ourselves, the tendencies in the world would also change. As a man changes his own nature, so does the attitude of the world change toward him. This is the divine mystery supreme. A wonderful thing it is and the source of our happiness. We need not wait to see what others do." This longer and more nuanced quote illustrates how, even as we are shaped by the world, by changing ourselves we also change the world around us.

By changing our mindsets, we can also be part of shifting the culture. When we start responding to winter differently, our perspective and behavior can spread. When we celebrate the end of daylight saving time, we show others that winter is worth anticipating. When we lean into the season of rest, we demonstrate how to adapt to winter. When we notice beauty and joy in the darkness, we help others see it too. When we talk about winter's delights, we encourage those around us to verbalize what they love about the season. When we embrace the calm tranquility of winter, we help our loved ones see how cozy it can be. When we

light candles, we model how to find comfort in long nights.
When we engage in seasonal rituals, we help others find mean-
ing in dark times. When we invite a friend to come on a winter's
walk, we communicate that getting outside in winter is a plea-
sure. When we jump in a lake or the ocean, we inspire passersby
to take a dip. And when we change our wintertime mindsets, we
help nudge the culture a little bit closer to embracing winter.
Maybe it starts small, spreading first to our close family mem-
bers and friends, but then it spreads to their family and friends,
to their colleagues, and out through our communities, until ev-
eryone is thinking about winter warmly.

PROTECTING WINTER

T'S STRANGE to write a book about winter during the hottest year the world has ever recorded. As I write this, winter slips more into danger. Some of the places I mention in this book are the most vulnerable. Tromsø's Polar Night is becoming rainier, icier, and less snowy. Svalbard's fjords, which used to freeze over reliably, allowing people to snowmobile across them, now freeze irregularly and unpredictably. When temperatures rise above freezing in the Arctic, the top layer of snow can melt and refreeze; subsequent snows fall on this slippery layer of ice, increasing risk and prevalence of dangerous avalanches in Svalbard and elsewhere. In Lapland, reindeer normally survive winter by eating the lichens that grow on the bottoms of trees, low to the ground. The reindeer easily nuzzle their way through snow to reach their mossy treat. But when it gets too warm and the snow melts, or when it rains and that water freezes, it encases their food in a layer of ice that is impossible for the reindeer to break through, effectively blocking them from their food. Many Sami herders have had to resort to feeding their reindeer hay rather than relying on the naturally abundant and more nutritious lichen, which also makes reindeer management more labor intensive than in the past.

We are still learning how precious winter is, how necessary. In Massachusetts, members of the Mashpee Wampanoag tribe have swum and caught fish at Santuit Pond for thousands of years. But recently, the pond has failed to freeze in winter, which usually kills cyanobacteria—a blue-green algae that can be toxic. Without the proper freeze cycles, the algae has multiplied, filling the pond with slime and killing fish, frogs, and other wildlife. In North America, allergy season in 2018 was twenty days longer—with 21 percent more pollen—than in 1990; shorter winters allow trees and flowers to bloom earlier and for longer, putting more pollen in the air and worsening allergies and asthma. Earlier spring warmth also melts existing snowpacks, lengthening dry seasons, increasing both the time in which wildfires occur and the amount of dry soil and plant life available to burn. Winter festivals are already feeling the effects of climate change: in 2024, The Great Northern had to close their ice bar early—a week of record-high February temperatures was too much for the frozen watering hole.

On my worst days, I feel the hopelessness of climate angst; I feel angry and sad and scared about what has already been wrought, how much there is to lose and the direction in which we are collectively headed. My fear is that winter is disappearing, and that one day Tromsø, and all wintery places, will be left with darkness but without the snow, ice, or a chill in the air: no more reflected light, no more skiing, no more delicate ice crystals adorning bare branches. At the same time, climate change is making weather patterns more unpredictable, unleashing polar vortexes and bringing winter storms to places that are unequipped to deal with them, that don't have the infrastructure to manage snow or ice.

But people fight for what they love. My hope is that helping people enjoy winter more will inspire more action to protect it; that reveling in winter's coldness reminds people that it's worth fighting for. This is how the US-based climate advocacy organization Protect Our Winters was born, founded by Jeremy Jones, a professional snowboarder, lover of the outdoors, and fierce champion of the environment. Like other winter athletes, Jones started noticing that many of the places he loved—resorts and mountains where he snowboarded—were closed for lack of snow. As the planet warmed, those good powder days were becoming less frequent. He looked around to see who was doing something about this. Where was the organization for people like him to help promote solutions to fight climate change? Where was the organization for winter athletes, outdoorsmen and -women, winter lovers of all types? When he didn't find one, he created Protect Our Winters.

Protect Our Winters—or POW as it's affectionately called—brings together professional winter athletes, resort owners, athletics brands, outdoor enthusiasts, and scientists to do what the organization's name suggests: protect our winters. (I'm one of the scientists on their Science Alliance team.) Their mission is to galvanize the public in support of policies and practices that fight climate change while also lobbying local, state, and national government leaders to support systemic action—through bills, laws, and regulations—to slow and reverse the effects of our warming and changing climate. The ultimate goal is to ensure that winter survives for future generations to enjoy, so that our children, our children's children, and their children can shred it up for decades to come.

While outdoor athletes more at home on mountains than in Congress might seem an unlikely group to spearhead a climate change movement, POW demonstrates that those who love something are the most motivated to protect it. In the US, POW is comprised of members of what they call the "outdoor state": fifty million Americans who treasure the outdoors and who self-identify as outdoor enthusiasts. Looked at this way, this group of Americans is the largest state in the nation, beating out the second most populous state, California, by about eleven million people.

POW's guiding principles emphasize progress over perfection and underscore the fact that it's better to have a lot of people who care about protecting the planet as best they can than a small group of intensely committed, hardcore overachievers who are zero waste and doing everything right. Potentially their top principle is to "embrace imperfect advocacy." This idea of imperfect advocacy can help offset some of the discomfort or hypocrisy we feel when we do things—by choice or by force—that aren't aligned with our values of protecting the Earth and fighting climate change. My intention to recycle goes out the door when I find the rental I'm staying in while traveling doesn't have recycling. I try to eat less meat, but love my dad's steak and Grandma Sandy's brisket. I care a lot about climate change, but fly frequently for both work and pleasure. Sometimes we can fall into the trap of all-or-none thinking, in which we feel like, *If I can't do it all perfectly, why bother trying at all?* Or worse, our cognitive dissonance kicks in: *If I care so much about the environment, why am I doing this thing that I know is prob-*

lematic? I must not care as much about the environment as I thought. Changing our beliefs or views of how much we value the environment is a lot easier than figuring out how to get from New York to Amsterdam without flying. But the idea of imperfect advocacy makes space for all of this: we don't have to be perfect, or perfectly consistent, to be part of the movement and take positive steps toward fighting climate change.

Just as cultivating our wintertime mindsets can help us enjoy and appreciate winter more—perhaps motivating us to champion and protect it by fighting climate change—so too can changing our mindsets give us the tools to tackle this global challenge. My time with POW counters some of the eco-anxiety and existential dread I feel when I think about Svalbard's ice melting, glaciers receding, California burning, and the bees dying. Practicing changing my mindset about winter has given me tools to intervene on my own eco-dread. Where are the opportunities in climate change? How is this a chance for greater empathy and connection with each other, for innovation and inspiration, for living more aligned with our values?

Rethinking our relationship to winter is practice imagining what could be instead of what is. When we look at the winter darkness and think "I could never love that," or consider going for a walk in the freezing rain and think "I could never do that," and then slowly learn to savor the darkness or enjoy a drizzly walk, we learn that some of our preconceived ideas are fallacies holding us back. We begin to wonder what else we could reimagine, what else could be different. Could we bike to work instead of drive? Could our plastics be made of corn, our cardboard made of mushrooms? Could we live more sustainably, in more community? Could we save a warming planet?

We can use our mindsets to imagine a world that isn't merely a continuation of what we have now, but is even better: with more equality for people, more protection for land, plants, and animals, and more joy. Where we've swapped monoculture grass lawns for mini wildflower meadows, so that even a walk through a suburban neighborhood feels like an excursion into nature. Where eating locally is supported by neighborhoods in which everyone has gardens and communities come together to swap produce. Where technology enables nature and brings us closer to it. Where farming innovations use less land, water, and fertilizer to grow crops, so we can feed more people and free up land for recreation and wilderness. Where homes are designed thoughtfully so that they stay warm in winter and cool in summer.

We have an opportunity to innovate, invent, and build the world we want to live in. If all of winter is a challenge we can make an opportunity, then the chance to protect winter may be our greatest opportunity of all, an opportunity to live more in tune with nature, the world, and the seasons, and to capitalize on the economics and possibilities of winter. We have a chance to dream and envision and be intentional. We can let winter happen to us—we can let climate change happen to us—or we can use our mindsets to channel our energy, finding opportunities in challenge and expanding what's possible.

THE IDEA OF YOUR FUTURE

In some ways, loving winter, hating winter, it seems like a small thing. What does it matter if some people want to grumble through the season? Is it really so bad if some people feel grumpy and down when it gets dark and cold?

But every day, we have the chance to embrace the world in front of us. We can celebrate what's there; find the delights; seize any chance for joy, big or small. When we write off winter, we resign ourselves to settling for crumbs of happiness; we decide it's okay to be miserable for one to six months of the year. We let the little unpleasantries, the pinpricks of cold and the annoyance of wet and the fatigue of dark grind us down without realizing it.

Reclaiming winter is a chance to find intentional joy; to let ourselves anticipate and rest. It's an opportunity to notice, with awe and wonder, what is really in front of us. It's a practice in talking about those delights; sinking into coziness, ritualizing the mundane. It allows us to know ourselves more deeply, breathe in crisp air, feel the wind on our face or the rain on our skin. It can propel us to adventure or help us find warmth. It can inspire us to make our cities better, to work toward the future we want. Embracing winter is about embracing our life: all of it, the dark parts and the light. Our winter story is, in part, our life story. What do you want yours to say?

Acknowledgments

Writing this book was an unbelievable joy and privilege.

First, thanks to my brilliant publishing team. Zoë Pagnamenta, my stellar agent, understood this book from the very beginning and has been my trusted sounding board throughout the entire process. Thanks also to Jess Hoare and the rest of the team at the Calligraph agency. Working with my insightful editor, Emily Wunderlich, has been a highlight of the writing process. Emily, thank you for constantly pushing me to make this book bigger and more useful. *How to Winter* is better in every way—more helpful, more readable, and more playful—because of you. Thanks also to Meg Leder, Penguin Life's editorial director extraordinaire, for your vision and enthusiasm. In the UK, thanks to Carrie Plitt for helping find the perfect British home for this book; to Carole Tonkinson for acquiring the book at Bluebird; and to Jodie Lancet-Grant for constantly championing *How to Winter* and for loving the word "machatunim" as much as I do. Thank you also to the many, many incredible team members at Penguin Life and Penguin Random House (US) and Bluebird and Pan Macmillan (UK)—the editorial assistants, copy editors, marketers, publicists, designers, and sales department—for bringing your energy and talent to getting this book out into the world. And so much gratitude to the many overseas agents, publishers, and translators making these words available for audiences worldwide.

SPECIAL THANKS TO some of the people and organizations that hosted me in winter locales all over the world. In Ii, Finland, Kaisa Kerätär and Antti Ylönen provided the coziest writing residency, helped guide my research in Finland, and introduced me to Finnish winter swimming and foraged porcinis. In Iceland, thank you to the staff and funders of Reykjavík UNESCO City of Literature and Gröndalshús for space to write, think, and explore. On the Isle of Lewis, thanks to Jon Macleod for guiding me around the island with such care and kindness, and to Grinneabhat and Tina MacPhail for hosting me and for a Burns Night I'll never forget. In Yamagata, Pure Water was the most thorough and enthusiastic host and translator I could have asked for; thank you for answering my many questions and arranging such a memorable excursion for us, and thank you to our hosts at Farmhouse Ajiki for a cozy stay and beyond-delicious food.

Science is a lot harder than it looks. Endless gratitude to the many psychologists and other scientists whose research scaffolds the ideas I've written about; I hope I've done your work justice. Many thanks to everyone who took the time to speak with me for this book—researchers, writers, thinkers, and winter-lovers all over the world. Special thanks to Taija Aikio at the Siida Museum for answering my questions about Sami language and spring-winter, and to Kelly Rohan for all your inspiring and integral work and for answering my questions about seasonal affective disorder. Erika Owen is the travel writer who unknowingly pointed me to Fischersund; Alix Hui is the fellow researcher who documented Norwegian shades of gray on her blog. Thank you to anyone who has invited me to speak or has attended one of my workshops, to my students (especially those from my Stanford Continuing Studies Mindsets Matter course, who continue to get in touch with their stories), and to readers all over the world who have been kind enough to write to me and share their thoughts and feelings about winter and the power of mindset— your responses encouraged me to write this book.

THE PROPOSAL AND first draft of this book were written during the Lighthouse Writers Workshop's two-year Book Project, and if you are looking for mentorship and community for your own book, I can't recommend the Book Project enough. Thank you to the staff and instructors at Lighthouse who make the Book Project possible and to Shana Kelly for feedback on early proposals and query letters. Excerpts of this book were workshopped in classes with Lauren Markham and Helen Thorpe; thanks to you both for your feedback. Simo Stolzoff took the time to speak with me and told me about the Book Project, and has continued to be a source of insider info and a kind ear ever since our first conversation. Vauhini Vara is the most incredible writing mentor I could have ever dreamed of; your suggestions for revision made my writing more vibrant at every turn, and you continue to be an endless source of inspiration, wisdom, and reassurance. Having you in my corner has made all the difference. A highlight of writing this book was forming friendships with the five amazing women in my Book Project cohort: Marisa Taylor Karas, Ladane Nasseri, Astha Rajvanshi, Susanna Space,

Angelique Stevens—thank you all for your insights and suggestions for my manuscript, for sharing your own work with me, and most important, for being a source of comfort and joy during the writing process.

I am forever indebted to Joar Vittersø for taking a chance on me and inviting me to work with him in the Arctic, as well as for his patience and mentorship; I am so grateful for our many conversations and our collaboration. Many thanks to the US-Norway Fulbright Foundation for funding my research year in Tromsø, and to the foundation staff, particularly Petter Næss, Rena Levin, and Kevin McGuiness. The magic of Tromsø was revealed to me, in part, through the kindness and friendship of many people in my northern home. Special thanks to Thor-Eirik Erikson for inviting me to join his meditation group, to Fern Wickson for her insight, to Ida Solhaug for her limitless warmth, and to the many faculty members in the psychology department at the University of Tromsø for welcoming me into your academic community and shedding light on how people in Tromsø enjoy the winter. And, of course, thank you to the Tromsø breakfast club for cabin getaways, potlucks, nighttime hikes in search of northern lights, and laughs. You made Tromsø feel like home, and never held it against me that I didn't make it to a single early-morning breakfast.

As an academic, my writing and thinking has been influenced by a long line of mentors. Thank you to all my teachers, from Ocean Township to Emory to Stanford. At Emory University, special thanks to Geshe Lobsang Tenzin Negi for showing me the power of the mind, and to Corey Keyes for showing me how and why to prioritize flourishing. Many of the ideas in this book were discovered or developed during my PhD. My eternal gratitude to the Stanford psych department for being a nurturing and challenging intellectual home for six years. Special thanks to Carol Dweck, Hazel Markus, Jeanne Tsai, Jamil Zaki, and Greg Walton for your research, wisdom, and mentorship. This book would not exist without the Stanford Mind & Body Lab: thanks to you all for constantly supporting me, pushing me, and inspiring me. And biggest thanks of all to my graduate mentor, Alia Crum. Ali, thank you for always encouraging me to throw my backpack over the fence and figure it out later (and for that metaphor). You opened door after door for me—in my career, but also in my mind and in myself. Your guidance and mentorship have given me the tools to craft the life and career of my dreams. I hope this book makes you proud.

Lauren Howe's close read of this manuscript bolstered the science throughout this book. Lauren, thank you for pointing me in the direction of overlooked research, helping to make my language more precise and nuanced, and for being a wonderful mentor, collaborator, and friend for the past nine years. Sabrina Kaplan helped organize years of winter-related writing and materials to prepare me for writing this book. Forrest Dollins assisted with background research and literature reviews. Carly Kaplan read early chapters and gave insightful feedback.

HERE IS WHERE I want to list every person I love, but I believe it's discouraged to have acknowledgments that are longer than the book, so I will restrict myself to those who have directly shaped *How to Winter.*

Thank you to all of my friends who have provided countless pep talks, endless enthusiasm, and an ever-flowing river of love and support: Camilla Griffiths for being my heart and my home, from near or from far; Sean Zion for being my forever academic sibling and for talking through all things mindset with me; Gregg Muragishi for shabu-shabu chats and sharing an office with me for six years; Danielle Zamarelli for daily check-ins, words of wisdom, and always hyping me up; Anna Kaufman for being *Wintry Mix*'s number-one fan; Rachel Klein for on-demand affirmations; Tyler Hayes for making Amsterdam feel like home; and Becky Lee for a long, long list of things, including naming this book and my newsletter, reading drafts, cover consultations, and continuous life chats. Your friendship is awe-inspiring.

The support of my two families makes everything in my life possible. Thank you to the entire Yaffe-Becker-Kaplan-Shapiro-Lyubinsky crew for your steadfast, unwavering love and support. Special thanks to Carrie, Gordon, Neal, and Ilana for being our New York landing pad, for schlepping us all over, and for always cheering me on no matter where life takes us. An enormous thank you to both sets of my parents for giving Zeus two loving homes and plenty of treats as Rob and I traveled the globe researching this book. Thank you to Aunt Karen for cozy Christmas memories and to Aunt Donna for modeling how to dress for all weather. Marcus and Shelby, thanks for letting your home be our home, and for all the laughs, all the time. I love you. Mom, thanks for reminding me I can always come home. Dad, thanks for reminding me there's always something else out there. Thanks to you both for the two sides of me. You have encouraged me to pursue every crazy dream I've ever had and sacrificed so that I rarely had to; thanks for all the trips to Newark airport.

And to Rob. Thank you for talking, and living, through every aspect of this book with me, being the best adventure partner, and for your patience and wisdom and gentleness and easy laugh. Every joy is made greater for sharing it with you. I love you.

Notes

A note on my notes: While academic convention encourages us to cite every source of verifiable information, in the age of the internet I have opted to focus on the citations that I feel are of greatest value to the reader, with an emphasis on the scientific research I rely on in this book. In cases where my source material is obvious—for example, when I reference books by their full title and author in the text—I have opted not to cite them here. In some places I have chosen to cite review papers or books that I think do a particularly excellent job of summarizing large bodies of literature, with the understanding that curious and inspired readers can use these sources to dig deeper as they wish.

Prelude: My Journey to the Land of Winter

3 **lack of daylight in winter:** N. E. Rosenthal, *Winter Blues: Everything You Need to Know to Beat Seasonal Affective Disorder* (New York: Guilford Press, 2012): 12–14.

3 **seasonal affective disorder should rise:** See, for example, Rosenthal, *Winter Blues*; Leora N. Rosen et al., "Prevalence of Seasonal Affective Disorder at Four Latitudes," *Psychiatry Research* 31, no. 2 (1990): 131–44.

3 **calls the latitude hypothesis:** Anthony J. Leavitt and Michael H. Boyle, "The Impact of Latitude on the Prevalence of Seasonal Depression," *Canadian Journal of Psychiatry* 47, no. 4 (2002): 361–67, doi.org/10.1177/070674370204700407; Greta Brancaleoni et al., "Seasonal Affective Disorder and Latitude of Living," *Epidemiology and Psychiatric Sciences* 18, no. 4 (2009): 336–43; Vidje Hansen et al., "Self-Reported Mental Distress Under the Shifting Daylight in the High North," *Psychological Medicine* 28, no. 2 (1998): 447–52.

4 almost nine thousand residents: May Trude Johnsen et al., "Is There a Negative Impact of Winter on Mental Distress and Sleeping Problems in the Subarctic: The Tromsø Study," *BMC Psychiatry* 12 (2012): 1–6.

12 Seasonal Beliefs Questionnaire: Kelly J. Rohan et al., "A Measure of Cognitions Specific to Seasonal Depression: Development and Validation of the Seasonal Beliefs Questionnaire," *Psychological Assessment* 31, no. 7 (2019): 925.

13 Carol's influential research: For a recent overview, see Carol Dweck and David Yeager, "A Growth Mindset About Intelligence," *Handbook of Wise Interventions: How Social Psychology Can Help People Change* (2020): 9–35.

14 These employees later experienced: Alia J. Crum et al., "Rethinking Stress: The Role of Mindsets in Determining the Stress Response," *Journal of Personality and Social Psychology* 104, no. 4 (2013): 716.

14 hotel room attendants: Alia J. Crum and Ellen J. Langer, "Mind-Set Matters: Exercise and the Placebo Effect," *Psychological Science* 18, no. 2 (2007): 165–71.

16 In our study, wintertime mindset: Kari Leibowitz and Joar Vittersø, "Winter Is Coming: Wintertime Mindset and Wellbeing in Norway," *International Journal of Wellbeing* 10, no. 4 (2020): 35–54.

1. Well, What Did You Expect?

28 One large-scale review: Ted J. Kaptchuk et al., "Placebos in Chronic Pain: Evidence, Theory, Ethics, and Use in Clinical Practice," *BMJ* 370 (July 20, 2020).

28 placebos can alleviate: Donald D. Price et al., "A Comprehensive Review of the Placebo Effect: Recent Advances and Current Thought," *Annual Review of Psychology* 59 (2008): 565–90; Damien G. Finniss et al., "Biological, Clinical, and Ethical Advances of Placebo Effects," *Lancet* 375, no. 9715 (2010): 686–95.

28 They can decrease asthma: Stefanie Dutile et al., "The Placebo Effect in Asthma," *Current Allergy and Asthma Reports* 14 (2014): 1–8.

29 They were pricked on the forearm: Lauren C. Howe et al., "Harnessing the Placebo Effect: Exploring the Influence of Physician Characteristics on Placebo Response," *Health Psychology* 36, no. 11 (2017): 1074.

29 men who were taking a medication: Nicola Mondaini et al., "Finasteride 5 mg and Sexual Side Effects: How Many of These Are Related to a Nocebo Phenomenon?" *Journal of Sexual Medicine* 4, no. 6 (2007): 1708–12.

30 A study on this switch: Kate MacKrill et al., "Evidence of a Media-Induced Nocebo Response Following a Nationwide Antidepressant Drug Switch," *Clinical Psychology in Europe* 1, no. 1 (2019): 1–12.

34 Light also helps: Kathryn M. Stephenson et al., "Complex Interaction of Circadian and Non-Circadian Effects of Light on Mood: Shedding New Light on an Old Story," *Sleep Medicine Reviews* 16, no. 5 (2012): 445–54. Gilles Vandewalle et al., "Daytime Light Exposure Dynamically Enhances Brain Responses," *Current Biology* 16, no. 16 (2006): 1616–21.

2. Leaning In, Lying Down

46 we might need more sleep: Aileen Seidler et al., "Seasonality of Human Sleep: Polysomnographic Data of a Neuropsychiatric Sleep Clinic," *Frontiers in Neuroscience* 17 (2023): 115.

48 The DSM-5: American Psychiatric Association, *Diagnostic and Statistical Manual of Mental Disorders*, 5th ed. (Arlington, VA: American Psychiatric Association, 2013).

49 official manual for seasonal affective disorder: N. E. Rosenthal, *Winter Blues: Everything You Need to Know to Beat Seasonal Affective Disorder* (New York: Guilford Press, 2012): 52–54.

51 **includes significant skepticism:** Vidje Hansen et al., "What Is This Thing Called 'SAD'? A Critique of the Concept of Seasonal Affective Disorder," *Epidemiology and Psychiatric Sciences* 17, no. 2 (2008): 120–27.

51 **Outside of the US:** Paul A. Mersch et al., "Seasonal Affective Disorder and Latitude: A Review of the Literature," *Journal of Affective Disorders* 53, no. 1 (1999): 35–48.

51 **more than five thousand Dutch:** Wim H. Winthorst et al., "Seasonality of Mood and Affect in a Large General Population Sample," *PLOS One* 15, no. 9 (2020): e0239033.

52 **were lower in Iceland:** Andres Magnusson and Jon G. Stefansson, "Prevalence of Seasonal Affective Disorder in Iceland," *Archives of General Psychiatry* 50, no. 12 (1993): 941–46.

52 **precise screening method:** Dan G. Blazer et al., "Epidemiology of Recurrent Major and Minor Depression with Seasonal Pattern: The National Comorbidity Survey," *British Journal of Psychiatry* 172, no. 2 (1998): 164–67.

52 **studies of American populations:** Megan K. Traffanstedt et al., "Major Depression with Seasonal Variation: Is It a Valid Construct?" *Clinical Psychological Science* 4, no. 5 (2016): 825–34; Steven G. LoBello and Sheila Mehta, "No Evidence of Seasonal Variation in Mild Forms of Depression," *Journal of Behavior Therapy and Experimental Psychiatry* 62 (2019): 72–79.

52 **And Rohan herself has been:** Yael I. Nillni et al., "Seasonal Trends in Depressive Problems Among United States Children and Adolescents: A Representative Population Survey," *Psychiatry Research* 170, no. 2–3 (2009): 224–28.

53 **she told The New York Times:** Cameron Walker, "Seasonal Affective Disorder Isn't Just for Winter," *New York Times*, June 1, 2021.

55 **parts of reindeers' eyes:** Karl-Arne Stokkan et al., "Shifting Mirrors: Adaptive Changes in Retinal Reflections to Winter Darkness in Arctic Reindeer," *Proceedings of the Royal Society B: Biological Sciences* 280, no. 1773 (2013): 20132451.

56 **2022 to 2023 season:** Drew Kann, "Feds Declare Disaster for 18 Counties with Huge Frozen Peach Losses," *Atlanta Journal-Constitution*, June 27, 2023.

61 **viewing leisure as "wasteful":** Gabriela N. Tonietto et al., "Viewing Leisure as Wasteful Undermines Enjoyment," *Journal of Experimental Social Psychology* 97 (2021): 104198.

3. What You See Is What You Get

75 **people who struggle with anxiety:** Andrew Mathews et al., "Cognitive Biases in Anxiety and Attention to Threat," *Trends in Cognitive Sciences* 1, no. 9 (1997): 340–45.

81 **Two years later:** Kelly J. Rohan et al., "Outcomes One and Two Winters Following Cognitive-Behavioral Therapy or Light Therapy for Seasonal Affective Disorder," *American Journal of Psychiatry* 173, no. 3 (2016): 244–51.

82 **most patients stop:** Paul J. Schwartz et al., "Winter Seasonal Affective Disorder: A Follow-Up Study of the First 59 Patients of the National Institute of Mental Health Seasonal Studies Program," *American Journal of Psychiatry* 153, no. 8 (1996): 1028–36.

82 **Rohan's CBT approach:** Kelly J. Rohan et al., "Change in Seasonal Beliefs Mediates the Durability Advantage of Cognitive-Behavioral Therapy over Light Therapy for Winter Depression," *Behavior Therapy* 54, no. 4 (2023): 682–95.

84 **In this intervention:** Holli-Anne Passmore and Mark D. Holder, "Noticing Nature: Individual and Social Benefits of a Two-Week Intervention," *Journal of Positive Psychology* 12, no. 6 (2017): 537–46.

85 **multiple randomized controlled studies:** Holli-Anne Passmore et al., "An Extended Replication Study of the Well-Being Intervention, the Noticing Nature Intervention (NNI)," *Journal of Happiness Studies* 23, no. 6 (2022): 2663–83.

85 **just twenty minutes is enough:** Mary Hunter et al., "Urban Nature Experiences Reduce Stress in the Context of Daily Life Based on Salivary Biomarkers," *Frontiers in Psychology* (2019): 722.

85 **"Moments, not minutes":** Miles Richardson et al., "Moments, Not Minutes: The Nature-Wellbeing Relationship," *International Journal of Wellbeing* 11, no. 1 (2021): 8–33.
87 **run with community participants:** Holli-Anne Passmore et al., "Wellbeing in Winter: Testing the Noticing Nature Intervention During Winter Months," *Frontiers in Psychology* 13 (2022): 840273.

4. Use Your Words

102 **One study looked at smells:** Phoebe R. Bentley et al., "Nature, Smells, and Human Wellbeing," *Ambio* 52, no. 1 (2023): 1–14.
105 **Lera Boroditsky is a cognitive scientist:** Lera Boroditsky, "How Language Shapes the Way We Think," TED.com, November 2, 2017, video, 14:02, ted.com/talks/lera_boroditsky _how_language _shapes_the_way_we_think.
105 **Russian speakers are significantly faster:** Jonathan Winawer et al., "Russian Blues Reveal Effects of Language on Color Discrimination," *Proceedings of the National Academy of Sciences* 104, no. 19 (2007): 7780–85.
106 **could also be east:** Information from Siida Sámi Museum map display in Open-Air Museum, Inari, Sapmi (Finland), visited on January 27, 2023.
106 **Hebrew-speaking children learn:** Lera Boroditsky, "How Language Shapes Thought," *Scientific American* 304, no. 2 (February 2011): 62–65.
106 **greater gender inequality:** Jennifer L. Prewitt-Frelino et al., "The Gendering of Language: A Comparison of Gender Equality in Countries with Gendered, Natural Gender, and Genderless Languages," *Sex Roles* 66, no. 3 (2012): 268–81.
106 **Boroditsky sums it up thusly:** Lera Boroditsky, "How Does Our Language Shape the Way We Think?" in *What's Next?: Dispatches on the Future of Science*, ed. Max Brockman (New York: Vintage Books, 2009): 116–29.
107 **As Boroditsky writes:** Boroditsky, "How Language Shapes Thought."
107 **cancer patients who were shown:** Sean R. Zion et al., "Changing Cancer Mindsets: A Randomized Controlled Feasibility and Efficacy Trial," *Psycho-Oncology* 32, no. 9 (2023): 1433–42.
107 **minor, not-dangerous side effects:** Lauren C. Howe et al., "Changing Patient Mindsets About Non-Life-Threatening Symptoms During Oral Immunotherapy: A Randomized Clinical Trial," *Journal of Allergy and Clinical Immunology: In Practice* 7, no. 5 (2019): 1550–59.
109 **white-throated dippers:** Siida Sámi Museum and Nature Centre, "The Sámi Homeland's Eight Seasons," siida.fi/en/visitors/a-learning-experience/the-sami-homelands-eight-seasons/.
114 **Words are so powerful:** Gregory M. Walton, "The New Science of Wise Psychological Interventions," *Current Directions in Psychological Science* 23, no. 1 (2014): 73–82.
114 **growth mindset interventions:** For one seminal example, see Joshua Aronson et al., "Reducing the Effects of Stereotype Threat on African American College Students by Shaping Theories of Intelligence," *Journal of Experimental Social Psychology* 38, no. 2 (2002): 113–25.
115 **this approach gets people to:** Eric Bettinger et al., "Increasing Perseverance in Math: Evidence from a Field Experiment in Norway," *Journal of Economic Behavior & Organization* 146 (2018): 1–15.
115 **Getting people to say something:** Hye Rin Lee et al., "Components of Engagement in Saying-Is-Believing Exercises," *Current Psychology* 42, no. 17 (2023): 14903–18.

5. In the Mood

129 **describe their ideal state:** Jeanne L. Tsai, "Ideal Affect: Cultural Causes and Behavioral Consequences," *Perspectives on Psychological Science* 2, no. 3 (2007): 242–59.
130 **This cultural difference in preference:** Jeanne L. Tsai et al., "Cultural Variation in Affect Valuation," *Journal of Personality and Social Psychology* 90, no. 2 (2006): 288.

130 ideal American job candidates: Lucy Zhang Bencharit et al., "Should Job Applicants Be Excited or Calm? The Role of Culture and Ideal Affect in Employment Settings," *Emotion* 19, no. 3 (2019): 377–401.

131 "best-selling storybooks": Jeanne Tsai, "How Culture Influences Our Emotions (and Why it Matters)," Stanford Alumni, December 15, 2021, YouTube video, 58:02, youtube.com /watch?v=ak8eVjpNpfE.

131 American storybook characters smile: Jeanne L. Tsai et al., "Learning What Feelings to Desire: Socialization of Ideal Affect Through Children's Storybooks," *Personality and Social Psychology Bulletin* 33, no. 1 (2007): 17–30.

131 Looking at the official pictures: Jeanne L., Tsai et al., "Leaders' Smiles Reflect Cultural Differences in Ideal Affect," *Emotion* 16, no. 2 (2016): 183.

132 influence our mindsets about aging: Jeanne L. Tsai et al., "Valuing Excitement Makes People Look Forward to Old Age Less and Dread It More," *Psychology and Aging* 33, no. 7 (2018): 975.

133 Finns don't usually display: Penelope Colston, "The Finnish Secret to Happiness? Knowing When You Have Enough," *New York Times*, April 9, 2023.

138 normal living-room lights: Joshua J. Gooley et al., "Exposure to Room Light Before Bedtime Suppresses Melatonin Onset and Shortens Melatonin Duration in Humans," *Journal of Clinical Endocrinology & Metabolism* 96, no. 3 (2011): E463–72.

147 Psychologists who study awe say: David B. Yaden et al., "The Development of the Awe Experience Scale (AWE-S): A Multifactorial Measure for a Complex Emotion," *Journal of Positive Psychology* 14, no. 4 (2019): 474–88.

148 people in their sixties, seventies, and eighties: Virginia E. Sturm et al., "Big Smile, Small Self: Awe Walks Promote Prosocial Positive Emotions in Older Adults," *Emotion* 22, no. 5 (2022): 1044.

149 reduced symptoms of post-traumatic stress disorder: Craig L. Anderson et al., "Awe in Nature Heals: Evidence from Military Veterans, At-Risk Youth, and College Students," *Emotion* 18, no. 8 (2018): 1195.

149 awe might even make you nicer: Paul K. Piff et al., "Awe, the Small Self, and Prosocial Behavior," *Journal of Personality and Social Psychology* 108, no. 6 (2015): 883.

150 positive awe experiences have been linked to: Amie M. Gordon et al., "The Dark Side of the Sublime: Distinguishing a Threat-Based Variant of Awe," *Journal of Personality and Social Psychology* 113, no. 2 (2017): 310.

150 After being primed to feel awe: Yang Bai et al., "Awe, Daily Stress, and Elevated Life Satisfaction," *Journal of Personality and Social Psychology* 120, no. 4 (2021): 837.

150 In our brains: Michiel Van Elk et al., "The Neural Correlates of the Awe Experience: Reduced Default Mode Network Activity During Feelings of Awe," *Human Brain Mapping* 40, no. 12 (2019): 3561–74.

150 awe is the strongest predictor of: Jennifer E. Stellar et al., "Positive Affect and Markers of Inflammation: Discrete Positive Emotions Predict Lower Levels of Inflammatory Cytokines," *Emotion* 15, no. 2 (2015): 129.

6. Nights, Lights, and Rites

160 thinking about darkness: Anna Steidle and Lioba Werth, "Freedom from Constraints: Darkness and Dim Illumination Promote Creativity," *Journal of Environmental Psychology* 35 (2013): 67–80.

163 video of fire: Christopher Dana Lynn, "Hearth and Campfire Influences on Arterial Blood Pressure: Defraying the Costs of the Social Brain Through Fireside Relaxation," *Evolutionary Psychology* 12, no. 5 (2014): 147470491401200509.

7. You're Not Made of Sugar

189 **college students thought:** Elizabeth W. Dunn et al., "Location, Location, Location: The Misprediction of Satisfaction in Housing Lotteries," *Personality and Social Psychology Bulletin* 29, no. 11 (2003): 1421–32.

189 **untenured college professors:** Daniel T. Gilbert et al., "Immune Neglect: A Source of Durability Bias in Affective Forecasting," *Journal of Personality and Social Psychology* 75, no. 3 (1998): 617.

189 **men and women inaccurately predicted:** Paul W. Eastwick et al., "Mispredicting Distress Following Romantic Breakup: Revealing the Time Course of the Affective Forecasting Error," *Journal of Experimental Social Psychology* 44, no. 3 (2008): 800–7.

190 **people substantially underestimate:** Elizabeth K. Nisbet and John M. Zelenski, "Underestimating Nearby Nature: Affective Forecasting Errors Obscure the Happy Path to Sustainability," *Psychological Science* 22, no. 9 (2011): 1101–6.

190 **"What I do is":** Anthony Taylor and Kari Leibowitz, *Great Northern Podcast*, January 2022, thegreatnorthernfestival.com/the-great-northern-podcast-2022/anthony-taylor-amp -kari-leibowitz.

195 **babies took longer naps:** Marjo Tourula et al., "Children Sleeping Outdoors in Winter: Parents' Experiences of a Culturally Bound Childcare Practice," *International Journal of Circumpolar Health* 67, no. 2–3 (2008): 269–78.

197 **book on Norwegian friluftsliv:** Annette R. Hofmann, Carsten Gade Rolland, Kolbjørn Rafoss, and Herbert Zoglowek, *Norwegian Friluftsliv: A Way of Living and Learning in Nature* (Germany: Waxmann Verlag GmbH, 2018): 23.

199 **Woolley asked people at the gym:** Kaitlin Woolley and Ayelet Fishbach, "For the Fun of It: Harnessing Immediate Rewards to Increase Persistence in Long-Term Goals," *Journal of Consumer Research* 42, no. 6 (2016): 952–66.

204 **Becky's first tattoo:** Simone Schnall et al., "Social Support and the Perception of Geographical Slant," *Journal of Experimental Social Psychology* 44, no. 5 (2008): 1246–55.

205 **Writing for The Great Northern blog:** Anthony Taylor, "The Opportunity of Winter," *Great Northern*, January 19, 2023. thegreatnorthernfestival.com/tgn-blog/the-opportunity -of-winter.

206 **In her thesis, Hurly shares:** Jane Hurley, "Sleeping Bags, S'mores and the Great Outdoors: The Role of Nature-based Leisure in Refugee Integration in Canada" (master's thesis, Royal Roads University, 2015).

8. Sink, Sweat, or Swim

212 **70 percent of people in Japan:** Yutaka Tochihara, "A Review of Japanese-Style Bathing: Its Demerits and Merits," *Journal of Physiological Anthropology* 41, no. 1 (2022): 1–14.

212 **93 percent of Japanese people:** Tadashi Yano et al., "Comparison of the Habit of Bathing Between Japanese Living in Kyoto and Japanese Americans Living in Los Angeles," *Journal of the Japanese Society of Balneology, Climatology and Physical Medicine* (2017): 80–92.

213 **high-frequency bathers:** Shinya Hayasaka et al., "Bathing in a Bathtub and Health Status: A Cross-Sectional Study," *Complementary Therapies in Clinical Practice* 16, no. 4 (2010): 219–21.

214 **naturally fed hot-spring onsen:** Hiroharu Kamioka et al., "Relationship of Daily Hot Water Bathing at Home and Hot Water Spa Bathing with Underlying Diseases in Middle-Aged and Elderly Ambulatory Patients: A Japanese Multicenter Cross-Sectional Study," *Complementary Therapies in Medicine* 43 (2019): 232–39.

214 **study of almost 900 participants:** Katsuhiko Kohara et al., "Habitual Hot Water Bathing Protects Cardiovascular Function in Middle-Aged to Elderly Japanese Subjects," *Scientific Reports* 8, no. 1 (2018): 8687.

214 **increased cardiovascular functioning:** S. B. Grüner et al., "Benefit of Warm Water Immersion on Biventricular Function in Patients with Chronic Heart Failure," *Cardiovascular Ultrasound* 7, 33 (2009); A. Michalsen et al., "Thermal Hydrotherapy Improves Quality of Life and Hemodynamic Function in Patients with Chronic Heart Failure," *American Heart Journal* 146, 728–33 (2003); A. Cider et al., "Immersion in Warm Water Induces Improvement in Cardiac Function in Patients with Chronic Heart Failure," *European Journal of Heart Failure* 8, 308–13 (2006).

214 **Daily bathing is also associated with:** Hiroharu Kamioka et al., "Association of Daily Home-Based Hot Water Bathing and Glycemic Control in Ambulatory Japanese Patients with Type 2 Diabetes Mellitus During the COVID-19 Pandemic: A Multicenter Cross-Sectional Study," *Diabetes, Metabolic Syndrome and Obesity* (2020): 5059–69.

215 **a 10- to 30-minute bath:** Shahab Haghayegh et al., "Before-Bedtime Passive Body Heating by Warm Shower or Bath to Improve Sleep: A Systematic Review and Meta-Analysis," *Sleep Medicine Reviews* 46 (2019): 124–35.

215 **took baths more frequently:** S. Yamasaki et al., "Association Between Habitual Hot Spring Bathing and Depression in Japanese Older Adults: A Retrospective Study in Beppu," *Complementary Therapies in Medicine* 72 (2023): 102909.

217 **A feature on Iceland's pools:** Dan Kos, "Iceland's Water Cure," *New York Times Magazine*, April 19, 2016.

220 **an astounding list:** Jari A. Laukkanen et al., "Cardiovascular and Other Health Benefits of Sauna Bathing: A Review of the Evidence," *Mayo Clinic Proceedings* 93, no. 8 (August 2018): 1111–21; Joy Hussain and Marc Cohen, "Clinical Effects of Regular Dry Sauna Bathing: A Systematic Review," *Evidence-Based Complementary and Alternative Medicine*, April 24, 2018, doi.org/10.1155/2018/1857413; Rhonda P. Patrick and Teresa L. Johnson, "Sauna Use As a Lifestyle Practice to Extend Healthspan," *Experimental Gerontology* 154 (2021): 111509.

220 **easing stress and promoting relaxation:** Joy N. Hussain et al., "A Hot Topic for Health: Results of the Global Sauna Survey," *Complementary Therapies in Medicine* 44 (2019): 223–34.

220 **sauna bathing can improve sleep:** Hussain et al., "A Hot Topic for Health."

220 **skin conditions:** Doreen Kowatzki et al., "Effect of Regular Sauna on Epidermal Barrier Function and Stratum Corneum Water-Holding Capacity in Vivo in Humans: A Controlled Study," *Dermatology* 217, no. 2 (2008): 173–80.

220 **lower blood pressure:** Earric Lee et al., "Sauna Exposure Leads to Improved Arterial Compliance: Findings from a Non-Randomised Experimental Study," *European Journal of Preventive Cardiology* 25, no. 2 (2018): 130–8; Tanjaniina Laukkanen et al., "Acute Effects of Sauna Bathing on Cardiovascular Function," *Journal of Human Hypertension* 32, no. 2 (2018): 129–38.

220 **improve lung function:** Nico J. M. Cox et al., "Sauna to Transiently Improve Pulmonary Function in Patients with Obstructive Lung Disease," *Archives of Physical Medicine and Rehabilitation* 70, no. 13 (1989): 911–13; Minna L. Hannuksela, and Samer Ellahham, "Benefits and Risks of Sauna Bathing," *American Journal of Medicine* 110, no. 2 (2001): 118–26.

221 **colds and viruses:** Setor Kwadzo Kunutsor et al., "Sauna Bathing Reduces the Risk of Respiratory Diseases: A Long-Term Prospective Cohort Study," *European Journal of Epidemiology* 32 (2017): 1107–11; Setor Kwadzo Kunutsor et al., "Frequent Sauna Bathing May Reduce the Risk of Pneumonia in Middle-Aged Caucasian Men: The KIHD Prospective Cohort Study," *Respiratory Medicine* 132 (2017): 161–3; E. Ernst et al., "Regular Sauna Bathing and the Incidence of Common Colds," *Annals of Medicine* 22, no. 4 (1990): 225–27.

221 **increases interleukin-10:** Małgorzata Żychowska et al., "Association of High Cardiovascular Fitness and the Rate of Adaptation to Heat Stress," *Biomed Research International* 2018 (February 28, 2018), 1685368.

221 **Regular sauna bathing lowers cholesterol:** Dorota Gryka et al., "The Effect of Sauna Bathing on Lipid Profile in Young, Physically Active, Male Subjects," *International Journal of Occupational Medicine and Environmental Health* 27 (2014): 608–18.

221 **increases insulin sensitivity:** Mark F. McCarty et al., "Regular Thermal Therapy May Promote Insulin Sensitivity While Boosting Expression of Endothelial Nitric Oxide Synthase–Effects Comparable to Those of Exercise Training," *Medical Hypotheses* 73, no. 1 (2009): 103–5.

221 **study of more than two thousand men:** Jari A. Laukkanen et al., "Combined Effect of Sauna Bathing and Cardiorespiratory Fitness on the Risk of Sudden Cardiac Deaths in Caucasian Men: A Long-Term Prospective Cohort Study," *Progress in Cardiovascular Diseases* 60, no. 6 (2018): 635–41.

221 **more than sixteen hundred men and women:** Tanjaniina Laukkanen et al., "Sauna Bathing Is Associated with Reduced Cardiovascular Mortality and Improves Risk Prediction in Men and Women: A Prospective Cohort Study," *BMC Medicine* 16, no. 1 (2018): 1–14.

221 **found that regular sauna:** Tanjaniina Laukkanen et al., "Sauna Bathing Is Inversely Associated with Dementia and Alzheimer's Disease in Middle-Aged Finnish Men," *Age and Ageing* 46, no. 2 (2017): 245–49.

222 **highly stressful jobs:** Kaemmer N. Henderson et al., "The Cardiometabolic Health Benefits of Sauna Exposure in Individuals with High-Stress Occupations. A Mechanistic Review," *International Journal of Environmental Research and Public Health* 18, no. 3 (2021): 1105.

225 **winter swimming releases endorphins:** Susanna Søberg, *Winter Swimming: The Nordic Way Towards a Healthier and Happier Life* (London: MacLehose Press, 2022), 79–88; Petr Šrámek et al., "Human Physiological Responses to Immersion into Water of Different Temperatures," *European Journal of Applied Physiology* 81 (2000): 436–42.

225 **and norepinephrine:** D. G. Johnson et al., "Plasma Norepinephrine Responses of Man in Cold Water," *Journal of Applied Physiology* 43, no. 2 (1977): 216–20.

226 **people report that cold-water swimming:** Didrik Espeland et al., "Health Effects of Voluntary Exposure to Cold Water—A Continuing Subject of Debate," *International Journal of Circumpolar Health* 81, no. 1 (2022): 2111789, tandfonline.com/doi/pdf/10.1080/22423982 .2022.2111789.

226 **cold-water swimming is beneficial for:** Pirkko Huttunen et al., "Winter Swimming Improves General Well-Being," *International Journal of Circumpolar Health* 63, no. 2 (2004): 140–44.

226 **reduces insulin resistance:** Magdalena Gibas-Dorna et al., "Cold Water Swimming Beneficially Modulates Insulin Sensitivity in Middle-Aged Individuals," *Journal of Aging and Physical Activity* 24, no. 4 (2016): 547–54; Magdalena Gibas-Dorna et al., "Variations in Leptin and Insulin Levels Within One Swimming Season in Non-Obese Female Cold Water Swimmers," *Scandinavian Journal of Clinical and Laboratory Investigation* 76, no. 6 (2016): 486–91.

226 **improves the immune system:** Anna Lubkowska et al., "Winter-Swimming as a Building-Up Body Resistance Factor Inducing Adaptive Changes in the Oxidant/Antioxidant Status," *Scandinavian Journal of Clinical and Laboratory Investigation* 73, no. 4 (2013): 315–25.

226 **increases prevalence of leukocytes:** B. Dugué and E. Leppänen, "Adaptation Related to Cytokines in Man: Effects of Regular Swimming in Ice-Cold Water," *Clinical Physiology* 20, no. 2 (2000): 114–21, pubmed.ncbi.nlm.nih.gov/10735878/.

226 **Cold-water immersion after exercise:** Jonathan DC Leeder et al., "Cold Water Immersion Improves Recovery of Sprint Speed Following a Simulated Tournament," *European Journal of Sport Science* 19, no. 9 (2019): 1166–74.

226 **enhances recovery:** Joanna Vaile et al., "Effect of Cold Water Immersion on Repeated Cycling Performance and Limb Blood Flow," *British Journal of Sports Medicine* 45, no. 10 (2011): 825–29, bjsm.bmj.com/content/45/10/825.

226 **development of brown adipose tissue:** Sara Shams et al., "Swimming in Cold Water Upregulates Genes Involved in Thermogenesis and the Browning of White Adipose Tissues,"

Comparative Biochemistry and Physiology Part B: Biochemistry and Molecular Biology 265 (2023): 110834; Søberg, *Winter Swimming*, 122–31;

227 **more brown adipose tissue:** Tobias Becher et al., "Brown Adipose Tissue Is Associated with Cardiometabolic Health," *Nature Medicine* 27, no. 1 (2021): 58–65.

227 **thought that only babies:** Andreas Paulus and Matthias Bauwens, "Brown Adipose Tissue: Metabolic Role and Non-Invasive Quantification in Humans," *Visceral and Ectopic Fat*, ed. Hildo J. Lamb (Amsterdam: Elsevier, 2023): 25–37.

229 **eleven minutes of cold-water:** Susanna Søberg et al., "Altered Brown Fat Thermoregulation and Enhanced Cold-Induced Thermogenesis in Young, Healthy, Winter-Swimming Men," *Cell Reports Medicine* 2, no. 10 (2021).

231 **help us wring meaning:** Sean Raymond Zion, "From Cancer to COVID-19: The Self-Fulfilling Effects of Illness Mindsets on Physical, Social, and Emotional Functioning" (master's thesis, Stanford University, 2021).

232 **mindsets can reframe difficult:** Danielle Z. Boles et al., "Can Exercising and Eating Healthy Be Fun and Indulgent Instead of Boring and Depriving? Targeting Mindsets About the Process of Engaging in Healthy Behaviors," *Frontiers in Psychology* 12 (2021): 745950.

9. Clearing the Way

237 **"seed" and "soil":** Gregory M. Walton and David S. Yeager, "Seed and Soil: Psychological Affordances in Contexts Help to Explain Where Wise Interventions Succeed or Fail," *Current Directions in Psychological Science* 29, no. 3 (2020): 219–26.

244 **This led to four major pillars:** WinterCity Edmonton, "For the Love of Winter: WinterCity Strategy Implementation Plan," City of Edmonton, Alberta, Canada, passed September 10, 2013, edmonton.ca/public-files/assets/document?path=PDF/TheLoveofWinter-ImplementationPlan.pdf; WinterCity Edmonton, "Winter Design Guidelines: Transforming Edmonton into a Great Winter City," City of Edmonton, Alberta, Canada, December 2016, edmonton.ca/public-files/assets/document?path=PDF/WinterCityDesignGuidelines _draft.pdf; WinterCity Edmonton, "Keep the Snowball Rolling: WinterCity Strategy Evaluation & Report," City of Edmonton, Alberta, Canada, May 2018, edmonton.ca/sites/default /files/public-files/documents/COE_WinterCity_Evaluation_Report_FINAL.pdf.

245 **Simon O'Byrne, the WinterCity Think Tank cochair:** WinterCity Edmonton, "For the Love of Winter: Strategy for Transforming Edmonton into a World-Leading Winter City," City of Edmonton, Alberta, Canada, edmonton.ca/sites/default/files/public-files/assets/PDF/COE -WinterCity-Love-Winter-Summary-Report.pdf.

252 **Oulu's bike culture:** Erika Benke, "The Cycle-Mad City in Finland that Doesn't Stop for Snow," BBC.com, January 20, 2023, video, 1:57, bbc.com/news/av/world-europe-64354089.

253 **Holland, Michigan:** Shandra Martinez, "Why Michigan City Spends Millions to Heat Its Streets during Winter," *MLive*, February 25, 2016.

257 **misleading and simplistic paraphrase:** Mohandas Gandhi, "General Knowledge About Health: Accidents: Snake-Bite," *Indian Opinion*, 1913; Mohandas Gandhi, *Collected Works of Mahatma Gandhi* 13 (Delhi, India: Publications Division, Ministry of Information and Broadcasting, Government of India, 1958).

Epilogue. Protecting Winter

260 **the Mashpee Wampanoag tribe:** Eve Zuckoff, "In a New England Pond, Toxic Algae Is Disrupting Tribal Heritage," New Hampshire Public Radio, August 28, 2023.

260 **allergy season in 2018:** William R. L. Anderegg et al., "Anthropogenic Climate Change Is Worsening North American Pollen Seasons," *Proceedings of the National Academy of Sciences* 118, no. 7 (2021): e2013284118.

260 **Earlier spring warmth also melts:** Anthony L. Westerling et al., "Warming and Earlier Spring Increase Western US Forest Wildfire Activity," *Science* 313, no. 5789 (2006): 940–43.

Further Reading

Dweck, Carol S. *Mindset: The New Psychology of Success* (New York: Ballantine Books, 2006)

Hersey, Tricia. *Rest Is Resistance: A Manifesto* (New York: Little, Brown Spark, 2022)

May, Katherine. *Wintering: The Power of Rest and Retreat in Difficult Times* (New York: Riverhead Books, 2020)

McGonigal, Kelly. *The Upside of Stress: Why Stress Is Good for You, and How to Get Good at It* (New York: Avery, 2016)

Partanen, Anu. *The Nordic Theory of Everything: In Search of a Better Life* (New York: Harper, 2016)

Søberg, Susanna. *Winter Swimming: The Nordic Way Towards a Healthier and Happier Life* (London: MacLehose Press, 2022)

Wiking, Meik. *The Little Book of Hygge: The Danish Way to Live Well* (New York: William Morrow, 2016)

For more about the research from the Stanford Mind & Body Lab, visit mbl.stanford.edu.

For more about Protect Our Winters, visit protectourwinters.org.